LETTERS WRIT BY A TURKISH SPY

LETTERS WRIT BY A TURKISH SPY

BY

Giovanni P. Marana

selected and edited by

ARTHUR J. WEITZMAN

1970

Temple University Publications

DISTRIBUTED BY

COLUMBIA UNIVERSITY PRESS

NEW YORK

ISBN 0 87722 000 x

Printed in Great Britain

CONTENTS

ACKNOWLEDGEMENTS

I wish to record my sincerest thanks to those who aided me in this project. I am very grateful to S. D. Goitein, Professor of Arabic at the University of Pennsylvania, who helped me identify many of the Arabic and Turkish references in this collection of letters. Professors Lawrence Berman of Dropsie College and Franz Rosenthal of Yale University also gave me assistance in Oriental matters. I thank the Trustees of Temple University for a grant of money for the summer of 1964, which allowed me the freedom to devote full time to this edition. And finally I thank my wife for her encouragement and editorial assistance.

INTRODUCTION

The seventeenth century was an age of terrible upheaval and violence. The religious wars in which Protestant fought against Catholic, Puritan against Royalist and Christian against Turk afflicted the countries of Europe as they had not suffered for many centuries. But as the century advanced, Europeans became appalled by the carnage perpetrated in the name of religion. Sectarian passions and religious fervour waned; the issues that divided Catholic and Protestant, while they were to remain issues for centuries, seemed less worthy to fight about than they had a century earlier. Hostility to non-Christian peoples diminished perceptibly as knowledge of new lands and new peoples was brought to the attention of curious Europeans eagerly seeking information of other political and religious systems which could be compared to their own. Weary of the strife of half a century, Dryden in 1682 voiced the general hope, 'Common quiet is Mankind's concern'. The spirit of the Enlightenment, consensus based on mutual interest rather than religious orthodoxy, the desire to find a set of principles every reasonable man could believe in, the subjection of passion to the firm guidance of reason, and the ardent hope for an orderly world where trade and peace would flourish: these finally were the ideals embraced in varying degrees by the intellectual community of the late seventeenth century. Although we have the works of Locke, the proceedings of the Royal Society in England, the writings of Bayle and Fontenelle in France, the popularization of Enlightenment ideals has never been so fully realized as in Giovanni P. Marana's *Letters Writ by a Turkish Spy*. But no other seventeenth-century work of its importance and charm has been so utterly neglected.

Immensely popular in the late seventeenth and eighteenth centuries, *The Turkish Spy* has been relegated to an unjust oblivion. Except for a few references in the scholarship of the Victorian and Modern Age – all laudatory – *The Spy* has gone unnoticed, its importance unappreciated. In his *Introduction to the Literature of Europe* the Victorian critic Henry Hallam cited it as no ordinary work and devoted some analysis to it.[1] Recently an American scholar demonstrated its importance in the cultural history of France and Europe.[2] But except for these appreciations and a number of studies on the authorship of the work – long a subject of contention – *The Turkish Spy* has lain forgotten on the shelves of rare book rooms and remained largely unread. It is certainly time that this collection of letters, or at least a portion of it, be made available to the public. The present edition hopes to remedy the neglect of the last century and a half.

The first volume of *Letters Writ by a Turkish Spy* – there are altogether eight volumes – was published in France in 1684 in French. From all evidence the author was Giovanni P. Marana (1642-93), an Italian journalist and Francophile, who resided for many years in France. Through extensive reading about Moslem culture, he conceived the notion of having a Turk visit Paris and write back to his friends and colleagues all that he saw and did. Marana gave expression to this highly original idea in a collection of letters in which a Moslem character finds his way in a European and Christian city. Marana may be said to have fathered the device of concocting a series of letters written by a visitor to a foreign country. This extraordinary literary invention, which later proved so congenial to Montesquieu and Goldsmith, introduces the genre of the literary letter of the foreign observer used so successfully in later history.

The editor and translator of the first volume of *The Spy* (Marana, but as was the custom in seventeenth-century journalistic work, the book was published under false pretences) claims to have discovered in Paris a packet of letters written in Arabic. Asserting to have had the letters translated into Italian and then French (to obfuscate the authorship), Marana discovered that they were written by a Turk named Mahmut,

1 (London, 1872), IV, 332-335.

2 Joseph Tucker, '*The Turkish Spy* and its French Background,' *Revue de Littérature Comparée*, XXXII (1958), 74-91.

sent to spy on the French for his master, the Sultan of the Ottoman Empire. The letters are Mahmut's reports to various officials of the Turkish Empire and His Majesty's ministers on the military and political activities of their Christian enemies. Ever since the Crusades an endemic state of war, which occasionally broke out into campaigns and battles, was the normal relationship between Moslems and Christians. The Turks in the seventeenth century had even threatened the security of Europe and had almost conquered Vienna. But not all of Mahmut's letters deal with these affairs of state; some are simply personal missives to friends and family.

Thus Marana by this stroke of brilliance was able to accomplish in the first volume what every good journalist dreams to do: bring to life with fresh insight the obvious and familiar aspects of everyday life. He was able to enjoy a certain degree of anonymity, since the letters were ostensibly a Turkish spy's writings; anything dangerous in them could be disavowed. Although it is true that the first volume of letters was finally passed by the censor (there was no freedom of the press during the reign of Louis XIV), Marana could never be sure what reprisals would be taken under that autocratic ruler. And the second advantage of this publishing ruse was the sensational element inherent in the revelations of a spy, which Marana ingeniously exploited and which forms one of the main appeals of the letters.

The problem of authorship arises with the publication of the next seven volumes of the collection. Since they first appeared in England between 1691 and 1694 in English, it has been held that an Englishman wrote them. Marana's first volume was Englished in 1687 by an unknown translator three years after its first appearance in France. This translator or printer may have had Puritan sympathies because the ninety-ninth letter of the first volume was suppressed. In this letter, which reveals Royalist support, Mahmut praised Charles I and the Royal cause, and condemned the dissensions in England caused by the Puritans. In subsequent volumes, however, Mahmut's monarchial bias is given full sway.

The second volume of *The Turkish Spy* appeared together with the first volume in 1691, with the notice of 'second edition' on the title page but no mention of Marana. Another deception was perpetuated in the (Preface) of Volume II. In it the editor reprinted a letter from a Mr. Saltmarsh (of whose existence there is no record), who claimed to have discovered an Italian edition of *The Spy* and brought it to England; this Italian version the editor asserts to be the source of the subsequent English edition, which comprises volumes two to eight. Yet no Italian edition of *The Turkish Spy* dating from the seventeenth century is extant, nor is there any record of one. The second volume of the English *Spy* could not have been translated from a French version, since the earliest French edition of the last seven volumes appeared in Cologne in 1696, five years after the English printing; and the Cologne edition purports to be a translation from the English. By 1696 Marana had been dead for three years.

If the remaining letters of *The Turkish Spy* are not of French or Italian origin, then Marana could not have written them, and the attribution points in the direction of England since the earliest extant version of the greater part of the letters is in English. So argues Joseph Tucker in a recent article.[3] However plausible Tucker's argument is, he was unable to find a definite English candidate, except for sixty-three letters of the 1718 *Continuation*, which was Defoe's. Working on the same problem of attribution, William McBurney came to the opposite conclusion.[4] He argues that perhaps Saltmarsh was a pseudonym for Hindmarsh, the bookseller, and that Marana did write a manuscript which was brought to England and translated by the translator of the first volume, probably the hack writer William Bradshaw. McBurney builds his case upon the internal evidence of the letters, pointing out the similarities of thought and taste reflected in *The Turkish Spy* and Marana's other writings, the pro-French bias of the letters, 'continuity of design, characterization and style throughout the contested work'. However persuasive McBurney's presentation of internal evidence is, he discovered no manuscripts, and he overlooked the fact that in the Saltmarsh letter printed in the second volume it is clearly stated that an Italian published edition existed and

[3] 'On the Authorship of *The Turkish Spy*: an *État Présent,*' *Papers of the Bibliographical Society of America*, LII (1958), 34-47.
[4] 'The Authorship of *The Turkish Spy,*' *PMLA*, LXXII (1957), 915-935.

was exceedingly popular. And if 'Saltmarsh' told the truth then it is more likely that an Italian edition of the letters, not a manuscript, would be found – but no such Italian edition has been found. Everything points to an elaborate ruse of the English bookseller to give credence to his publication. And it is even more likely that the 'Preface', and Saltmarsh's letter and the events described in them were entirely fictitious. Booksellers in the eighteenth century often resorted to such deceptions.

Yet the dilemma remains, for McBurney is certainly right in his assertion that there is continuity of design, characterization and style throughout the work, which gives it coherence. Whoever the author or authors were, the Oriental machinery of the letters is never allowed to lapse; one is always aware that the letter writer is a Moslem, a foreigner, and moreover, a spy who is not particularly comfortable in the Parisian milieu, but is resigned to his duty, which he stoically accepts.

In this regard, Montesquieu's *Persian Letters* and Goldsmith's *Citizen of the World*, which owe their form to the invention of Marana, were not as consistently and carefully written in respect to the characterization of their letter writers. When a literary device or mask such as this is used, there is always the danger of discarding the mask when it inhibits the author. Occasionally Montesquieu and more often Goldsmith allow their masks to slip, and speak out in their own voices. Marana and the collaborator of *The Turkish Spy* were exceedingly careful to keep the mask tightly on. Furthermore, the correspondent discerns carefully to whom he writes. To a political officer in the Ottoman Empire a letter would be about politics; to a dervish or imam the subject might be religion or philosophy; to his family and friends more personal affairs were communicated. The letters contain a tremendous scope of interests and subjects, but imbedded within the historical and political reportage are the fictional features, the events of Mahmut's life in Paris and the political intrigues affecting him at Constantinople.

Mahmut resided in Paris from 1637 to 1682, and in the course of these years experienced many difficulties. In his youth he fell in love with a Greek woman named Daria, who was married but encouraged his advances. She proved to be a coquette. Mahmut resolved to abstain from all women. Twenty years later he meets her again and his passion is rekindled by the now-widowed woman. She is again false to him, and he resolves for the second and last time never to pay court to a woman. He learns to his horror, however, that he had been responsible for her husband's death. Three years earlier Mahmut was attacked in an alley by an unknown man bent on murdering him. Fortunately Mahmut was able to master the situation and turn the tables on his attacker. Learning of the assailant's identity from his widow, Mahmut is shocked by the knowledge of having killed the husband. These adventures are the least of his difficulties. All during his stay in Paris his enemies at home have been intriguing at the seraglio to blacken his reputation. We learn from his defences in his letters that these enemies have impugned his faith in Islam and reported that he has converted to Christianity, which he strenuously denies. Moreover, his stay in Paris is punctuated by narrow escapes from detection, an occasion of imprisonment, the buying of information from informers, locating hidden papers, and so on – all the cloak-and-dagger conventions of international spy stories.

Mahmut has an unusual character and is a new protagonist in English literature, if one for a moment expropriates him from the French. Unlike the garrulous war-like hero of the heroic play or romance of the late seventeenth century, Mahmut is 'of low Stature, of an ill-favour'd Countenance, ill-shap'd, and by Nature not given to Talkativeness', evincing a philosophic turn of mind, which shows itself in his reading of European philosophers, particularly Descartes, who has a decisive influence on his thinking. He is sensitive to the hypocrisy and fanaticism around him, but does nothing to effect changes. And he can be a warm advocate of liberal sentiments. In an eloquent passage he defends the liberal education of women. 'Their Senses are generally as quick as ours, their Reason as nervous, their Judgments as mature and solid. Add but to these natural Perfections, the Advantage of acquir'd Learning, what polite and charming Creatures will they prove.' These sentiments – considering that a Moslem uttered them – add to the attractiveness of his character. He reveals himself a vegetarian, the result of his benevolent impulses. Tender-hearted about the treatment of animals, he writes some letters against the prevailing notion that animals have no souls. He insinuates himself quietly, the observer of society and events rather than the initiator of them, the ideal of the Renaissance. In this respect, he is closer to Goldsmith's cosmopolitan citizen and MacKenzie's man of feeling than to the past ideal man, the heroic doer. Mahmut, while remaining a comic figure, is an inchoate man of sentiment. We both laugh at and admire him for his comic blundering but good-natured heart.

As satire, *The Turkish Spy* impugns Christian and European insularity. The Oriental machinery of the letters is effectively used as a counterpoint to European complacency of belief in religion and morality. Marana, who undoubtedly read travel accounts of the Middle East and Turkish Empire, ironically undercuts the intolerant Christian observer of Moslem religion and manners by creating a Moslem observer of Christian religion and manners. Mahmut, by turns the devout Moslem and then the sceptic, views Christianity and the Christian nations as, for example, earlier Christians did the nations of Islam. But the irony goes deeper, for in the early years of his European sojourn Mahmut was as naïve about his own religion and nation as the Christians were about theirs. For instance he comments on the war between France and Spain in the 1630's: 'These two Nations do the Duty of the Mussulmans in destroying one another; and when this is done, they give God thanks for the Evil they have committed. Whence we may judge of the Wisdom and Piety of the Mahometans amongst whom there's seldom been an open War; and if it should happen, 'tis generally condemned.' Yet any reader who knew anything at all about Middle-East history must have realized how untrue Mahmut's statement was, for there was constant strife between the Turks and Persians, not only over imperialistic ambitions, but also over religious differences between the Sunni and Shi'a sects. The Moslem is as complacent and sure of the righteous conduct of the Islamic nations as the Christians are naïvely of theirs. In the discussion of religion Mahmut speaks of Christian ritual and belief as superstition, but of his own Muhammadanism all is reasonable and enlightened, at least when he is not in one of his sceptical moods. All of these opinions must have come as a shock to Christian readers used as they were to such language being applied to Islam. Mahmut's defence of his own religious beliefs is a knife that cuts two ways. On the one hand it boldly rips the fabric of Christian self-righteousness by having a foreigner hold up a mirror to its hypocrisy and inconsistencies; while on the other hand, it subtly cuts the inner lining of all dogmatic and absolute opinions. In doing so, Marana and his successors in this genre attempted to destroy the whole cloth of dogmatic religion and preconceived beliefs and substitute scepticism and relativism in their place. To the extent that *The Turkish Spy* attempted to ridicule religious dogma and ritual, it may be said to be in the central tradition of the eighteenth-century deists and *philosophes,* who also believed that they were bringing enlightenment to Europe by their direct attacks on Christian orthodoxy. Marana and his English collaborator were indeed sensitive to the avant-garde movements of European thought and probably did much, judging from the enormous success of the letters, to spread the new doctrines of the Enlightenment through England and France.

Mahmut's embrace of Cartesian philosophy adds another dimension to the letters. At the same time that he is or attempts to be a devout Muslim, he is profoundly influenced by Descartes's scepticism, which leads him to many doubts of the various points of belief and religious practices of his forefathers. In a letter to the Mufti he writes: 'Thou wilt tell me, the Alcoran speaks with great clearness; yet how many obscure Passages do we find in the words of our Holy Prophet, wherein we need their exposition?' He begins to doubt the efficacy of Moslem ritual and even sees some advantages to Christianity under the impact of the new tolerant attitudes. In the course of the letters, however, the doubts give way to scorn of organized religion and especially the Roman Catholic clergy, who receive tremendous abuse, for which reason the letters were placed on the Church's *Index* soon after they appeared. As a result of his contact with Western religion and philosophy, the spy turns to deism. The deists, Mahmut explains, 'deserve the Title *Philosophers* or Lovers of Wisdom and Truth. And 'tis from them I have learn'd this unwillingness to be impos'd on in Matters of Religion'. Mahmut concludes that the only value religion has, beyond that of keeping the vulgar in obedience to established authority, lies in the ethics and moral principles it advocates. Revelation, prayer and priestcraft are superfluous superstitions which enlightened philosophers may discard. The attitude towards religion in *The Turkish Spy* foreshadowed the main developments of eighteenth-century religious liberalism.

As a part of the Oriental vogue in fiction, *The Turkish Spy* inaugurated the genre of the Oriental letter writer, which was managed so effectively by Montesquieu, D'Argens and Goldsmith. *The Turkish Spy* provided a link between travel writings and the vogue of Eastern fiction. Marana was able to write his work because of the enormous backlog of information about the Middle East brought to Western Europe by travellers and Oriental scholars. Echoes of travellers' attitudes found their way into the letters. Recurrent criticism of the lack of education of Moslems is answered by the spy, who claims that Christians are misinformed, for the Moslem young are taught Arabic and Persian from infancy, 'In which two *Languages,* how many famous *Histories* have been writ! There is no point of useful Wisdom, which is not compriz'd in the *Writings* of the Eastern Sages'. The oft-repeated charge that learning is not encouraged in Moslem countries because printing is forbidden is answered satirically by Mahmut. He defends the suppression of printing – and yet at the same time lets fly a dart – by pointing out that books printed in the vulgate languages only disseminate lies and errors, and that the deleterious effects of printing can be seen in the fomenting of discontent and rebellion among the people, in the creation of religious sects and in the disrespect shown towards superiors. The prohibition of printing in Moslem countries avoids these evils. In spite of his sceptical and tolerant attitudes, Mahmut remains a strong monarchist and believer in established religion and the state. For the peace and security of the realm, those who have doubts should not spread them abroad.

In general the Islamic countries are portrayed in a favourable light in the letters. Mahmut plays alternately the role of the dogmatic nationalist and then the cosmopolitan sceptic; at one moment is convinced of the superiority of his religion and culture, but at the next finds difficulties and inconsistencies. And yet these vexing inconsistencies and troublesome doubts about Moslem culture are precisely the same kind irritating the critics of European culture. In such measure Marana has shown more of the kinship of the two cultures than of those features which divides them, and to a degree has attempted to bridge the cultural chasm that earlier travellers and religious dogmatists had channelled between Christians and heathens. In spite of the satire of European culture which is often veiled in the discussion of Turkish practices, the letters depict with some accuracy Muhammadan ritual, domestic life and politics. Such knowledge may have been gained through first-hand contact, but it was more likely acquired through a wide reading of travel books and histories. There is no record of Marana's ever having been in the Middle East. Mahmut, as a Moslem, furthermore, is shown in a favourable light, notwithstanding the occasional epithets he hurls at Christianity. In the preface 'To the Reader' of the first volume, the editor claims that Mahmut is no barbarian, the usual European opinion of the Turk: 'he reasons not as a Barbarian, but like an able Statesman and wise Philosopher . . . . Though these Letters be neither Greek nor Latin, nor written by a Christian, they contain nothing Barbarous, and though the Ignorant be in great Numbers amongst the Turks, there are yet Men of great Understanding that write the Annals of the Ottoman Empire.' *The Turkish Spy* did make a contribution to place the Moslem in a more favourable light.

As an influence on subsequent literature, *The Turkish Spy* is the seminal work for the genre of the foreign observer. The debt that Montesquieu, D'Argens and Goldsmith owe to Marana has already been mentioned. Immediately after the publication of Marana's letters an extraordinary number of 'spy' books appeared, all of them based in some degree upon Marana's innovation. Gatien de Courtilz's *French Spy* appeared in English in 1700; Ned Ward's *London Spy* enjoyed seven editions (first ed., 1698-1700). *The Northern Atalantis: or York Spy* of Captain Bland was published in 1713; and thereupon followed *The German Spy* in 1738, *The Jewish Spy* in 1739, and Samuel Madden's *Memoirs of the*

Twentieth Century (1733), which is also in the mode of *The Turkish Spy*. And in 1709 there appeared Charles Gildon's *The Golden Spy* with the interesting subtitle, 'A Political Journal of the British Nights Entertainments of War and Peace, and Love and Politics,' a significant cross breeding of *The Arabian Nights* with *The Turkish Spy*.

Besides the direct effect on other 'spy' letters, an indirect influence may be perceived in the periodical essay. Addison and Steele may have imitated some of the techniques and features that Marana used in his letters. The basic unit of both *The Turkish Spy* and the *Spectator* is a short essay; plot and characterization are superimposed on both collections to provide a fictional appeal. In both, a shy, inactive observer who is not given to talk provides a mask behind which the author may satirize, convey information, theorize, and in general comment on his culture. The range of topics in both is wide – from the most ludicrous and trivial to the central questions of the day; and finally a clever vein of satire runs through both collections, in which the affectations of contemporary Europeans are ridiculed by an acute, somewhat removed observer. Moreover, Addison wrote two satiric letters in the manner of *The Turkish Spy*. In *Spectator* No. 50 we are told that four American Indian (Iroquois) kings had visited London a few years before (1710); one of them, King Sa Ga Yean Qua Rosh Tow, left behind a manuscript of letters containing his impressions of the metropolis. Like Marana, Mr. Spectator claims to have found a bundle of papers written by a foreigner, which are translated into English for the edification of his audience. The king's letter, redolent of Marana's satire of Paris, directs its attack on the dismaying absurdities of Addison's London. The other pseudo-letter in the Marana strain is a letter of the Ambassador of Bantam, who served in Charles II's court. In *Spectator* No. 557 Addison made it serve as a satirical vehicle for his desire for plain and truthful speaking. The Ambassador interprets the civilities of social intercourse at their literal level and creates embarrassment when his host offers him his house, and the Ambassador takes his English host at his word by carting away the furniture.

The evidence is perhaps too slight for us to assert positively that *The Spy* influenced the periodical essay form which

Steele and Addison perfected. However, there was an obvious need for some kind of journalistic commentary on the society of Queen Anne, and *The Turkish Spy* no doubt prepared the taste for the genial satire and ironic mode of the *Tatler* and later the *Spectator*. We can at least claim that Marana's letters either directly or indirectly influenced Addison's pseudo-letters.

One of the main reasons for the neglect of *The Turkish Spy* is its vast length – 600 letters in eight volumes. Naturally, these letters are not of equal merit. Some are tedious recitals of the events of Europe set down in chronicle fashion; others are long-winded explanations of Christian or Moslem dogma and ritual. But there is a rich vein of satire, fictional intrigue and adventure, and philosophic rumination, which, if carefully extracted, might give the reader a flavour of the whole without slighting the spirit of the work. The principle of selection employed here has been based upon the assumption that the greatness and wide appeal of *The Spy* lies not in its historical reportage, which constitutes more than half of the collection, but in its literary merit, its satire and fiction. As an historical source for the seventeenth century, *The Spy* is in many instances inaccurate and superficial; it can only be of passing interest to the historian. But as a literary document, *The Spy* has obvious attractions.

In fact, there are strains of subjects or themes – similar groupings may be found in the *Spectator*, Montesquieu's *Persian Letters* and Goldsmith's *Citizen of the World* – which can be extrapolated without harming the continuity of the whole. The purpose then of this edition is to separate the more significant letters, especially those which have some kind of unifying theme from the less exciting and routine in the collection. The organization here follows the chronological pattern laid down in the original. The letters may be classified, however, by their themes. The most satiric deal with religious matters: Mahmut's contrasting of Christianity with Islam. Another group deals with his discovery of Descartes and the sceptical philosophy of antiquity and the seventeenth century. A third concerns his personal adventures: his love affair, narrow escapes from the law, his melancholy old age and increasing difficulties with intrigue in the Turkish seraglio. And a fourth group contains legendary materials, like the Wandering Jew legend or the story of the man washed up on the coast of Holland. The last type of essay may be termed humanitarian or polemical, in which Mahmut argues against the Cartesian view that animals have no souls, or where in certain letters he rhapsodizes over his love of nature.

The basis for this edition has been the first complete English edition (1691-94), which is in the British Museum. I have checked this against later eighteenth-century editions which were available to me. I have excluded Defoe's *Continuation of the Turkish Spy* because it is not an integral part of *The Spy* and therefore deserves no place in this selection. The text in this edition has been modernized; I have taken the liberty of updating the spelling, punctuation and paragraphing but have been scrupulously careful to keep the original sense of each sentence. The syntax of the English version is occasionally weak or grammatically incorrect, yet I have made no editorial improvements, except where the meaning was distressingly ambiguous or obscure, or where there was an obvious typographical error. As to the annotations, I fall back to Dr. Johnson for my defence:

> It is impossible for an expositor not to write too little for some, and too much for others. He can only judge what is necessary by his own experience; and how long soever he may deliberate, will at last explain many lines which the learned will think impossible to be mistaken, and omit many for which the ignorant will want his help. These are censures merely relative, and must be quietly endured.[5]

ARTHUR J. WEITZMAN
Northeastern University

[5] 'Preface to Shakespeare', in *The Works of Johnson*, (London, 1801), II, 127.

Mahmut the Arabian, and the vilest of the Grand Signior's slaves, to Hasnadarbassy, Chief Treasurer to His Highness at Constantinople

Volume I, Book I, Letter I

I have at length finished my journey after one hundred and forty days march, arriving at Paris the fourth of this present moon, according to the Christian style.[1] I made no stay in Hungary, yet sojourned one and forty days at Vienna, where I observed all the motions of that court, according as I was ordered; of which I shall not now speak, having given a full account to the ever-invincible Vizier Azem. Being but newly arrived, I scarce know anybody and am as little known myself. I have suffered my hair to grow a little below my ears, and as to my lodging, 'tis in the house of an old Fleming, where my room is so small that jealousy itself can scarce enter. And because I will have no enemy near me, I will therefore admit of no servant.

Being of low stature, of an ill-favoured countenance, ill-shaped and by nature not given to talkativeness, I shall the better conceal myself. Instead of my name, Mahmut the Arabian, I have taken on me that of Titus the Moldavian; and with a little cassock of black serge, which is the habit I have chosen, I make two figures, being in heart what I ought to be, but outwardly and in appearance what I never intend.

Carcoa at Vienna furnishes me with bread and water, supplying me with just enough to live, and I desire no more. The eggs here are dearer than pullets with you. It is to him that I will address my letters.

[1] Marana introduces an exotic colouration here by the use of moon instead of month. He is probably referring to the custom of the Chinese and other Orientals who divide the year by the moon instead of the calendar. At the end of each letter, he gives the number of the moon, which in this letter corresponds to our ninth month, or September 11, 1637.

Eliachim, the Jew, came to see me, who seems to be sufficiently informed of what passes in the world and will be a useful man to me. Yet I will never trust him more than I need. Although I have a dispensation from the mufti for lying and false oaths, which I shall be obliged to make, yet I have still some qualms on my mind. However, our sovereign must be served, and I can commit no sin, so long as this is my sole end. As for the intelligence which I shall send, none shall come from me but what is true, unless I be first deceived myself.

It will be hard for me to mention anything considerable of a city which is not to be viewed in one day, I having been there but seven. 'Tis peopled like the borders of the sea with sand, the inhabitants lodging to the very cock-lofts; and houses are built on the bridges.

This great city is divided by a river, and both parts of it are joined by a great bridge of stone, well built and very stately. In the midst of it is seen a horse of brass with the statue of Henry IV, which bestrides it; whose heroic actions have justly surnamed him the Great. He seems still to command this capital of the kingdom. The other bridges being full of houses are not seen, appearing as if they had been made for the city, not the river.

The king's palace is an ancient building, yet retains a certain majesty, which denotes the grandeur of its master. Within it appears a desert, for the court is always abroad or in the army.

A church-man, termed at Rome a cardinal, is the principal minister of state; his name is Armand du Plessis, Cardinal of Richelieu. He is esteemed a great politician, a man of wit and action, and every way fitted for the place he holds.

All the people make vows to heaven that their king may become a father, for the Queen has been barren these many years.

I go into the churches as a Christian, and when I seem attentive to their mysteries, I hold our sacred Alcoran in my hands, addressing my prayers to our Holy Prophet; and thus behaving myself, I give no offence. I avoid disputes, mind my own concerns and do nothing which may endanger my salvation.

Preserve thy health and expect to hear from me as oft as

the interest of our great and mighty monarch requires, who is the master of my life and affections.

I make thee no present of my services, for they be devoted to that Lord, whose slave thou art, as well as I. The letters I write for the future shall be directed to the ministers of the divan. [2]

Live with the piety of a good Mussulman and the prudence of an able minister, and preserve the treasure as thine heart, which thou knowest is the last expiring.

Paris, the 11th of the 9th moon of the year 1637, according to the Christian style.

To Muzlu, Reis Effendi,[1] Principal Secretary of the Ottoman Empire

Volume I, Book I, Letter VIII

This is the second letter which I have writ to thee. My dispatches hitherto have not been filled with things of great importance, by reason I have not yet had time to learn them. I wish greatly to write what may please thee. Receive therefore what I offer kindly and be persuaded that I fear thy censures as much as if I did not deserve them.

I live here according to the instructions which were given me, and live easy enough. The country is good and fat, the men are good companions, frank and seem discreet. I have not as yet any acquaintance with the women, and yet it is necessary I find means to introduce myself into their companies. It is a sex that will not pardon when they think themselves neglected. They are proper to discover things one would know and to say them when one would have them published; and likewise, they as much penetrate into the secrets of hearts as the most refined and spiritual courtiers. Further, there are many of them that can conceal nothing but what they do not know.

2 'The Grand Signior's Privy Council'.
1 Foreign minister of the Ottoman Empire.

I frequent not the monks but when necessitated. If I see them, it is to seem devout, upon design of being introduced by them into the house of a minister of state, when I teach his son the Greek language.

We must not expect to find here the great tranquillity which is at Constantinople. The town is so full of coaches, of horses and wagons that the noise surpasses imagination. Thou wilt certainly find it strange that men who are in health and have no fore legs, should find themselves to be drawn in an engine with four wheels. But I more wonder to see the same men can resolve to suffer the inconveniency of the noise and of the expense which they throw away out of vanity. The more moderate French, who do not approve of this luxury, say that in the time of Henry III there were but three coaches in Paris, where of two were the king's. But the number is now so great that they are not to be counted.

I can tell thee no more of the genius of the French; thou knowest it perfectly. There is in all their actions a spirit very delicate and an activity like that of fire. It seems as if none but them knew the short duration of man's life; they do everything with so much haste, as if they had but one day to live. If they go on foot, they run; if they ride, they fly; and if they speak they eat up half their words. They love new inventions passionately. I can say nothing certain of their fidelity, though methinks we might suspect such who do not read as they write, nor write as they speak. They love monies, which they look upon as the first matter and second cause of all things; they well nigh adore it, and that is the original sin of all nations.

Paris ought to be destroyed to enrich many cities in Europe in order that thou mayest comprehend her greatness her traffic, how rich she is, and how all sorts of arts do flourish in her.

The French nobility is always ready to get on horseback at their king's command; they love war so well that it is to be supposed we should have enough to do with them if we were so near them as the Spaniards, and they did not want infantry.

I shall hereafter observe every circumstance with so much care, as well in this kingdom as elsewhere, that nothing shall escape me. In the meantime, I shall endeavour to get acquaintance but shall want more money than is allowed me to answer what is expected from me. Two sequins[2] a day are more than enough to support a man that will live like a cynic,[3] but not sufficient to introduce me into their houses, to dive into their secrets and enable me to discover the affairs of most importance, according to my commission, so that thou must assist me to obtain more.

I hope to succeed in my employment if thou dost not refuse me thy assistance, finding no difficulty in the execution of my orders but the necessity of lying when I pass for a Christian. I fancy I see Muhammad in a rage and believe my soul lost, though I am from my heart more faithful in my religion than all the Muhammadans put together. Seeing I am resolved to do a thing to which I have so much aversion, thou mayest be assured I will bear all the evil imaginable that can happen to me with firmness, though in all appearance I ought to hope nothing but good.

Deliver, I beseech thee, this enclosed letter into the hands of the most venerable mufti and extort from him, if possible, a solution of my doubts. There is nothing that touches me nearer than what regards my religion and with my religion the service of my emperor.

Paris, the 15th of the 11th moon of the year 1637.

To the Mufti, Prince of the Religion of the Turks

Volume I, Book I, Letter IX

I will die a true Mussulman, though I should see all the crosses of the Carthaginians set up for my punishment and had before my eyes all the instruments of the most cruel tortures that the enemies of holy religion could invent. But seeing there is no question at present of dying but of living to serve my emperor, I beg thee, sovereign prelate, that thou wilt be pleased to conserve my innocence in giving me an

[2] A sequin was worth about eight shillings.
[3] That is, a life of extreme asceticism.

ample absolution or in imposing a penance that may cancel all my crimes.

Paris hath always been the residence of the kings of France; whence it is that the exercise of no other religion but the Christian is suffered there. And those who acknowledge the Bishop of Rome for their head have the principal management of the affairs of religion; and 'tis with these that the rites of the Latin Church are more strictly observed.

I live here in appearance as if I were a Christian and a Catholic. I enter into their churches, assist at their ceremonies, kneel before the cross; and I appear with great devotion and humility before the images, which are had here in veneration. I know well enough (if the life which I lead be not permitted me as advantageous to the affairs of state and the person of the Grand Signior) that I commit sacrilege, acting as I do contrary to the precepts of Muhammad expressed in his Alcoran.

I am guilty of violating the law which is prescribed me and deserve death, if thou dost not by approving this life I am obliged to lead, assure me of both my salvation and life. 'Tis true, thou hast already given me absolution from all the false oaths I shall be necessitated to take when they are for the service of my master; but I am not assured this absolution extends far enough to secure my conscience when I abuse holy things.[1] 'Tis thy province to decide this point, which is of such importance to my repose; which makes me expect thy resolves with impatience, if thou thinkest a faithful Mussulman, who conserves his religion in his heart and lives as I do among the enemies of the law, worthy this grace. The interest of my conscience obliges me to demand after what manner I ought to govern myself, when I see them who are effectually what I seem to be, practise the same acts of religion.

The French will in a little time celebrate their carnival or shrove-tide. As soon as it is done, the Catholics think of fasting, having first assisted at a ceremony where ashes were put upon their foreheads to make them remember they were formed out of the dust and shall return to dust again. It is at this time they go to hear sermons, their priests explaining

[1] A veiled attack on the Catholic practice, particularly among the Jesuits, of absolving sin for political expediency.

that which they call the Gospel, and they frequent the church more than ordinary. They apply themselves oftener to works of piety; and having purged their conscience by penances and secret confessions, which one man makes to another, they eat of a certain bread, which they call the sacrament of the Eucharist, where, after certain words pronounced by their priest, they will have the body of their messiah to be really present under those apparent species.

This ceremony is an obligation that good Christians cannot dispense with, it being ordained by their law and by their great prelate, the Bishop of Rome. They commonly call it confession and communicating and keeping Easter. Ought I to hazard myself in committing so horrid a sacrilege and tempt, as I may say, God by so great a superstition and so irritate our great Prophet? It may be said, perhaps, that many Jews have done the same thing and do it every day to preserve themselves more securely. But how many of them have been chastised by visible miracles from heaven and undergone terrible punishments by the ordinances of the Judges?

All these reflections trouble my spirit, O Holy Primate of the most divine law. I do not think it lawful to mock the mysteries of any religion whatsoever. The God of the Christians is the same that we adore, but their religion is quite opposite to ours. There is a great difference between their Jesus crucified with all the ignominies possible, as these infidels do believe, and a Muhammad immortal and triumphant, a great legislator and the angular stone of the first empire of the world.

Give me then positive orders, to the end I may be eased of my scruples and may believe that what thou permitest may be an effect of thy justice and not of a toleration which may be pernicious to me.

It is true, I may wave all these things in feigning to have done them; but it will be more advantageous for my affairs not to exempt myself, if that may be without a crime.

Teach then a most obedient slave what thou shalt believe most conducible to the glory of God, and most profitable for the service of our sovereign Lord. I do not send thee my doubts to puzzle thee but to draw from thy great and sublime genius such lights as may dissipate the darkness I live in.

This done, Sovereign Prelate, remember thy humble servant and pray our Holy Prophet that he will keep me from perishing.

Paris, the 15th of the 11th moon of the year 1637.

To Bedredin, Superior of the Convent of Dervishes[1] of Cogni in Anatolia

Volume I, Book I, Letter XI

I write to thee who art venerable by thy age and hast made so many long voyages. Thou hast been so many times in pilgrimage to Arabia, Tartary, Persia and the Indies, always barefoot and begging out of pure devotion to the Saint of Saints, our great Prophet Muhammad. I address this letter to thee: Thee who bearest the scars of twenty-five great wounds: Thee who hast prayed fifty-nine times in the most retired sanctuary of Mecca and hast lived more than seventy years of religion amongst the dervishes, where thy merit caused thee to be elected Superior of the Convent in Anatolia.

Thou knowest well that I serve him who is arbitrator of the destiny of the universe; I mean the sultan, sovereign of the world. Learn what I heard here from the mouth of the Christians, and pardon me if I have not sufficiently answered them. Do not accuse me to have deserved death for having seemingly cursed our holy law and Him that gave it us; and if I have seemed to reject His successors, Ali, Osman and Omar,[2] it was expedient that I should commit some evil, not to lose the opportunity of doing much good. Thou knowest well I am destined to serve, and that being absolved from all the perjuries I shall commit, I may transgress the law by being permitted to lie. That suffices: read my letter and learn

[1] Equivalent to a Christian order of monks.

[2] Islam is divided into two great sects, the Sunni and Shi'a. Mahmut like most Turks was a Sunni, while the Persian were generally Shiites. The Sunnis claim that the first three Caliphs, Abu Bakr, Omar and Osman were the legitimate heirs of the Prophet; the Shiites believe that these Caliphs were usurpers, and that the true heir was Ali, the cousin and son-in-law of Muhammed. Mahmut seems to reject all of the heirs by taking a Christian disguise.

how far their malice does extend who are enemies to our religion.

To instruct thee better in what has happened to me, I must tell thee that amongst these infidels there is an order of religion much in vogue called the company of Jesus; wherein there is an infinite company of men, some more capable than others in all sorts of sciences, sacred and profane; and, according to appearance ought to be very recommendable for the holiness of their manners. These religious ones, who are ordinarily called Jesuits, have the education of the youth in almost all the cities of Europe as well as in the Indies. Many excellent wits are brought up on the seminaries they have established. When they preach, the people crowd to their sermons. They are the confessors of almost all the princes and monarchs of Christendom, who discover to them their weaknesses, their sins and the vices whereunto they are inclined; and receive from them upon their (the prince's and monarch's) knees like slaves such penance as they (the Jesuits) think fit to impose on them.

A man may say of them that being dispensers of penances, they are also the masters of recompenses. They are habited in a long vest of black wool, which descends to their heels. They go not barefoot, but their vestments are simple. They observe great modesty in all their actions; they march with gravity, never go alone and suffer not their beards to grow. They apply themselves to edify the good and to correct the bad.

The founder of this order was a soldier called Ignatius. The Spaniards will have him to have been of their nation, and the French affirm that he is of that part of Navarre which is subject to the crown of France. If thou wouldst have me speak the truth, I think this founder was a good man, seeing all his disciples are men of good example, of great modesty in their actions and very discreet in all their undertakings. This Ignatius began to study his grammar in his thirty-seventh year, which would make one believe he took less pains to become a saint than a scholar. His enemies call his disciples the politicians of the Church; and I on the contrary call them the camels of Esau, because in bearing the burden of the affairs of their religion, they are loaded more than others and forced to couch under their burdens. There is one thing seems strange in them, to wit: that they should name themselves, the Religious of the Society of Jesus, as if they had a design to distinguish themselves from other Christians. This title, which is particular to them, ought not only to agree to all the other religious persons but to all the followers of the Nazarite.

If they follow the precepts of their father Ignatius, thou must needs approve their way of living. He has taught no other way than that of obedience to those who profess his order. He ordains that those who enter into his Society do abandon themselves to the discretion of their superiors. And they affirm that if the Pope commands them to pass the sea in a vessel without oars, without sails and without a rudder, they would obey and must pass. And some having reproached them that there was folly in such blind obedience, they answer that wisdom ought to be observed in the Commandments, and that it ought not to be searched in obedience.[3] Make reflections upon this sentence, which is conformable to our laws.

To inform thee of the power and greatness of this order, it suffices to tell thee that during the sixteen years that this soldier governed it, he saw a hundred colleges in Italy, in Germany, in France and in Spain; and that in Rome, which was founded by Borgia, hath been, as may be said, the parent of all the rest. Judge thereby the number of their houses and disciples.

Having one day met with one of this society who understood the Oriental languages and who, conversing with me, did not believe he discoursed with a Mussulman, I heard him vomit injurious and fearful imprecations against Muhammad, against his law and against all true believers. I have so much horror to write to thee all he said that I will tell thee but some few of them, the rather to divert thee by the knowledge of the errors of our enemies, and also that thou mayest not be afflicted at some things not very reasonable which are observed in many of the precepts of the law we follow. Let this be said, as if I had not spoken it, seeing I pour frankly the secrets of my heart into thy bosom, no way doubting that thou knowest to be silent in what may cause my death. This Jesuit maintains that Mussulmans are not wise in following the

[3] That is, we are truly obedient when we do not examine too closely the Commandments.

precepts of a drunkard who forbad drinking of wine and committed excesses himself, when he thought he was unobserved. He maintains further that it is foolish to give credit to such a fellow who makes a paradise to consist of beautiful women, where one may abandon himself to all sorts of pleasure and debauchery; and that he hath not foreseen a hell where he and all his followers ought to suffer the pains due to their crimes. He adds further that one must be very foolish to adore a blasphemer who hath commanded his law should be maintained by the sword, when it could not be supported by reason.

The father did not leave off so. He said that seeing the Alcoran is filled with dreams, with bestialities, with blasphemies and impurities, the muftis, doctors and interpreters of the law must be in a great blindness not to condemn a possessed, an enchanter who gives for the precepts of his religion the committing of violence, robberies and all that may satisfy, the most irregular appetites. What extravagancy, urged he, to adore the hell of so vile a slave as Muhammad, and to believe upon his report that Jacob's father was his porter, to defy his camel and to place it in heaven? He adds further that there is nothing so absurd as to command the Turks to wash their bodies when their souls are defiled with filth; to give them at the same time charity by precept and to command them robberies by devotion. It seems also to him foolish to believe that Muhammad is the only true prophet, the only agreeable person to God, and to swear afterwards by 124,000 prophets. He still entertains me with this sort of discourse.

But all this, O great Dervish, is nothing; he vomits yet this damnable heresy: that the wickedest wretches and the most detestable that ever lived were Judas, Muhammad and Luther; that these two last, as most impious, are the more tormented in hell. Judas, he said, suffered less pains, because if he betrayed his Lord, he was one of the instruments of the redemption of all mankind; whereas the others in damning themselves, damned also an infinite number of other people. This Jesuit would have continued his blasphemies if Cardinal Richelieu in whose antechamber we were, had not come out of his closet to go to the king.

I had been silent all this while, because he gave me not a moment's liberty to speak. At length he asked me at parting, if I was not of his sentiments? And I answered precisely thus: 'My father, if thou art a good man, I approve what thou sayest, because thou speakest out of true zeal; but if thou beest a hypocrite, I disapprove all, because thou shalt be damned with Muhammad and all the Mussulmans.'

The Jesuit smiled, not comprehending the venom which lay hid in my answer. But dost thou not believe, thou, who art a dervish, the most illuminated, that a man, of what religion soever he be, provided he be a good man, may be happy after his death? Tell me, I pray thee, thy opinion herein, it is a point very important to be decided.

As for me, I begin really to think that there may be saints, even amongst the Christians, as there are amongst us. I have seen and understood many things that denote true piety in some of them, and we must acknowledge that the precepts of their law have somewhat of justice; and if they be well observed, they seem no less holy to me than our own. They have one article that puzzles me. They affirm there is but one truth, so that we are lost if we are not Christians, or they are damned if they are not Muhammadans.

And this is what I had to say to thee in this matter; but I shall not end this discourse without some violent scruples of conscience. Pray the great God with me that he will illuminate my understanding with inward light until the man promised by our Holy Prophet, the man I say who ought to be born of his race, be descended upon the earth, and who is to see all kings humbled in his presence and to unite with Jesus the two religions that they may make but one.

In the meantime let us live as honest men who have sin in horror like the plague, which poisons the soil and apply ourselves, as much as in us lies, to what is truly good. And above all things, let us carefully observe this precept, writ in the book of their law, but is not always imprinted in their hearts: never do to others, no not thy enemies, that which thou wouldst not have done to thyself. A duke of Guise [4] gave an example of this to all France, and 'tis what thou oughtest to preach in the vast empire of the Mussulman. This prince sur-

[4] Probably François de Lorraine, Duc de Guise, 1519-63.

prised a villain that would have assassinated him, who confessed that the interest of his religion (which was that of Calvin) had obligated him to form a design to take the duke away, to deliver the Calvinists and those of his party from so great an enemy. The duke instead of causing him to suffer the pains due to so black an enterprise, pardoned him, contenting himself (the duke) to tell him: 'Friend, if thy religion obliged thee to kill me without hearing me, my religion obliges me to give thee thy life and liberty now I have heard thee. Go thy ways and amend thyself.' This prince was then general of Charles IX's army.

Sage Bedredin, our Muhammad never showed such generous sentiments when he prescribed in his law this precept against Christians that had never offended him: when you encounter the infidels kill them and cut off their heads; imprison them and keep them in chains until they have paid their ransoms or till you find it requisite to set them at liberty. Persecute them until they have all submitted or are entirely overthrown.

Observe in this letter what may be of use to thee. Pardon my friendship, the frank manner of writing and remember in thy prayers, who personates a Christian and is in his heart a most faithful Mussulman. If it be in thy power to succour me, never do me any injury. God protect and govern thy great age to the last moment.

Paris, the 28th of the 2nd moon of the year 1638.

To the Kaimakam [1]

Volume I, Book I, Letter XXVIII

That which hath been so long expected is at length happened: the queen is brought to bed of a dauphin. [2] The king is a father; thy kingdom seems to desire nothing more, and the people witness their joy by a thousand differing festivities.

[1] Kaimakam means officer; in the seventeenth century a kaimakam was appointed to rule Constantinople in the Sultan's absence.
[2] The future Louis XIV.

The men, the women, the children and the aged run through the streets as at bacchanals. They rejoice with their friends; they go to church and thank God, as if a messiah had been born to them.

All the priests praised God in their temples for such a present, and the monks not so content deafen the people with the noise of their bells and do more than the drums and trumpets of the soldiers and all the cannon of the citadel and arsenal. I did in company of others what I should not have dared to perform if I had been alone or had not been observed.

Those who affirmed the queen would be brought to bed of a son pretend now they had been advertised by some divine revelation and will pass for prophets; amongst these are many religious people. Observe how far their superstition extends.

The Court has dispatched many expresses into all the provinces of France, and others have been sent to all the ambassadors to give notice of his birth to their respective princes.

A priest who is a bishop hath baptized this child without any ceremony in presence of the chancellor of France, the princes, princesses and grandees of the kingdom, the farther solemnity being reserved for another time. The king commanded *Te Deum* to be publicly sung, being the hymn which is usual to all Christians to thank God for extraordinary successes.

Nothing is seen in the streets of Paris but bonfires and fountains of wine, which run day and night. The people testify their joy and the fires are so great on all sides that it looks as if the city were to be reduced to ashes.

Amongst so many subjects of joy, the king has wherewith to afflict him, having been for some days tormented with a violent tertian ague. It cannot be but he must have his spirits agitated with so many wars at once. He has armies against Spain, in Flanders, Italy, Burgundy and the Empire in Germany, without mentioning his naval forces and the designs and pretensions which he doth not yet declare. Thou mayest be confident that leagues will be formed against him and conspiracies against his state. The great ones of the kingdom are not asleep, having long since had designs to humble the favourites and ministers whose deportments displeased them, and to make themselves masters of affairs and the government.

I have a piece of news to tell thee, but receive it as coming from a woman, not Mahmut. I seldom send that for assured which in appearance is not truth. What I am going to say will undoubtedly seem ridiculous.

The women give out that the dauphin has teeth and the nurses will witness it. Those who easily believe wonders publish this as a most certain truth. The people, who add faith to the most incredible things, raise stories upon this and are full of pretended auguries. But there being no law that obliges us to believe that which we find incredible, thou mayest therefore receive this news as thou pleasest and look upon it as useless, and excuse me.

They give the king the title of Saint, which they add to that of Just, because of his great piety in devoting his son before he was born to the Virgin (whom the Christians say is the mother of their Messiah) with his kingdom, people and person. He hath put them under the protection of the Mother of God, whom he has made appear by prayers, processions and extraordinary alms.

This ceremony is ordinary enough with these infidels, who by an inexcusable idolatry devote their towns and dedicate their temples to men that are dead, whom they call saints, worshipping them afterwards upon their altars and invoking them in their distress.

I have nothing more at present to write to thee; God give thee always the grace to be just to thyself and others.

Paris, the 16th of the 9th moon of the year 1638.

To Melec Amer

Volume I, Book II, Letter IX

Paris, where I live, is a very healthful city, and so are all the places thereabouts free from pestilential airs; and yet there oft happens sudden deaths, as well as at Constantinople; and they die here likewise of joy. I will relate to thee what I have partly seen, and not what I have heard, to happen in London, the most ancient and chief city of the kingdom of England. A rich old man falling sick and lying on his deathbed sent to his only son living in Paris, where he spent his time in pleasure, to come over that the old man might with his estate give him his blessing. Think what news this was to a young man to whom the life of a father was troublesome as being an obstacle to his liberty; and who waited his father's death to take his swing of all the pleasures which his corrupt nature makes him respect as his sovereign good. This young man intending to get upon horseback to run where he was called found himself embarked for a voyage which he did not design to make; he fell dead on the place, and I saw him in the same instant wherein he was living and healthful to expire. Were I of the sect of our philosopher Muslaadin Saadi, [1] I would tell thee, it matters not whether one dies suddenly or languish a long time, whether a man dies in his bed or at the gallows. But I being none of Zeno's disciples and knowing no peripatetic or philosopher amongst so many sects that were in Greece who disputed whether life or death is to be preferred: so, expect not from me any arguings on the morals of those Greeks, nor yet of the Persians. But if death be such a terrible thing, endeavour to live in such a manner that it may never affright thee when it shall approach thee or when thou shalt see it invade others; expecting it at all times and in all places. Dost thou know by what herb or by what secret magic charm I do not fear it? 'Tis by the leading of an innocent life.

Here is published, and that with great reason, the last words of a man of great birth, who died when he was very old by a wound he received. He had served divers kings in places of the highest trust, and being mortally wounded in a battle, mark what he said to those that exhorted him to die like a good Christian and with the same courage he had showed in life. His reply was that a man who had lived well fourscore years cannot be to seek how to die well for a quarter of an hour. This great man, who was a famous soldier, was also a true philosopher, and I might say he was a saint, had he been of our religion. I believe he was a most edifying spectacle and

[1] A reference to the great Persian poet Muslih-al-Din Sadi of Shiraz. He is no doubt termed philosopher because of the practical moralistic intent in his writings.

the more considerable inasmuch as the example he gave of dying well is more valuable than that which he gave in so many battles of courageous fighting. He was called Anne de Montmorency, Constable of France, whose life I had the curiosity of reading, being found in the history of the civil wars of that kingdom.

But before I end this letter, let me denote to thee the difference there is between the effects of grief and joy. The messenger from England of whom I already spake finding at his return the old man whom he had left dying still alive, he gave him such a strange stroke by telling to him the death of his son, that grief having vanquished the assault of death, restored to this unhappy old man that strength he had lost in his health; so that coming himself some days after to Paris, I saw him bewail the loss of his only son.

He that said heretofore, 'A man should learn all his life to die well,' uttered no strange doctrine. Our days will last long enough if we be ready to say at all times, 'We have lived enough.' And if we love as we ought our great emperor, who is invincible, holy and the most just among men; and if we observe what a French peasant said to all those that passed before his door, 'Never deny your assistance, nor never do anybody any hurt.'

Let thou and I number our days (as was preached heretofore in the seraglio to the white eunuchs[2] by the Persian, whose eyes were put out because he saw too clearly). He always insisted on the shortness, uncertainty and vanity of human life. He said, "'Twas short, considering what we had to do in it; uncertain as to what we shall do in it; and always mixed with what we have done and what remains for us to do.' Teach not thy son Mehemet yet, for whom thou hast so much affection, these precepts. Children have not that ripeness of judgment as is necessary to hear discourses of death; they are too hard bits for their stomachs, which indeed old men can hardly digest, and which they swallow not without feeling all the bitterness of them.

[2] In the Moslem palace there were two orders of eunuchs, white and Negro. The Negro eunuchs superintended the harem, while the white served in the palace grounds. Even so, the white eunuchs were looked upon with suspicion as being attractive to the sultan's concubines. The white eunuchs were therefore warned about their prying eyes.

I pray God keep the imperial city with those that dwell in it and shelter it from the storms which fall on infamous cities; and I beseech Him thou mayest live without offence, that thou mayest never fear death.

Paris, the 25th of the last moon of the year 1638.

To Enguruli Emin Mehemet Sheik, a Man of the Law

Volume I, Book II, Letter X

When I parted from Constantinople, I gave thee a stone of excellent virtue against the gravel, and thou presented me with a paper which was to secure me against all bodily evils. Time only can decide which of us two made the best present to his friend. Thou hast pretended to teach me in a few words how to live amongst the infidels, and I thought in giving thee a stone to give thee a remedy against the distemper thou art troubled with. I never turn myself towards the place where Mecca lies but I remember where thy amity began and how far since it has been extended towards me. Absence has not lessened thy kindness, nor hindered thee from sending me thy grave counsels; but I am as yet too young to set about preparing myself for the other world and too vigorous and healthful to hearken to thy serious and melancholy discourses.

I wish thou were but at Paris, where thou wouldst see a great number of people who sell a most precious thing to purchase a vain and fantastic title. How many with great earnestness sue for places from the king that they may seek their deaths! Perhaps thou never thoughtest there were any such kind of people. What dost thou think then of soldiery in general? – are they any other than martyrs of ambition, to whom one would think life is a burden? 'Tis a sad spectacle to see how many dead lie in the streets or carried on the shoulders of their friends or kinsmen to their graves. Yet this is so common a thing in Paris that the people make no wonder of it.

This way of living obliges me to do as the rest. I begin to

consider that what happens to another may happen to me; there's no avoiding one's destiny. This preface is only to bring in a story of this king's goodness, which ought to be an example to all princes. The French have need of fresh soldiers to fill up so many troops as they continually entertain. Not long since then there came a man full of years and overwhelmed with despair who desired to be lifted in this prince's service. To obtain what he desired he told the king that he was the father of twelve children, seven of which were daughters who were marriageable; that he could no longer live, being not able to maintain such a great family; and that being ignorant as yet how to die he would learn it in the king's service. The prince having appointed him to wait upon him one day privately in his closet, thus spake to him:

'Thy despair makes thee desirous to be lifted amongst my soldiers, and charity obliges me to retain thee amongst the citizens. Those that are fools when they enter into troops commonly come out wiser, because they learn several things of which they were before ignorant. But as to thy part, what time hast thou to learn who art ready to fall dead at the same moment thou enterest into the school? Yet I receive thee. Take this sword; go and combat thy folly and take this purse to succour thy family and be cured. But if thou art wise say not from whom thou hast received thy cure.'

I know not what sum was in the purse, no more than I do of what metal the sword was. But I have this story from an officer of the king's closet, with whom I have that strict converse, that he told me this passage as soon as ever it happened.

I'll tell thee, if thou wilt, some of the principal passages of my life, for I conceal nothing from the ministers and the most venerable mufti, who knows all that I do. I adore the Sovereign Master of the universe and have a great veneration for His Holy Prophet. I never defiled my hands in blood; neither have I ever violated any man's bed. I easily forgive my enemies and hate above all things the crime of slandering. If this be not sufficient to merit salvation, I do not know what is. These are all my virtues; as to other qualifications, I have none. I have no knack at thieving; my talents lie not that way. Were I qualified, I might, as most do, devise means to put my art in practice. But living according to these aforementioned maxims, I doubt not but I shall find entrance into that paradise where faithful souls will enjoy a perfect happiness and set their feet on the necks of the enemies of our holy law, where they shall suffer neither hunger, thirst nor nakedness – free from the parching heats of the sun and the pinching sharpness of the colds caused by the moon – where under the agreeable shade of trees they shall gather the most precious fruit, standing, sitting or lying, and drink in cups of gold or emerald the most delicious liquors which spring from a clear fountain and be served with inconceivable magnificence. In this divine place, they shall be more beautiful and shining than the stars in the firmament whose brightness enlightens the darkest night; their robes shall be of finest silk, of a colour more green and pleasing to the eye than the herbs which spring up in May; and shall further receive from the hands of God a portion more sweet and delicious than can be imagined as a recompense for the good they have done during their abode amongst men. Thou knowest 'tis impossible for me to go on pilgrimage to Mecca, seeing I am obliged to abide at Paris. Thou knowest also, I cannot give myself to contemplation, being forced to lead an active life. Serving in France, as I must do our puissant and invincible emperor, I must not remain among the dervishes, who pass their days in solitude. Thou seest here what my condition will bear; accuse me not therefore for neglecting the pious advices thou givest me. I forget not so much death as I forget that I must die.

Be informed of this from me, there's not a town in the world where people do learn better to live ill than at Paris; neither is there any place where they are better taught to die. I need not tell thee, here are public academies (as were heretofore amongst the Egyptians) wherein dead bodies lie exposed to public view to make men remember the indispensable necessity of dying. But I may tell thee there's no day wherein in this great town a great quantity of fools do not teach wiser than themselves things they have been ever ignorant of, for the gibbets and scaffolds set up for the punishment of the guilty, hinder the destruction of a great many people whose innocency is preserved by these kinds of spectacles. Here the poor, who had heretofore plentiful subsistences, teach good husbandry; the proud, humility; the debauched with women, chastity.

I believe there is no part of the world where there are more thieves and pickpockets who do their work with greater art and subtilty; they exercise their craft in all places – in the churches as well as the streets, markets and bridges; so that our people of the Morea,[1] who are thought by us to be such great masters in this science, are mere asses to them. Adieu.

Paris, the 10th of the 1st moon of the year 1639.

To the Venerable Mufti, Prince of the Religion of the Turks

Volume I, Book II, Letter XII

Thy decree is very cruel to separate me without having committed any crime from the communion of the faithful. I have read the holy answer thou hast made me with great veneration, but this has not been without many tears. Thou hast not untied the knot of the difficulties which perplex me but made it indissoluble, so that I only live in the certainty of having no certitude, and my soul, which is encompassed with fear, will be in dread till death. If I do what thou proposest, how shall I be sure of not failing, seeing I do not understand what I ought to do? I am so dull that I cannot distinguish whether thou exhortest me to do what I have ever done or whether thou forbiddest me what I asked of thee.

I entreated thee to let me know whether I might live amongst the Christians and do in appearance what they do effectually in the observance of the ceremonies of their religion. Thou answerest me that the circumcised or faithful should have no doubt in his law and needs no other precepts to observe it than the law itself. Moreover, that the true Mussulman must be willing to lose his estate, his life and honour in the sultan's service; that the Christians are enemies to the true God, the emperor and religion; and that in fine one ought to sacrifice all things not to betray this God, who is our chief

[1] The Peloponnesian peninsula, known during the Byzantine Empire as Morea.

master. Tell me, I entreat thee on my bended knees, cannot a man be a true Muhammadan without hating eternally the followers of Jesus? And in living amongst them secretly a true Mussulman, must one show oneself to be of another religion or pretend to be of theirs? Thou wilt tell me the Alcoran speaks with great clearness, yet how many obscure passages do we find in the words of our Holy Prophet wherein we need thy exposition?

I have no belief for Tagot,[1] neither will I give credit to the devil; my law expressly forbids it. For I believe in one only true God who knew the intention of our Holy Lawgiver and sees what we cannot discover. And the Prophet cries out that he that has such principles leans on the strongest prop he can ever meet with, there being nothing which is able to overthrow it.

Disperse, reverend sir, as much as thou canst the darkness of my spirit. I conjure thee by the Almighty Father, who can make live flesh come on the dry bones of the ass which died an hundred years past.

I do not discontinue here my usual prayers which I make in the manner they are prescribed me by the law with my face always turned to the side of Mecca. When I fast I eat only at night and I continue my repast till Aurora advancing the day gives me light enough to distinguish black thread from white,[2] and I pass over the day without taking any nourishment till the darkness be so great that I cannot see the eye of a needle. 'Tis true I give no alms to the poor because I doubt whether it be lawful to do good to those who continually move heaven against us.

The bishops here are in great veneration. They have not an absolute authority because they depend on the Roman prelate and the king. Yet their jurisdiction is very large, the kingdom being full of churches, and these churches frequented by millions of people. They wear about their necks a golden cross. They live in public good lives, are obliged to know all the points of their law; they must be doctors, are

[1] A reference to Taghut, a devil or idol mentioned in the Koran (Sura II, 257).

[2] The usual Moslem form of fasting, which is enjoined upon all Moslems during Ramadan, is to abstain from eating during the day but to resume a normal diet at night.

obliged to celibacy, to be sober, hospitable, prudent, irreprehensible without coveting others' goods. They must never be drunk or shed human blood. Their habit is a long vest reaching to the ground of black silk or violet. They go little on foot but are carried in coaches to avoid the wearisomeness which would oppress them in a town which seems the greatest in the world; which thou wouldest do too perhaps, wert thou designed to be their sovereign prelate.

The great Arbiter of the world, favour by His mercy or by an effect of His justice the inconceivable honour of suffering thee to sweep during thy life His most holy and only temple of Mecca in the company of Ishmael and Abraham that thou mayest keep it clean without any filth of what kind soever.

Paris, the 10th of the 1st moon of the year 1639.

To Bekir, Bassa,[1] Chief Treasurer to the Grand Signior

Volume I, Book II, Letter XVII

Eliachim the Jew, whom thou thoughtest so wise and virtuous a man, concealed his qualities at Constantinople to discover them more advantageously at Paris. It was not his fault that my affairs were not entirely ruined. The villain gave marks of his treachery in the very moment he saw me receive the money from Carcoa of Vienna upon thy order. I wrote to thee I thought this man would be faithful in instructing me in the things which were necessary for me to know, and that I would be upon my guard in those things wherein he might do me mischief. Thou mayest easily imagine how I am vexed at present, for I can neither accuse him nor draw from him a just revenge.

He made me believe that a lawyer's son at Paris, a young man of great hopes, having received some displeasure from his relations, was resolved to be circumcised and embrace the Muhammadan religion, and that he would not lose so happy an occasion of doing me service. He therefore had contrived

[1] Bassa is an European corruption of *pasha,* which was a title given to those in high government posts.

to hide this young man in a close cellar underneath the house where I lodge without discovering to him the place where he should be. He added he had promised him money and to procure him a considerable employ in Constantinople; and that he had in fine filled him with all the hopes which are wont to be given to those that through fickleness or temporal advantages forsake the religion of their fathers to profess another. He also assured me I should have no trouble by this business, having taken all necessary care to transport this convert immediately to Tunis or Algeria and from thence to Constantinople. I yielded to the reasons he alleged, and this young man was brought in the night to the house where I lay and hid without my seeing him. But the next day was not opened without a strange scene in the house. I was astonished to see a woman in a great rage stand before me demanding satisfaction for violating her daughter and taking away her life, charging me with having forcibly carried her away, and then murdered her. She made me all these reproaches in the company of a great many officers of justice.

Think then the confusion I was in; the more I denied the crime, the more fiercely they charged it on me. I was threatened with death if I did not confess it and give the satisfaction required of me. At the same time this sly Jezebel gave a sign to one of the rogues her companions to go down to such a place and bring up her daughter, who was found alive in man's clothes and melted into tears. It signified nothing to allege reasons to prove my innocency, so that I was forced at last to throw out to these hungry wretches all the money I had, and they withdrew not till they had abused and reviled me in a most bitter manner. They got from me about an hundred and eighty-four sequins of gold and about an hundred piasters of silver.

Eliachim has the confidence to affirm he knew nothing of the cheat and thinks to justify himself in saying that if he who is a Jew was deceived by this young man who pretended to become a Turk, there were a thousand French people who had been cheated in like manner. I shall not here mention what I alleged to him to make him own his perfidiousness, this being fruitless.

On the other hand, reflecting on the employ I had and my

present circumstances, it appeared to me necessary to dissemble this truth and to wait for some favourable occasion to send this villain out of Paris and to lay some snare for him at Constantinople. I give thee notice of this event for two reasons: that I may have more money and to provide for my safety, believing myself in great danger as long as I live where such a fellow comes. I shall not mention the interests of Mahmut's life, for I shall ever think it well spent should it be lost in the sultan's service, who is the only prop of the universe.

Thou wilt not want opportunities wherein thou mayest draw out of Eliachim's purse the money he has robbed me of; neither wilt thou want means to remove from me so dangerous a companion. Thou shouldst know what the Christians, who are always irreconcilable enemies to the Jews, say of them. They affirm that these infamous wretches are the slaves of all nations, excepting Turkey and especially in Constantinople, where they are masters; they are at the same time caressed and cursed in the midst of abundance. They appear always miserable and yet they lay hands on all others' properties. They add that they be vagabonds like Ulysses, yet in whatever place they are, they find a country like Homer; that they are all perfidious and in public affect to appear religious but live in grievous disorder and luxury in their own houses, sticking at no sort of crimes, bragging that though it be not permitted them to purchase lands, yet they have found means to get into their hands a great part of the gold in Europe. The Christians also say their number must needs be great, seeing they never go to war, and there is none amongst them that do not marry. They are, say they, ever cowards and poltroons where there's any danger or pains, but bold when they foresee any certain gain in the markets they make. They never speak the truth but when 'tis to deceive; they are ever liars, and there's no impiety or sacrilege at which they will scruple; and these same Christians affirm they will commit one time or other some horrid crime in our great imperial city, being the Turk's concealed enemies, though the Christians put great confidence by them; and that we are willing to be deceived by them. I have written to Carcoa to send me speedily some assistance. I have been forced to borrow money of this same Eliachim, that traitor who has brought me into the condition I am in. He could not deny me, though he pleads (like a rogue as he is) extreme poverty.

This trick which has been put upon me will oblige me henceforward to keep a valet, but I will take one so little that no man shall reproach me with choosing much of an ill thing. Abandon not the poor Mahmut, who prays God that he would give thee all sorts of prosperities and make thee live in perfect health, and wishes that all the monarchs of the infidel nations may become slaves to the sultan, who shall be ever invincible. And that their riches may increase the treasure thou guardest.

Paris, the 15th of the 2nd moon of the year 1639.

To Dgnet Oglou

Volume I, Book III, Letter XI

Should I tell thee I am in health I shall write an untruth, for I am really out of order and expect a fit of sickness, which I wish 'twere in my power to avoid, though it may prove short and mortal. A hectic fever puts me oft in mind how frail and brittle a thing is man, and that he ought in multiplicity of business in times of prosperity as well as adversity to think of dislodging hence. The bread I eat has no relish; solitude appears dismal to me, and company wearies me, for I cannot attend to what's discoursed, and yet I do not like they should say nothing. There's nothing pleases me but drink, yet all the sea will not quench my thirst. I am restless in bed and find myself more tired thereby than if I sat up, and that which I loved yesterday, I hate today. Thou knowest how I loved books; this humour is quite changed. If the sun shines into my chamber, I as soon shut my windows, being not able to endure it, and having remained a minute in obscurity, I am impatient for the light. Paris, where one may say strangers come from all parts to see the varieties and diversions there to be met with, appears to me now an hospital of fools. I long for nothing more than Constantinople and to be with my friends, imagining I shall find ease in their company. And this is the unhappy condition of thy friend without hope of seeing any more turbans and Mussulmans. I loath as much the sight of an ignorant physician as the Emperor Severus did a corrupt judge, and I look on a little valet that serves me as a necessary evil. Yet I'd a little divert thee maugre the illness which has seized one.

'Tis not above six months since I entertained this enemy in my house, who is a French valet, who makes himself a fool. Of a pigmy's stature, yet a giant in roguery, he is clad like the graces, being half naked and wears buskins like the poetical divinities. His ordinary function is to sweep every day my chamber, which yet is as nasty as Augea's stable. When I am awake he is asleep, and he's always awake when I am asleep. For these thirteen years that he has seen the light, he cannot remember he has been two hours without eating. When he eats, not openly and before folks, lest he should shame me, he will yet be sure to keep his chaps agoing on something in corners. When I went abroad, I was forced to follow him; and now that I keep my bed, 'tis hard to judge which of us two is the master, for he never parts with his hat from his head. He's moreover a politician as much as any Florentine. When he's to do any good office, he falls into the Spanish pace, but to perfect a bad one, he's as nimble as Caesar was in the quickest of his expeditions. Whence it is that I am a debtor to my own arm and hand for the service I draw from him, being like certain drugs which never yield an odour till well beaten. As to his religion, a man would imagine he held the metempsychosis, so carefully does he preserve the lice that eat him, lest in killing them he act contrary to the precepts of Pythagoras. He is moreover an irreconcilable enemy to all neatness, to water and to truth; and he is more stinking than a synagogue, drunker than a Swiss and a greater liar than any oracle. In the meantime my illness increases and my domestic enemy is so well that he assuredly awaits my death to live more honourably on my spoils. I differ much this day from what I was yesterday, and I know not whether I shall not tomorrow go to my long home. Pray the Immortal for me and remember we were once in slavery together. Should I escape I shall have the joy of never seeing thee in the sad condition I am; and if I cannot escape death at this time, I shall have the satisfaction of suffering it before thee. However, believe I do not despair, though I much complain. I cease writing to thee but I'll never cease loving thee. Mahmut embraces thee in this country of infidels, having thee always in his heart and praying for thee continually.

Paris, the 12th of the 4th moon of the year 1639.

To Dgnet Oglou

Volume I, Book III, Letter XIX

The lovely Greek, after whom thou enquirest so earnestly, is long since retired into France and has been married eighty moons to a great French merchant, with whom I am not acquainted but am informed is very rich and fortunate in his dealings; but infinitely more fortunate in being the husband of Daria Lena Maani, by whom he has several fine children.

This charming Greek does now profess the Roman religion, which is the only fault I find in her. I never knew a woman, whose whole carriage is so graceful, who does all things with such a careless exactness and whose virtue is less morose. Mere chance brought me acquainted with her, whom I no sooner saw but was struck with admiration. She came to Paris the last year to solicit a lawsuit against a stranger about an estate. It was at court and in the presence of the king himself that I first saw Daria. She spoke to him so sweetly that she soon obtained what she desired. At the same instant I felt such inexpressible passions and longings after acquaintance – suffer me, my dear Dgnet, to tell thee that never any creature made such deep impressions in the heart of a man as this charming Greek did in mine.

I drew near to her as soon as I could; I spoke to her in her own language, telling her I was an Arabian; and she answered me with as great modesty as benignity. I went the day following to give her visit in her own lodgings, where this adorable person received me with the greatest civility, not forbidding me a return, being pleased perhaps to meet with one that could speak her own language, which is very rare in these parts.

Since then, I could not for my life forget her. I have served her with the greatest diligence and so doted on her that I forgot myself and thee and if I may dare to say so, the Grand Signior too. Pardon this infidelity on the account of a passion, which knows no moderation, being not able to withstand the force of so invincible an enemy.

Daria is young, of a generous temper and in whose whole deportment there's no grace wanting. Her virtue is far above Lucretia's, for this Roman Lady killed herself, having first endured the violence of a tyrant, whereas she would die before she would come to such a trial. If you have seen her at Constantinople you must have known her perfections. I for my part, who only knew her at Paris, have remarked four beauties in her person, which I believe is not to be found in any of those ladies kept in the seraglio. Her eyes, her mouth, her teeth and her hands seem to have been made only to furnish the god of love with darts. She is sure to strike where she will with her fine black eyes full of fire; and she has also the secret of healing the wounds she makes when she pleases. As soon as ever she opens her mouth, the three graces are seen to sit sporting in her countenance; and her body is moreover so proportioned in all its parts that had she lived in the time of Phidias,[1] he had certainly taken her for the model of his Venus, which was the admiration of all the world.

I have plied this fair Greek with visits, loved her even to idolatry; my respect has been ever equal to her virtue. The greatest favour I obtained from her was to suffer me thus to speak to her: 'I love you, Daria. Daria, I adore you.' But she would never suffer the least expression which might make her understand anything else.

This incomparable beauty often said to me, 'Mahmut, I have a great respect for thee, because thou art discreet and virtuous and should also love thee wert thou not a man. Live on still as thou hast done, and thou wilt thereby oblige me to respect thee yet more, but thinkest not to obtain from Daria any more than an innocent affection. I owe all to my husband, and I will never be unfaithful to him.'

If I ever attempted to snatch any small favour, it was always in vain, having ever repelled me in such a manner, as made

[1] Phidias (*c.* 490-32 B.C.) was one of the greatest of Greek sculptors.

me lose all hope and at the same time feel a new increase of passion. Consider, dear Oglou, what passed then in my heart, and what a war I was to sustain.

In my great inquietudes and sharpest and cruellest pains, philosophy supplied me with no other remedies but patience; she set before me the examples of the esteem which the ancients had for pudicity. But she hindered me not from also remembering that we find in history almost all the philosophers more transported with venereal pleasures than retained by the precepts of wisdom. Diogenes and Aristotle, became they not fools hereby? – and Seneca, whose morals are the rules of the wisest, was not he driven out of Rome for his adulteries? I tell thee plainly, the precepts of philosophy have influenced me not a whit; I derided them and was resolved to love on and that more excessively than all the philosophers together. Daria's soft severity has laid on me stronger laws than all the dogmas of the stoics, so that nothing can make me change my resolution of loving her eternally. If it be true that love is a weakness, only men, who are noble creatures, are thereunto subject, it being certain that mean souls cannot love, because they have no heart. Nature's original is far higher than reason's; one is the work of God, whereas the other comes from man. Be not then astonished if reason does so oft yield to nature.

Daria had a mind to learn Italian, which she thought a better language than others. I taught her a great deal of it in a little time, but business quickly deprived an unhappy master of the most perfect of scholars. She said once to me: 'Mahmut, let us have a perpetual amity for one another, but let us love and esteem virtue far before friendship. Teach me history and geography to the end that knowing kingdoms, towns and provinces and those that govern them, I may know into how many parts the earth, which appears so admirable, is divided; I may now learn the forces, methods of government, manners, religions of nations, the differences of seas and of mountains, of lakes and rivers, of inhabited places, islands and deserts that I may not confound the barbarous with the civilized nations, and republics with monarchies.'

My worthy friend, so noble an inclination joined with a singular grace and attended with so many rare qualities, as well spiritual as corporal, have reduced the poor Mahmut to a slavery, more rigorous than that which he suffered with thee in Sicily. How many nights have I passed in horrible restlessness, and how many times have I vainly believed I was with Daria, whom I sought in my chamber, when sleep succeeding long watchings, represented her to me in a dream more complaisant than ordinary. In a word, Daria so filled my thought that I forgot my books, and avoiding also the company of my friends; she alone was my daily study, and I renounced all other divertissements. The finest ladies were nauseous to me; the finest gardens seemed horrible forests which serve for a retreat to savage beasts. In fine, my passion, friend Oglou, comes to that excess that I can find no remedy. My tears were of no effect to soften Daria, and I have cast myself a thousand times in vain at her feet; all my cares and respects have served only to give me proofs of her virtue. Receive as thou oughtest the confidence I put in thee, and if thou hast not an heart that can love so ardently, at least have some complacency towards a man whose passion has no bounds and reproach me not with having had too much weakness for having been vanquished by a woman. 'Tis women that have always won the greatest victories; it is their trade to conquer and even those too who subdue all things. It is impossible for me to comprehend how I could love so strongly without dying; neither can I imagine how I shall live, if I be long deprived of the sight of her I love.

Daria has left Paris and is distant thence above three hundred miles. Consider then the condition I am in. I reckon myself in a solitary place, although there be above a million of inhabitants in the town where I dwell. I stir not out of my chamber, and as to my books, they will yield me no comfort. My only care is to nourish my distemper; whereby I study to make myself more miserable, because it is not in my power so much as to seek the way to the only happiness I wish for. Mahmut may be said to be the son of sorrow; my beard is nasty and overgrown; I am out of love with myself, comfortless, avoiding all society and become invisible to all people. I have no hope amongst so many causes of despair but the assurance which Daria has given me that I possess a place in her heart; and I believe it because she says so. Heaven has given her a frank and generous soul and promises her great things in the course of her life. I have secretly drawn her horoscope; as far as I could find, all the planets are favourable to her; she is to live a great while. Fortune will second her intentions; she will enjoy an uninterrupted health, and this lovely person will ever gain the advantage on all that shall oppose her. Happy is he that shall be of the number of her friends, but more happy is he that shall be beloved of her, for he may assure himself of being beloved of the handsomest and most deserving lady in the world.

Read my follies with some indulgence and be not angry with me when thou knowest I was all ready to renounce my religion for that of Daria; she began to convince me, and I began to believe that the religion of the most perfect and most virtuous of women was the best. If thou hast interest enough in the grand vizier or the Kaimakam, obtain for me the permission of leaving Paris for six moons only, but by no means let them know the occasion. I love much, absent from Daria, but it seems to me I do not yet love enough. I would have more violent transports during her absence than those I suffer whilst I see her; to the end I may say that all times and in all places never anybody loved so much. I have discovered to thee my whole heart; excuse my passion if thou wilt not excuse thy friend so horridly tormented with it, and remember what the beautiful Roxalana said to the Great Solyman: [2] 'The pleasure of commanding and making oneself obeyed is to be reckoned but in the second rank of pleasures; whereas that of loving and being beloved is the first.'

Henry IV was one of the greatest kings of France, and no man ever more greatly loved. When he reproached the Duke de Biron with the love he had for a lady, mark what this cavalier told him: 'Great king, how is it possible thou shouldst not be indulgent to lovers, who hast so often said when thou wast in love, thou forgetest thyself, thy kingdom and subjects?' And this, dear Oglou, is what has happened to me at Paris with this admirable person whom thou couldst no longer find

[2] In the long reign (1520-66) of Solyman or Suleiman I (sometimes called the Magnificent) the Ottoman Empire reached the height of its glory and power. Roxalana was Solyman's concubine; the custom of the Turkish sultans was not to marry. However, Solyman became so attached to Roxalana that he gave her the status of a legal wife and settled a dowry upon her.

at Constantinople. But alas, I should be an unhappy friend if with such a love as mine I would prove thy rival. I will not imagine it; yet I must tell thee that rather than yield thee Daria, I will sacrifice to thee all the time I have to live. I have given my picture to this charming Greek, who has received it very courteously, yet rather as the work of an excellent painter than the picture of a lover.

But being full of goodness and perfectly discreet, she said thus to me when I gave it her:

'Mahmut, thank heaven thou art not handsome. Such sort of men have not ordinarily all the success they pretend to in their amours. Wise ladies think these kind of people dote too much on themselves, and those that are disdainful find them not submissive enough and respectful. Such as fear evil tongues dare not look upon them, and also these gentlemen imagine ladies' favours are granted them because they cannot withstand them, and they expect oftentimes to be entreated to receive them; whereas those to whom nature has not been so liberal of her favours do more than bear love, they adore their mistresses, they are always humble and know how to gain the coyest beauty by their respectfulness. As to thy part, who art none of the fairest, thou wilt be happy if you changest not thy manner of living with me.'

It is impossible for me to say whether Daria has any considerable imperfections, being too greatly prepossessed by my passion to discover defects in a person whom I regard as an angel. Time and her promises will one day show me whether she has the vices usual to those of her nation, which are commonly an infidelity covered over with the most specious pretences and a continued dissimulation.

However, send me a cask of the white balm of Mecca and of the best sort for scent thou canst get. And at the same time, send me also some of that precious Eastern wood, whose scent is admirable to perfume the body. I have promised the fair Daria this present; let me soon have it to the end I may accustom Daria to the neatness and delicacies of the Muhammadans. Preserve also thy health; and if thou enviest me, love as much as I do. But love with continence, if thou wilt love long and be long beloved.

The great God preserve thee from loving however so excessively as thy friend Mahmut does; the dolours being therein always certain and fruition uncertain.

Paris, the 10th of the 1st moon of the year 1641.

To Dgnet Oglou

Volume I, Book IV, Letter VII

I say not that those are fools who are in love, but I must needs think that those who believe lightly are not overladen with discretion. 'Tis hard for a man always to keep himself from falling into a passion, but 'tis not hard for a man to keep himself from believing things with too great facility and from being caught with falsehoods, which are the most constant attendants of women.

Thou hast spoke the truth to me in sending me the balm and aloes I wrote for, and I shall not answer thee with lies in speaking of Daria, who is the subject of the letter which I received from thee. Let me thank thee without saying anything of the present thou madest me, which is very magnificent and acceptable, and suffer me to complain to thee freely of the hurt which another has done me. I need not consult my register to remember whatever I wrote to thee about this Greek; my heart, which is yet full of it, reproaches me every moment for having said too much to thee on that subject.

Never anything appeared to me so desirable as that herb which Homer called nepenthe to cure me of the cruel distemper with which I am tormented. This prince of poets makes a queen of our Egypt to present this admirable simple [1] to Helena, which has the virtue of appeasing immediately all dolours and makes us forget the vexations and offences offered us. But thou wilt not understand me unless I tell thee clearly that Daria has forgotten all the promises she made me as soon as ever she was from me, not remembering in any sort my love. 'Tis true she wrote twice to me since her departure but in so cold a style that it is plainly seen her heart is as cold as ice to me. As soon as ever she saw herself in the arms of her husband,

[1] A medicine or anodyne.

she made him a sacrifice to my passion, and better to make her court to him and persuade him of her fidelity, she delivered to him my letters. The husband laughed in reading them and said to her in a jeer to me, 'A man then so desperately in love has only sighed and wrote?'

'He has done something more,' replied this dissembling woman, 'having promised to send me a box of white balm of Mecca and aloes wood to perfume me, which yet I do not expect to receive so soon and perhaps never. For if Mahmut be not become a fool, he will as soon forget me as I shall certainly forget him.'

'And what hast thou promised this barbarian?' replied immediately the husband.

'I promised,' replied Daria, 'to send with my picture that of the most chaste of all women, which yet I do not pretend to do without your consent, nay, and command.'

What I now inform thee comes from a place which makes me not at all doubt the certainty of it. But having learned by what I related the virtue of this woman, now hear what the husband's was, who having seen my picture, commended the painter that drew it, embraced tenderly his wife whom he respected as a most singular example of conjugal fidelity. Thou wilt wonder at Daria's weakness in showing him my picture; she did do it, and her confidence has turned to account, she having received a thousand chaste embraces for a recompense. Thou seest here the happiness of the Christian women who have husbands who take so favourably the offences done them during their absence.

In the meantime Daria's picture does not come; she returns no more answers to my letters, which has discouraged me to write to her for some time. My passion begins not to be so violent, and this great fire which consumed me will soon turn into ashes. I have been mightily mistaken, for it is only amongst persons of an equal condition where true and lasting friendships are to be found. Let us love, my dear Dgnet; let the bonds of our friendship be such as will never break nor be dissolved. Daria is really a great example of fidelity to her husband, but she is also an example of inconstancy and treachery to a lover who had sacrificed all to her.

I am resolved henceforward to love no woman, and I am

certain, my dear friend, that my resolution shall hold. Rejoice with me at my cure and believe that if a fine and charming woman disordered my brains, the good humour and patience of her husband has brought me again to my senses. My adventure should make thee careful to avoid the inconveniences, but thou canst not run that risk, being happy with the other Mussulmans of Constantinople, who have laws which retain and hinder them from falling into the like irregularities.

I hope also thou wilt give over being my rival if thou hast ever had any kindness for this ungrateful Greek. If men must love once in their lives, let them have a care of falling into those excesses which deprive them of their reason and make them repent of their love all the days of their lives. My repentance is great, and though my passion be not wholly extinct, yet I feel a joy which makes me know I shall by degrees lose my passion for her.

Thou mayest well be tired with this long discourse but I shall end it in sending thee a description which one of the greatest wits in Spain has made of women. He says:

'They be the sources of life and death, that they are to be considered as fire because they use all that come near them as that element does; yet they give men a certain necessary heat. They are fine things, bring joy to families and whole towns, but are dangerous to keep, enflaming all that comes near them and reducing them commonly into ashes. They usually give a great lustre, but this lustre is never without such a smoke as darkens the understanding and makes them often shed tears who only behold them. He that has no commerce with women spends his life in melancholy, and yet they are seldom seen without danger. The way to manage them is not to do excessive things for them, no more than wholly to neglect them. A man oft obtains them easily and commonly loses them more easily. Fire and a woman are exactly the same, and he that said women are fires which burn all things has said likewise, that fire is like women, which consumeth all things.'

But our religious Arabians have spoken yet more elegantly when they wrote that God made a particular paradise for them, because say they, should women enter into that of men, they would soon change it into a hell.

Eve played her part so well when she was seduced by the serpent in the terrestial paradise that she deceived her spouse also that he might lie under the like condemnation. But, however, this sex having amongst so many defects something that is amiable, let us love them at least because of their usefulness for continuing the species but not for their beauty, whose enchantments corrupt the mind and hinder all the excellent operations of it. For men perhaps would be angels were there no women; I mean bad ones, for good women as well as good men can do no hurt. Adieu.

Paris, the 20th of the 10th moon of the year 1641.

To William Vospel, a Christian of Austria

Volume I, Book IV, Letter XVIII

God be praised, thy Patriarch Elias and his companion, forasmuch as I see thou art a saint and content in religion of the bare-footed friars which thou hast embraced.[1] Thou stirrest me up to do good and encouragest me to suffer and become serious enough to renounce the pleasures of the world, seeing thou tracest me a way so necessary to walk in in order to arrive at heaven. I did not believe indeed, I confess it, thou wert endued with that constancy and was afraid thou wouldst change, but seeing thou has the courage of keeping thy resolution and enduring all the incommodiousness which is to be met with in that kind of life which thou hast embraced. I am sorry for my suspicions and profess I have all due esteem for thee. I love thee as much as one honest man ought to love another who having found out the true good has ran impetuously after it; and who has passed immediately from a soft and voluptuous life to the severities of an austere religion in search of an assured port, which is more usually found in sufferings and macerations than in delights and pleasures.

There is one thing amongst others which extremely pleases me in the order thou hast entered: all things are in common

[1] In an earlier letter (Volume I, Book I, Letter XIV) Mahmut tried to dissuade Vospel from entering a monastery.

amongst you; one key opens an hundred doors. You have no *meum* and *tuum*; all clad in the same fashion and all go barefooted. You eat at the same table, and nobody has better or worse fare than another. In fine your prayers are the same and so are your vows of poverty.

But, prithee tell me, what would a thief have found in thy cell whom I saw yesterday hanged with a key about his neck? He had the dexterity of opening with this key all sorts of locks and has done a thousand roguish exploits which have at length brought him to the gallows. He told the people he died a most happy man as having practised with great success an art inferior to none; that the only crime he thought he had been guilty of for this thirty years was his committing but small thefts; that had he found the doors always open he had never entered into any house, and he exhorted magistrates to chastise only those who suffered themselves to be robbed.

Spanish authors have written there's no law which allots penalties to those that rob with prudence and ingenuity; thus call they those who steal wherewithal to appease the envious who would accuse them, the witnesses which might serve to convict them and the magistrates by whom they are to be judged. So that the thief that shall have stolen for himself and for all others I now mentioned shall be ever sent away absolved. Which makes me think that theft is of the nature of women, for both one and the other seem at this day to be necessary evils, just as keys seem only good nowadays to preserve what may be stolen and not to hinder it from being so.

How many things has the injustice of some people authorized for the safeguard of a town? 'Tis not enough to have a strong garrison of soldiers; three elements are not sufficient to defend it against a greater power that would oppress it. The earth is raised to make hereof trenches; the deepest ditches are dried up whatever quantity of water may be in them, and fire is enclosed in cannons, the effects of which are terrible. If thou surveyest Italy, thou wilt find in several towns, palaces which have more gates than Thebes had heretofore; and if thou countest the keys which serve to open them, thou wilt find the iron they are made of to cost more than the doors themselves.

Men are not contented to use these keys according to the

common use they seem to be designed for; their ambition makes them serve for marks of honour in several princes' courts, where they be recompenses for services, for virtue and valour. The golden keys in Spain which the great lords wear denote that they know how to open the gate of favour. And 'tis the same in Germany and especially in the emperor's court.

Happy was ancient Rome, whose citizens were so wise that being advised to turn the front of their houses on that side where they could not be observed by the neighbours, they answered the architect: 'We rather desire our houses may be overlooked into, because we do nothing wherein we fear a surprise?' Whereas modern Rome, on the contrary, may be termed unhappy, wherein there are not enough gates and porters of them to conceal what is done in the most retired places of their palaces. It is in this city, where luxury grew to that height under the first emperors that all men's studies were to find out new pleasures.

But I must end this discourse of keys, of doors and door-keepers; I must not expect to reform the world, nor would I weary thy patience. Pardon me my passing from the cell [2] to the story of the thief whom I saw executed, and from the thief to a discourse of keys and other things with which I have entertained thee. I was so full of it that I could not forbear the discourse, no more than I can now to speak of the subtilty of the Spaniards who have vaunted of the worth of their Escurial by the great number of the keys which belong to it; like that foolish emperor who valued the greatness of Rome by the great weight of spiders' webs which were there. The Spaniards affirm there are so many doors to this stately edifice that the keys which serve to open them weigh above ten thousand weight.

But 'tis time to end this tiresome letter. Let me then counsel thee to watch over thy conscience as the Parisians do over their shops to prevent violences. Here are so many great and small thieves that should they be punished as they were chastised in Syria, where the same punishment is imposed on him that is robbed as him that robs, this great town would

[2] That is, passing from a discussion of monasticism to that of robbery.

be soon unpeopled or become a prison to an infinite number of people who would be found faulty.

May it please the Great God, who should be adored by all creatures, to encline the great prelate (after thou art delivered from the burden of the flesh) to place thee amongst the number of those for whom the church has a pious veneration, and respect thy ashes in such a manner as I hope thy holy and exemplary life will deserve.

Paris, the 24th of the 4th moon of the year 1642.

To Berber Mustapha, Aga[1] at Constantinople

Volume I, Book IV, Letter XXIV

I cannot tell whether thou hast knowledge of the use of defiances which are made amongst the Christians when they be dissatisfied or offended with one another, which they term acts of honour or the marks of a gallant spirit. This custom of duels is become so common in Italy and especially in the kingdom of Naples that the greatest affairs as well as the smallest are therein decided by the sword. The gentry affirm this to be the best way of terminating their disputes and quarrels, which belong only to them and cannot be referred nor so well determined by the grave and cool proceedings of courts of justice.

This invention of deciding these differences by arms either with the sword or pistol alone in a close or open field naked in their shirts, so that one has no treachery to fear, is a way of drawing satisfaction for the injuries received, found out by men of great courage, who more esteem their honour than their lives. The offended person sends a challenge to him from whom he has received the injury; this note of defiance is expressed in choice and elegant words which invite and press the offender to fight in such a place on horseback or on foot, clothed or in their shirts, single or attended by an equal number of friends, which they call seconds, with sword and dagger or sword alone or pistol. If the challenge be received,

[1] Chief or master; in the seventeenth century the title aga was usually reserved for military leaders or those in government service.

he is civilly treated who brings it, and it may be has rich presents given to him. But before they fight, the enemies embrace as if they were reconciled, and then in an instant following the inclinations of their hatred and revenge, they wound one another, they spill each other's blood, and oftentimes their souls go out furious through the wounds they have made.

Those that have the honour of dying in these combats do oft refuse their lives, which a generous enemy would give them, believing they cannot live with shame should they receive their life from an enemy.

But the Roman Church, as a note of the horror she conceives at these combats, shuts heaven's doors against the souls of those who leave this life without doing penance, denying burial to those who die in the field of battle, or yield them only that which is granted in some parts of the East Indies to certain women who prostitute themselves, whose corpses are thrown as prey to the birds of the field and other animals who live on carrion.

It is not only in Italy people kill one another in single combats, 'tis the same in France among the nobility who manage these combats in a different sort. The best friends tear one another on the smallest occasion, and they prepare for a duel in such a manner as will appear to thee without doubt ridiculous.

These enemies sup together the night before the combat and often lie together in the same bed. The friends which serve as seconds do the same; and when they are come to the place where they be to fight, a friend is forced by the maxims of honour to cut his own throat with the man he perhaps most loves. Nothing happens more frequently in Paris than these kinds of combats, and they produce several adventures of which I would give thee an account, had I not a particular story to tell thee on this subject. It is of a challenge of a Spanish prince sent to a king, whose crown could not exempt him from a letter of defiance.

Thou hast without doubt heard of what has happened in Lisbon, where Don John de Braganza has been elected and proclaimed King of Portugal as the true heir of the royal race. Thou knowest also he drove the Spaniards out of his kingdom.

The Duke of Medina Sidonia, a Grandee of Spain and this new king's brother-in-law, could not hinder himself from being suspected of having underhandedly assisted this prince to ascend the throne; whether it be true or an artifice of his enemies God only knows. But, however, it's certain that the Count Duke d'Olivarez, the King of Spain's chief minister, sent an order to him to appear at court to justify himself from this suspicion. He thought to clear himself perfectly from the jealousies of the Catholic king by sending a challenge to Don John of Braganza to oblige him to fight with him, which letter of defiance was conceived in these terms:

> D. Gaspar Alonzo Peres Gusman the Good, Duke of the town of Medina Sidonia, Marquis, Count and Lord of the town of St. Lucar of Barameda, Captain General of the Ocean and Gentleman of his Catholic Majesty's Chamber. I say that John of Braganza who was never but a Duke calls himself King of Portugal; that his treason known to all the world is detestable and an abomination for having thrown a stain on the faithful house of Gusman, which has never failed in any duty to her sovereign, and for this reason defy and challenge to a single combat body to body with seconds or without seconds this Don John hereafter Duke of Braganza, leaving all this to his choice, as also the arms or weapons and place of combat. Written near Valencia d'Alcantara, where I shall expect fourscore days news of him, and the last twenty days I shall transport myself into the place he shall appoint accompanied or alone with such arms as he shall prescribe.
>
> Not only the tyrant of Portugal shall be advertised of my challenge but all Europe and the whole world. I pretend to be made known in this combat the infamous action of Don John, and in case he does not accept of this defiance, I desire this king, who is only a phantasm, may perish in some sort or other. I promise to give my town of St. Lucar, the principal seat of the Dukes of Medina to him that shall kill him.
>
> In the meantime I entreat my lord the King of Spain to give me no command in his armies but to grant I may only serve him as a volunteer with a thousand horse, which

I will maintain at my own charge, till that serving him in this manner, I may help to recover the kingdom of Portugal and may bring along with me and cast at his Majesty's feet the Duke of Braganza, if he will not fight with me in the manner I proposed.

If thou showest this letter of defiance to the Janissaries, that militia which is terrible to all nations, whom nothing can resist, when they execute the Grand Signior's orders, they will tell thee what such a challenge requires from men of courage and explain to thee the laws which people of valour prescribe to themselves. For my part who am ignorant of the art of war and the maxims of such as make profession of arms, I shall not make any judgment hereupon; only take the liberty to ask of thee, if the King of Portugal accepted the combat and killed the Duke of Medina, which of the two would have been declared infamous? [2] Whether there be any certainty in the decisions made by arms? I am willing to think justice is on the side of the conqueror, but if on the contrary the event of the duel uncertain, I take it to be a foolish thing for the duke to expose himself and thus affront the king, his brother-in-law. In short, the duke's prudence is not to be admired in this occasion, and Braganza has had the advantage on his side, seeing he has showed by his conduct that he is effectually King of Portugal.

I cannot but call these Christians fools, who suffer such customs among them and yet adore a Messiah who is a God of Peace, and they call us barbarians, when they are the only people that teach us and all other nations the arts of single combats, which is the most pernicious custom that can be introduced amongst men, who cut one another's throats oftentimes on slight occasions and become prodigals of that trea-

[2] The upshot of this challenge, which curiously enough Marana did not relate, was that the Duke of Medina in due time transported himself and his seconds in the appropriate armour to an appointed place on the Spanish-Portuguese border where he waited vainly for the King of Portugal. Moreover, it is not quite the full truth to say that Medina was suspected only of helping his brother-in-law; his crime went deeper than that. He had conspired after the example of the Duke of Braganza to detach Andalusia from the kingdom of Spain and set up a realm over which he would reign as king. After the humiliating duel episode, Medina sank into such obscurity that history makes no further mention of him.

sure with which the Immortal has intrusted them. Neither can I anymore approve of kings and princes of the same beliefs making war with one another, as we see every day amongst those who profess the Christian religion, which yet, as far as I can find, scarcely permits any wars but such as are defensive.

Pardon this tedious letter, excuse my conjecture in it and honour me with thy commands, which will be respected by me as so many obligations.

Paris, the 25th of the 6th moon of the year 1642.

To Dgnet Oglou

Volume II, Book I, Letter XII

I know thy genius and have observed with what complacency thou wert wont to peruse thy uncle Shela Raphim's travels, a journal writ in Arabic and full of profitable and wise remarks, especially that part of it which treats of France. I will not pretend to add to his observations but only acquaint thee with a novelty, which France itself never knew in his days.

The women of quality here of late addict themselves to the studies of philosophy as the men, the ladies esteeming their education defective if they cannot confute Aristotle and his disciples. The pen has almost supplanted the exercise of the needle, and ladies' closets, formerly the shops of female baubles, toys and vanities, are now turned to libraries and sanctuaries of learned books. There is a new star risen in the French horizon whose influence excites the nobler females to this pursuit of humane science. It is the renowned Monsieur Descartes, whose lustre far outshines the aged, winking tapers of peripatetic philosophy and has eclipsed the Stagirite with all the ancient lights of Greece and Rome. 'Tis this matchless soul has drawn so many of the fairer sex to the schools. And they are more proud of the title Cartesian and of the capacity to defend his principles than of their noble birth and blood.

I know our grave and politic Mussulmans will censure the indulgence of the French to their women and accuse them of weakness in giving such advantages to that witty sex. But notwithstanding this severity of the Eastern parts, I cannot altogether disapprove the Western gallantry. If women are to be esteemed our enemies, methinks it is an ignoble cowardice thus to disarm them and not allow them the same weapons we use ourselves. But if they deserve the title of our friends, 'tis an inhumane tyranny to debar them the privilege of ingenuous education, which would also render their friendship so much more delightful both to themselves and us. Nature is seldom observed to be niggardly of her choicest gifts to that sex; their senses generally are as quick as ours, their reason as nervous, their judgments as mature and solid. Add but to these natural perfections, the advantage of acquired learning, what polite and charming creatures will they prove, whilst their external beauty does the office of a crystal to the lamp, not shrouding but disclosing their brighter intellects. Nor need we fear to lose our empire over them by thus improving their native abilities, since where there is most learning, sense and knowledge, there is observed to be the greatest modesty and rectitude of manners. I see no reason therefore why we should make such bugbears of women, as not trust them with as liberal education as ourselves.

I believe thou sometimes bestowest a compassionate thought on the exiled Mahmut. Wouldst thou do something to alleviate my melancholy? The next time thou goest to the Atmidan[1] transcribe what is engraven on the pedestals of the obelisks and columns standing there and send it enclosed in a letter.

He that is Lord of the East and the West, from whose throne hang millions of stars in chains of gold, increase thy virtues and blessings and preserve thee from the poison of ill eyes and malicious tongues and bring thee to the fields of endless light.

Paris, the 6th of the 8th moon of the year 1642.

[1] Atmidan is the modern square at Meydani in Istanbul, the site of the ancient hippodrome of the Byzantine Empire. In the square are three columns with Latin and Greek inscriptions, which have no significant import except to explain the history of their erection and the personages involved. The inscriptions are reproduced in George Sandys's *Relation of a Journey Begun An: Dom: 1610* (London, 1615) and in subsequent editions.

To the Venerable Mufti, Prince of the Religion of the Turks

Volume II, Book I, Letter XXIV

I received the dispatch of thy sanctity, wherein thou hast renovated my soul and restored me to a sound consistence of spirit. My doubts are vanished, I am no longer racked with torturing scruples about my conduct. Thy absolution has obliterated the sentence my fears had pronounced on me.

As to the penance thou hast enjoined me, it is rational and adapted to the quality of my crime. I have counterfeited a Christian that I might the better perform the duty of a Mussulman. I have seemed devoutly attentive to the Roman missal that I might be instrumental to propagate the Alcoran. And for this religious fault thou requirest that I should inform thee how the Christians behave themselves in their temples, where I have been so often a spectator of their ceremonies. I submit with an absolute resignation and a willing compliance to thy venerable injunction and will briefly relate what I have observed.

These infidels seem to be ambitious of imitating the undefiled religion, and yet they prove but bad mimics; for as we are taught to wash our bodies before we enter the sacred mosque, so they at the entrance of their churches dip their fingers in certain vessels filled with water and salt and sprinkle their foreheads therewith, as though their purity lay in a swoon and was thus to be recovered to life again, or that the uncleanness of their whole bodies were contracted into the face. They esteem the water holy and yet they trifle with it as an indifferent thing. One would think they should be desirous to bathe themselves all over and let every pore in their skin imbibe the sanctified liquor. But they seem rather to use it as a charm, for after they have sprinkled a few drops on their faces and muttered to themselves two or three words, they think they have chased all impurity from them in a fright and boldly present themselves before the altars. Herein also they deviate from the practice of former Christians, who (if their own church histories be true) were accustomed to wash their arms and feet in certain cisterns before they entered the temples, whereof the fountains and lavatories remaining yet on the south side of the holy and magnificent mosque of Sancta Sophia at Constantinople are a standing testimony. For the Greek inscriptions show that some of them at least were contrived by the builders of this glorious temple in the time of Justinian the emperor for the purification of such as came thither to worship. By which 'tis manifest that these modern infidels degenerate from those more ancient ones.

Another thing offends me also, which is this: They believe the divinity is present in their temples after a peculiar and extraordinary manner, and yet they suffer dogs to profane them with their vilest excrements. They spare for no costs to adorn their churches, and their altars are enriched with invaluable treasures of silver, gold and precious stones, and yet after all they must become the receptacles of the dung of sordid animals.

These wicked wretches also walk up and down in these sacred places talking of their common affairs as though they were on the exchange or in the market place.

But that which is to be had in greatest admiration is that it is common for men to make love to the women in churches. They present themselves before the altars, but the saint whom they invocate is some beautiful female. She engrosses all their devotions; to her they make their vows. The amorous youth adores his mistress that kneels by him laden perhaps with more sins than himself. His eyes may be fixed on the altar or on the pictures and images but his tongue addresses to the more charming idol near him; or if his eyes are attentive on his prayerbook, he teaches it to speak nothing but the soft and effiminate things of love. Thus assignations of lust are made in the house of prayer, and the affairs of Cupid managed under the mask of religion. They fight the battles of Venus under the banner of their God.

I tell thee, venerable interpreter of the divine law, that the sight of these things has sometimes inflamed my zeal to that height, had it not been for an earnest desire to do some extraordinary service to the Grand Signior (which obliged me to take care of myself), I should certainly have transfixed these profane mockers of God on the spot and sacrificed them to a zeal which thou, who art piety itself, wouldst not, I believe, reprehend.

I fold my arms, most venerable sovereign of religion, and wrapping myself in profound humility, I fall prostrate to the earth, begging thy effectual blessing and intercession that I may be admitted into the number of the happy in paradise.

Paris, the 26th of the 9th moon of the year 1642.

To Abdel Melec Muly Omar, Superintendent of the College of Sciences at Fez[1]

Volume II, Book I, Letter XXVI

When I write to thee, 'tis with a respect equal to that which I pay to the emirs, the descendents of our Holy Prophet, since thou art sprung from the noble stem of the ancient Saracens, the blood of the celebrated Omar,[2] successor to the divine lawgiver streaming in thy veins.

I revere the banner carried into Egypt by thy renowned progenitor, before which the Grecians fled astonished, as at a sign sent from heaven of their approaching ruin. This sacred piece of antiquity I have seen at Medina, where 'tis reposited in the chancel of the Babylonian Caliphs. I have honoured it with a pious veneration, but much greater is my regard to thee, who are a living relic of that illustrious house.[3]

Permit me, venerable sage, to converse with thee a little after the manner of a pupil, with thee, I say, who art a fountain of sapience. For besides thy perfect knowledge of the

[1] Fez in Morocco had at one time enjoyed the reputation as the most important seat of learning in the Moslem world.

[2] Omar or Umar, the second Caliph of Islam, who was converted in the sixth year of Muhammad's mission, ruled from A.D. 634 to 644. His daughter became the third wife of the Prophet.

[3] The house of Omar and descendents. By his statement of veneration, Mahmut reveals himself a follower of the Sunni sect of Moslems, who trace their tradition to the first four caliphs as the rightful successors to Muhammad.

divine law, thou art accomplished with all humane literature.

There is a man in these parts of a large soul and elevated speculations who stiffly maintains that the earth moves and the sun stands still. He is not the first that broached this doctrine; it has had several learned patrons, but he has highly improved the theory. His reasons for it have almost the force of mathematical demonstrations, and nothing seems to oppose him but the authority of Moses and the Hebrew Scriptures. The Christians will not approve of any philosophy which interferes with that which they call the Bible; and yet their practise gives a perpetual lie to the contents of that book. Surely there is no envy in the Diety, and He that is omniscient will not punish men for improving their knowledge. The study of nature is full of innocent delights, and He that gave to man an appetite of science has not forbid him to gratify it with its proper objects. Nor can I see how this new philosophy contradicts any more than the bare letter of their Bible (for I have read it in several languages). And the Jews, who are guardians of the original Hebrew, allow a cabbalistical interpretation far different from the literal. So does the Arabian prince and philosopher Avicenna interpret those versicles in our holy Alcoran which treat of paradise in a sense far more refined than the letter seems to import. In reading such mysterious books, it is necessary to practise a learned chemistry to sublimate the gross internal sense of the words and to extract the spirit and soul of the discourse.

That the sun is the centre of this our planetary world and that the earth with the rest of the planets move round about it, is a thesis which keeps exact touch with human reason and seems naturally to square with our intellectual faculties. It sets all the wheels of this great and wonderful machine in a regular and proportionate circulation. It gives the truest account of the retrograde motions of the planets. Ptolemy's system of the world seems to romance upon the sun, moon and stars in assigning them hourly such prodigious journeys through the heavens as are inconsistent with the laws of motion. And Tycho Brahe was but a botcher in patching up the orbs with his eccentrics, epicycles, etc. The former keeps the fixed stars in an endless and unconceivable hurry; the latter involves the planets in a heavenly perplexity. Both come far short of Copernicus, that excellent astronomer, who by placing the sun in the centre of the world, has solved all the appearances of nature with the most exact analogy to truth. Nor is the argument taken from our sense of any force, since it invalidates the motion of the sun as well as that of the earth. Nay, it is more incongruous that the sun should move so many hundred thousand miles every hour and we not perceive him to stir a hairsbreadth at a time. But I will not intrench farther on thy patience, nor run the risk of a vertigo by pursuing the swift orbicular motions of nature. It matters not much whether the sun stands still or the earth, provided we run the race that is appointed us so as to gain the prize. Yet I will ask thy judgment on another point, which men of high reaches have started.

There are some learned men who say the moon and rest of the planets are habitable as our globe is. For my part to speak freely I could wish it were true; it is a sociable doctrine. It has made me melancholy sometimes, when I have cast my eyes upwards, to think all those ample tracts in the firmament should be void of inhabitants, and yet scarce a turf of our dunghill earth to be found without its domestics. It is demonstrable to the eye that the moon is an opaque body like this globe wherein we tread, having no other light but what it borrows from the sun. Where is the heresy then in supposing that it is created for a like use? I hope the sacred empire of the Mussulmans will not stain itself with such a barbarous murder as was committed on Vergilius, a certain Christian bishop who was burnt by the decree of the Roman Church for asserting the antipodes,[4] a truth which all nations are now sensible of since the improvement of navigation and traffic. And yet Galileo had like to have undergone the same sentence at Rome within these ten years for maintaining the earth's motion and that the sun is the fixed centre of the world; nothing but his recantation being sufficient to have saved him. Such severities choke the growth of learning and

[4] Irish missionary (*c.* 710-84) and later appointed bishop of Salzburg in Austria, Vergilius asserted that the earth was round and men lived on the antipodes or other side of the world, a doctrine which the Church since the time of St. Augustine found heretical. There is, however, no evidence except legend of Vergilius' having been burnt for his beliefs; he was in fact canonized by Pope Gregory IX in 1233.

stop progress which would otherwise be made in arts and sciences.

Happy are the students that live under thy suspicious patronage in that fruitful seminary of philosophers, where the mysteries of God and nature are taught free from the profane licentiousness of the ancient pagans or the superstitious rigours of modern infidels.

I pray the sovereign intelligence not to withdraw from thee his divine influence, nor restrain the flood of light that has been let loose on thy soul. But that thou mayest overflow like Nilus and enlighten not only Africa but the whole world with some new discovery.

Paris, the 29th of the 9th moon of the year 1642.

To Cara Haly, the Physician at Constantinople

Volume II, Book I, Letter XXVII

The Western philosophers, especially those who follow the sentiments of Monsieur Descartes, maintain that the souls of all living creatures (except men) are material and mortal, that a beast is but a machine like a watch or clock, not actuated or informed by any spirit distinct from the body, but moved to the performance of all natural actions by a mere corporeal mechanism, set on work by various impulses from external objects.

In this they oppose Aristotle and all the sages of the East. And thou knowest that our Arabian doctors are of a contrary opinion, who ascribe reason, discourse and immortality to the souls of beasts as well as to those of men, having assigned particular apartments for Al Burak, the beast which carried our Holy Prophet from Mecca to Jerusalem,[1] for the ram which Abraham sacrificed instead of his son Isaac, for the cow of Moses, the pismire of Solomon, the whale which saved Jonah, the raven which fed Elijah, the ass which rebuked Balaam

[1] A vision of a journey recorded in the Koran, Sura XVII. Al Burak was the fabulous animal which according to legend (but unmentioned in the Koran) carried Muhammad to the heavenly Jerusalem.

and in general for all the camels which have the honour to carry the sacred Alcoran to Mecca.

I will suspend my belief of their being entertained in paradise till I shall have the happiness to see them there, but I cannot however acquiesce to the opinions of these modern philosophers who assert their souls to be mere matter. The bodies of both men and beasts, I own, perform all motions by mechanical rules, but that mechanism is guided by a higher principle than the fortuitous impulse of external agents in beasts as well as men.

All animals seem to me to be endued with a faculty which if it may not be called reason, yet is something analogous to it, for which we want a proper name. And of this mind were Empedocles, Pythagoras, Plotinus and Porphyry with many other ancient sages, though this faculty is more eminently conspicuous in some kinds of beasts than in others.

I cannot but admire the regular architecture of bees, their industry and politic economy, vying with the most excellent form and administration of government among men. 'Tis with no less pleasure I behold the spider, when with exquisite art she builds her little silken palace and lays her fine-wrought trains to catch the unwary fly. 'Tis equally pleasant and diverting to observe the conduct of the pismires, their prudent forecast; how they trudge up and down all the summer to lay up a sufficient stock of provender for the barren winter. There is no kind of bird, four-footed beast or fish which does not confute this Cartesian hypothesis.

It is credibly reported by Porphyry [2] that in the East Indies there is a beast which they call a hyena, which approaching near the villages will imitate a man's voice and calling the inhabitants by their names, if they come out of their houses, it will seize on the first that comes to hand and devour him. The dog, the ape, the elephant with many other four-footed beasts afford us manifest specimens of reason or something very like it.

Who has not heard of the love which dolphins bear to men? Pliny relates a pretty story [3] of a dolphin that frequented the lake Lucrinus in Italy, and being often fed from the shore

[2] Porphyry's *De Abstinentia,* Book III, Section IV.

[3] *Naturalis Historia,* Book IX, Chapter 8.

by a certain school boy, grew at length so familiar as to come at a call. We also read of another who took the musician Arion on his back (when cast into the sea by cruel sailors) and carried him safe to shore.[4]

Can all these actions proceed from mere matter? In my opinion 'tis as easy to defend that human nature itself is but matter so and so modified, and that all the bustle men keep in the world is but the effect of a better composition of body, the result of a more perfect and refined machine. I easily agree that we far excel the other living creatures in all the operations of our souls and exercises of our reason. Yet we have our defects as well as they, and this I esteem as one of the greatest: to deny them any share in reason who so far excel us in sense. It is a culpable pride and envy in men thus to blast the reputation of their animal kindred, from which vices I know thou art free.

God, that has made use of the tongue of a silly ass to reprove the folly of a wise man in his own conceit, illuminate our understandings in the mysteries of His Law.

Paris, the 24th of the 10th moon of the year 1642.

To Cara Haly

Volume II, Book I, Letter XXXIV

Suffer me to converse with thee after the manner of friends with freedom and familiarity. I have often discovered to thee the distempers of my body; now I will reveal those more dangerous ones of my mind. And I know not whether they are distempers or cures of such. I have writ to the mufti on the same subject in part but with caution and reserve. With thee I will deal frankly and pour into thy bosom the secret of my heart.

I am dissatisfied in many things pertaining to religion. 'Tis true I cannot think or speak of our Holy Prophet but with infinite attachment and veneration; yet I owe something to my reason. I will believe the Messenger of God was true

[4] Herodotus's *Histories,* Book I, Sections 23 and 24.

and perfect, but is it a crime to think his successors were but men subject to frailty and error? Their divisions immediately after the death of our Great Lawgiver justify this reflection, since the fatal schism continues to this day.[1] Either the Persians or we must be in the wrong. Grant which thou wilt, it follows that the truth was no sooner sown in the world but it sprang up immortal heresies. I find no other assurance that we are in the right but the assertion of our doctors, the followers of Osman and Abu Bakr, who for aught I know are no more exempted from error than the disciples of Ali. Both sides believe the Holy Prophet, yet both at infinite distance in their interpretations of His law. Each party boasts they have the true sense of the divine oracles and curses the opposite for heretics. Truth cannot be repugnant to itself.

From his original schism well near a hundred several sects have sprung, each maintaining different interpretations of the law. While truth can be but one, where shall a man be sure to find it amongst so many pretenders to it? Think not I am going to turn Christian because of this liberty I take to search for truth. For the case is the same or worse among them.

Jesus (whom our Holy Prophet calls the breath and word of God, the reformer of the law of Moses, knowing the secrets of hearts and working miracles) preached to the Jews repentance, good works, the resurrection of the dead, the day of judgment, the joys of paradise and the torments of hell. He chose twelve disciples to disperse his doctrine over the world. But they likewise had dissentions among themselves, after that God had taken the Messiah up to paradise; each apostle leaving different traditions behind him in the countries where he taught. Hence sprung the differences between the Churches of the East and West and those in Ethiopia, one following Peter and Paul, another believing John, the third defending the traditions of Matthew. And from these greater schisms have sprung innumerable smaller sects and heresies, each church and party excommunicating, damning and cursing all the rest; yet all believe they shall be saved.

Thus is the world at odds about religion, persecuting, biting and devouring one another, because they cannot all

[1] See note 2, page 8.

think alike: a singular argument of religion and a special encouragement to gain proselytes.

These considerations have made me a sceptic in controverted points of faith and matters of opinion. Only in this I am fixed: that I believe in One Eternal God and reverence His Holy Messengers and Prophets. But if an angel from heaven should tell me monstrous and incredible stories of things repugnant to the common sense and reason of all mankind, I would desire him to excuse me if I suspended my belief.

I admire the golden age when the infant world had not yet learned bigotry, when human reason was not corrupted with divine fables, and natural conscience was the oracle to which all resorted for solution of their doubts, before superstition had begun to dress the Deity in frightful, uncouth shapes. Then harmless innocence could show her naked face which now is fain to go disguised. No man was put to death for words or thoughts of things above his reach. No crafty Numa then had fobbed upon the credulous people his feigned Egeria,[2] nor golden-tongued Pythagoras could impose the forged whispers of his eagle on the silly Crotonians for sacred oracles.[3] No wonder-working magician had led the rabble by the nose with his infernal juggles, but pure and undebauched reason taught men to lead immortal lives on earth.

Tell me, O learned Holy, canst thou believe that the Divine Architect had no other way to make man than by laying him a thousand years broiling in the sun? Or that there is an apple tree growing very near the throne of God? Or that the angels can stride some hundred thousands of miles at once? Can we not go to paradise unless we swallow these strange notions? Is it not enough to believe in God and Muhammad His Prophet, except we will receive all for truth which the doctors tell us? I fast and pray at the appointed times and sometimes oftener; I give alms; I love all the creatures of God that remain in His love. I am not guilty of theft, murder nor adultery; I never forswore myself nor bore false witness. Yet

[2] A legendary king of Rome, Numa Pompilius was instructed by the prophetic nymph Egeria in the rites of religious worship, which he in turn taught his subjects.

[3] Pythagoras settled at Crotona in Italy, where he was able to establish a secret society or brotherhood to advance his theories.

when I am recollected, I think myself the worst of all man; I think of every peccadillo I commit with inexpressible regret. If all this is not sufficient to acquit me a true and good Mussulman, no man I hope will blame me if I join with an eminent man in these western parts and wish my soul among the philosophers.

Paris, the 25th of the 11th moon of the year 1642.

To Ibrahim Hali Sheik, a Man of the Law

Volume II, Book III, Letter I

Here is a man come to this city, if he may be called a man, who pretends to have lived above these sixteen hundred years. They call him the Wandering Jew. But some say he is an impostor. He says of himself that he was usher of the divan in Jerusalem (the Jews call it the Court of Judgment), where all criminal causes were tried at the time when Jesus, the son of Mary, the Christian's Messiah, was condemned by Pontius Pilate, the Roman president. That his name was Michob Ader, and that for thrusting Jesus out of the hall with these words, 'Go, why tarriest thou?' the Messiah answered him again: 'I go, but tarry thou till I come'; thereby condemning him to live till the day of judgment.[1] He pretends to remember the Apostles that lived in those days and that he himself was baptized by one of them; that he has travelled through all the regions of the world and so must continue to be a vagabond till the Messiah shall return again. They say that he heals diseases by touching the party affected. Divers other miracles are ascribed to him by the ignorant and superstitious. But the learned, the noble and the great censure him as a counterfeit or madman. Yet there are those who affirm that 'tis one convincing argument of the reality of his pretence that he has

[1] In the traditional legend, the Jew was a shoemaker named Ahasuerus, who spurned Christ. While bearing the cross to Calvary, Jesus tried to rest on the shoemaker's doorstep. Ahasuerus told him to move on, and thus Christ punished him by dooming him to wander through the world until the last judgment. For a discussion of the legend and its sources see Moncure D. Conway, *The Wandering Jew* (London, 1881).

hitherto escaped a prison especially in these countries where the authors of all innovations are severely punished. He has escaped the inquisitions at Rome, in Spain and in Portugal, which the vulgar will have to be an evident miracle.

One day I had the curiosity to discourse with him in several languages, and I found him master of all those that I could speak. I conversed with him five or six hours together in Arabic. He told me that there was scarce a true history to be found. I asked him what he thought of Muhammad, the Prophet and Lawgiver of the Mussulmans? He answered that he knew His father very well and had been often in his company at Ormus in Persia, that Muhammad was a man full of light and a divine spirit but had His errors as well as other mortals, and that His chiefest was in denying the crucifixion of the Messiah; for said he, 'I was then present and saw him hang on the cross with these eyes of mine.' He accused the Mussulmans of imposture in making the world believe that the tomb of their Prophet hangs miraculously between heaven and earth, saying that he himself had seen it and that it was built after the manner of other sepulchres. Thou who hast been at the holy place[2] knowest whether this be true or false. He upbraids the Persian Muhammadans with luxury, the Ottomans with tyranny, the Arabians with robbery, the Moors with cruelty and the Mussulmans of the Indies with atheism. Nor does he spare to reproach the Christian churches: he taxes the Roman and Grecian with the pompous idolatry of the heathens. He accuses the Ethiopian of Judaism, the Armenian of heresy and says that the Protestants, if they would live according to their profession, would be the best Christians.

He told me he was in Rome when Nero set fire to the city and stood triumphing on the top of a hill to behold its flames. That he saw Saladin's return from his conquests in the East, when he caused his shirt to be carried on the top of a spear with this proclamation: 'Saladin, Lord of many rich countries, conqueror of the East, ever victorious and happy when he dies shall have no other memorial left of all his glories but only this poor shirt.'

He relates many remarkable passages of Solyman the Mag-

[2] Medina, where Muhammad is buried.

nificent, whereof our histories are silent, and says he was in Constantinople when Solyman built that royal mosque which goes by his name. He knew Tamburlaine the Scythian and told me that he was so called because he halted with one leg. He pretends also to have been acquainted with Scanderbeg, the valiant and fortunate Prince of Epirus.[3] He seemed to pity the insupportable calamity of Bajazet, whom he had seen carried about in a cage by Tamburlaine's order. He accuses the Scythian of too barbarous an insult on the unfortunate sultan. He remembers the ancient caliphs of Babylon and Egypt, the empire of the Saracens and the wars in the Holy Land. He highly extols the valour and conduct of the renowned Godfrey of Bouillon.[4] He gives an accurate account of the rise, progress, establishment and subversion of the Mamalukes in Egypt. He says he has washed himself in the two head springs of the river Nile which arise in the most southern part of Ethiopia. That its increase is occasioned by the great rains in Ethiopia, which swell all the rivers that fall into the Nile and cause that vast inundation which has so much puzzled philosophy to find out the origin. He says that the river Ganges in India is broader and deeper than the Nile, that the river Niger in Africa is longer by some hundreds of miles. And that he can remember a time when the river Nile overflowed not till three months after the usual season.

Having professed himself an universal traveller and that there was no corner of the earth where he had not been present, I began to comfort myself with the hopes of some news from the ten tribes of Israel that were into captivity by Shalmaneser, King of Assyria, and could never be heard of since. I asked him several questions concerning them but found no satisfactory answer. Only he told me that both in Asia, Africa and Europe he had taken notice of a sort of people who (though not Jewish in profession) yet retained some characteristics whereby one might discover them to be descended of that nation.

In Livonia, Russia and Finland he had met with people of

[3] Scanderbeg or Iskender Bey (1403-67) is a national hero of Albania for freeing parts of Albania from Ottoman rule.

[4] Godfrey of Bouillon (1060-1100) was an important military leader of the first Crusade and played a prominent part in the capture of Jerusalem.

distinct languages from that of the country, having a great mixture of Hebrew words, that these people abstained from swine's flesh, blood and things strangled. That in their lamentations for the dead they always used these words: 'Jeru-Jeru Masco Salem.' By which he thought they called to remembrance Jerusalem and Damascus, those famous cities of Palestine and Syria. In the Circassians also he had traced some footsteps of Judaism, their customs, manner of life, feasts, marriages and sacrifices, being not far removed from the institutions of the Mosaic Law. But what is most remarkable, he said, that he had conversed with professed Jews in the north parts of Asia, who never so much as heard of Jesus, the son of Mary, or of the revolutions in Judea after his death, the siege and destruction of Jerusalem or any other matters wherewith all histories abound concerning that nation. He said, moreover, that these Jews had only the Pentateuch, not having heard of the rest of those books which compose the greatest part of the Old Testament, and that this Pentateuch was written in a sort of Hebrew far different from that which is now commonly spoken by the rest of the dispersed Jews throughout the world. That the number of these Jews was infinite. And finally he thought that these, if any, were the true posterity of those ten captive tribes.

Having mentioned the destruction of Jerusalem, I asked him where he was at that time. He told me in the court of Vespasian at Rome and that he had heard the emperor say when he understood the Temple of Solomon was burnt to ashes, he had rather all Rome had been set on fire. Here the old man fell aweeping himself, lamenting the ruins of that noble structure, which he described to me as familiarly as if he had seen it but yesterday. He says that Josephus wrote partially of the seditious in the city, being related to one of the chief ringleaders, whom therefore he spared, being loath to stain the reputation of his own family to all posterity.

I tell thee, sage Sheik, if this man's pretences be true, he is so full of choice memoirs and has been witness to so many grand transactions for the space of sixteen centuries of years that he may not unfitly be called a living chronology, the protonotary of the Christian's hejira or principal recorder of that which they esteem the last epoch of the world's duration.

By his looks one would take him for a relic of the old world or one of the long-lived fathers before the flood. To speak modestly, he may pass for the younger brother of time.

It would be endless to tell thee how many other discourses we had of his travels and memoirs; till tired with his company and judging all to be a cheat, I took my leave.

I tell thee he seems to be a man well versed in all histories, a great traveller and one that affects to be counted an extraordinary person. The common people are ready to adore him, and the very fear of the multitude restrains the magistrates from offering any violence to this impostor.

Live thou in the exercise of thy reason, which will not permit thee to be seduced into errors by the subtle insinuations of men. Continue to love Mahmut, who honours thee without a fiction.

Paris, the 4th of the 11th moon of the year 1644.

To Dgnet Oglou

Volume II, Book III, Letter XVIII

One would think it an easy matter for a stranger to conceal himself in so vast and populous a city as is Paris. Especially one who makes so mean and contemptible a figure as does the supposed Titus of Moldavia. I little thought that the lowness of my stature and the deformity of my body would have attracted any curious eyes, but that my habit would have protected me from all suspicion and that I might have passed an age undiscovered among the infinite crowds of people who throng both the houses and streets of Paris. Yet there are some critical moments of our lives wherein fate delights to sport with us, to throw stumbling blocks in our way, to entangle us in difficulties and perils. This is a necessary discipline of heaven to rouse men from the lees of security and confidence in their own strength and abilities and to instruct us that providence alone can extricate us out of the labyrinths we often fall into.

I was walking yesterday before the great temple of this

city, which is dedicated to Mary, the mother of Jesus,[1] when on a sudden I was accosted (by one whom I little imagined to have seen in Paris) with these words:

'Mahmut! How came you by this habit? What make you in this place? Are you a Christian or do you thus disguise yourself for other ends?'

Thou mayest easily imagine what a terror seized me when I knew that he who spoke to me was my old master at Palermo.[2] It brought to my remembrance all the cruel blows and stripes I had received during that irksome captivity, and I could almost have fancied myself ready for the bastinado. However, dissembling my confusion, I answered briskly:

'Sir, you are mistaken in the person; my name is not Mahmut but Titus. I am a Christian and a Catholic; if you are such yourself, you have no reason to upbraid my habit since I wear it as a badge of my profession, being a student and candidate of the priesthood.'

This answer, instead of satisfying him, did but augment his jealousy, and being of a passionate temper, he broke out into fierce language calling me Turk, infidel, slave, dog and all the ill names his fury could suggest. He spoke so loud that it was taken notice of by the people as they walked by, who began to gather about us to learn the occasion of so much noise. I then condemned myself for not rather owning myself to him and inviting him to some more retired place where I might give him an account of my circumstances. I looked upon myself as a dead man and would gladly have sustained seven years of servitude again in Sicily to have been rid of the fear I was now under of a more terrible punishment.

While I was in this confusion of spirit, thinking of nothing but racks and tortures, the noise of the rabble who flocked about us had alarmed the people that were at their devotions in the church, who came running out to inquire the cause of such a tumult. Among the rest a friar, eminent for his learning and virtue and who had a particular esteem and friendship for me, perceiving the matter, came up close to me and taking me by the hand, spoke aloud these words:

[1] The Cathedral of Notre Dame.
[2] In his youth Mahmut had been a slave to this Christian master, from whom he had received brutal treatment and attempted to escape.

'Sirs, forbear to injure a stranger in the court of the mother of God. I know this man very well and will be responsible for him; he is a Catholic clerk and a servant of the Living God.'

The rabble gave a great shout at the end of this harangue, and had not my Sicilian master made a narrow escape, they would have endangered to tear him in pieces. I know not what became of him afterwards, but I attended the friar into the temple where we stayed during the celebration of their Mass, and then he conducted me through the inner parts of the temple by private ways into the lodgings of the priests, whence we issued out by a postern, and taking boat we crossed the river Seine into the fields. The friar congratulated my escape from the hands of the multitude, and I returned him a thousand thanks for lifting me out of the mire.

Thou seest, dear friend, that the Arabian proverb speaks not in vain when it says that the habitation of danger is on the borders of security, and that a man never runs greater hazards than when he least fears them.

He that turns the scales of life and death, good and evil, grant that some happy emergency may always arise to divert the perils which thou shalt incur in this uncertain life.

Paris, the 7th of the 9th moon of the year 1644.

To Dgnet Oglou

Volume II, Book III, Letter XXIII

It is, thou knowest, a considerable time since I was love-smitten with the beautiful Daria, who was fair as an angel and discreet above any mortal creature. It's hard to say whether the beauty of her mind or that of her body struck deepest impressions on my soul. How long were the nights and how short my slumbers and what a general distraction of thoughts were I in. I could not abide my chamber, and when I went out, no other place could please me. I knew not what I said or thought, whether I dreamt or was really awake, stood or sat, went backwards or forwards, all postures and places being alike, seeing none of them could afford me the relief I sought after.

I imagined no less but that I must thus languish on; yet I find that time and absence have at length made way for reason. Marvel not, dear Oglou, I have suffered these transports. Our passions are not in our power; we cannot love and hate when and whom we please. There is a conformity of blood wherein the stars, they say, work wonders. It's true no man can love and be wise at the same time, but prithee tell me, didst ever know any wise man who was not one time or another in love? Remember thine own passion for the same object, which will make thee the easier to excuse mine. I'll tell thee a story which I have somewhere read, which if it does palliate, yet will not aggravate my weakness.

A certain country man having lost his ass came to the muazzin or crier, desiring him to give notice at the door of one of their mosques, which he did for three several festivals. But no news being heard of the animal, the owner urged the muazzin to continue his proclamations with the regard of a fat pig to the finder.[1] The muazzin being an arch wag and tired with the fellow's importunity, one day when the ceremonies of their superstitious worship was ended and people flocked amain out of the mosque, he made this following proclamation: If there be any man here amongst you who will come forth and solemnly profess he never was in love, he shall have a fat pig.

An ungainly loobily fellow, who was leaning listening on his staff, bawled out that he could safely take his oath he was the person who had never been in love. Whereupon the muazzin taking him by the sleeve presents him to the country man, saying, 'Here, friend, I have found your ass, the pig is mine.'

Rejoice with me for the recovery of my liberty and believe an experienced man when he tells thee that a man's love to his friend, though it be not so violent and strong as that to his mistress, yet is more solid and lasting.

Paris, the 12th of the 11th moon of the year 1644.

[1] This is a curious oversight by the author. Moslems are not allowed to eat pork.

To Dgnet Oglou

Volume II, Book III, Letter XXV

It appears by thy melancholy letter thou hast not forgot the loss thou formerly sustained by fire but still continuest to disturb thyself with dismal apprehensions of spending thy days in ignominious poverty. I am afraid thou didst set thy heart too much on thy wealth, which makes thee so uneasy under thy misfortune. Perhaps thy money was thy master, and God in removing it from thee has made thee free and thereby fitted thee for the contemplation of the universe.

Never fear want. The same providence which took care of thee before thou camest into the world will never be wanting to thee now thou art in it. It is but a little that we need, and it will not be long before it will be impossible for us to want anything. Poverty never meets the thinking and industrious. And a man may satisfy nature without the least obligation to fortune, who when she seems most angry with us scarce ever denies us necessaries. The belly, indeed, is a troublesome creditor, yet is quieted with a little. Seneca tells us that Epicurus confined himself to a narrower allowance than that of the severest prisons to the most heinous offender and found himself at ease too in a stricter diet than any man in the worst condition needs to fear. But the misery of it is we are governed in all things by opinion and everything is to us as we think it to be.

The same great man tells us of one Apicius who poisoned himself for fear of starving, when he had two hundred and fifty piasters in his coffers. And another more modern philosopher relates that a rich man, an acquaintance of his, falling mad snatched up a straw and complained he must perish with hunger, for he saw there was no grain in the empty husks.

It's said of the Emperor Galba that he was wont to weep when he saw his table better covered than ordinary. And I have read of a certain Christian mufti who was so wretchedly covetous that he would steal privately into the great mosque of Rome and put out the lamps there to save charges.

But methinks I hear thee murmuring me an answer, that this was never thy humour, and these citations make little impression on a man that has had his house and goods burnt and narrowly escaped in his own person.

I shall tell thee then what happened lately in these parts, which will perhaps make thee more contented and thankful for thy life, seeing what was these poor people's lot might have been thine.

Certain considerable merchants coming to this town and lodging at an inn not far from my quarters, the house being full of guests, they were forced to be content with an upper room; where entertaining one another with pleasant discourse to pass away the time till supper, on a sudden the kitchen was all in a flame, unfortunately increased with combustible matter lying near the chimney. Some say there was great quantity of oil and gun powder (an odd storehouse to lay such commodities in). However, the fire appeared so suddenly and violently that in a moment all the floor under them was seized with it.

These gentlemen who were two stories high in a chamber towards the street as soon as they heard the cry of fire, began to make towards their trunks and portmantles, which were locked up in a large coffer, the key of which hung at their hostess's girdle. They were for going down to fetch it but the fire had in a manner consumed all beneath them. Whilst they were busied in trying to break open the coffer and to take out every man his own, their chamber became instantly so full of smoke as was like to choke them. They could neither save themselves by going up or down, the house being all over in flame. Moreover, their neighbours seeing their own houses in danger were so concerned for themselves that they had no time to pity others. So that few people attempted to succour these poor gentlemen, who on their side endeavoured with great pieces of wood to force a passage, but the walls and windows were too strong to give way to their efforts, being secured with thick iron bars fastened in the stone. In this lamentable condition, having this inexorable flame before their eyes, which had already seized on the chamber, tearing the hair off their heads and stamping on the ground, they set forth such dreadful shrieks, as moved all that heard them to extreme compassion.

They threw their gold and silver into the streets in vain crying for help; the fire being so increased that before the people could bring ladders and other instruments to break a way into the chamber these poor wretches miserably perished in the flames.

Thank God thou hast still thy life and senses. Turn these last the right way and thou wilt find thou hast lost nothing.

Paris, 21st of the 11th moon of the year 1644.

To the Kaimakam

Volume II, Book III, Letter XXXIV

I need not apologize for my long silence. Eliachim assures me he has acquainted Nathan Ben Saddi with the occasion of it, by whom the news of my imprisonment might be transmitted to the sublime Port. When I was first seized upon I had not the liberty to send for Eliachim or see anybody that I desired to speak with. But that honest Jew soon heard the news and writ to Vienna to prevent any dispatches that might come from thence or from Constantinople. He has now fully convinced me of his fidelity, which I so long suspected,[1] and I dare trust him henceforward with the most important concerns of my commission. His sagacity and conduct in this occurrence is worthy of acknowledgment and reward, having dextrously blinded Cardinal Mazarin, who is an Argus, baffled his severest scrutinies and been highly instrumental in procuring me the liberty I now again enjoy.

The Arabian proverb says, the camel that travels often to Mecca will return lame at last. I had for a long time essayed to penetrate into the drifts of this cardinal as well as those of his predecessor Richelieu, yet found nothing but riddles. One might as soon trace Arethusa in her wanderings underground or pursue a man in the intricate mazes of Dedalus as discover the intrigues of this state serpent. His designs are a perfect

[1] Cf. letter to Bekir Bassa (pp. 23-26).

labyrinth. However, walking one day in one of their churches, I cast my eye on a stone in the pavement just before the image of the Virgin Mary, which by the perpetual kneeling of many thousand votaries was worn away half a cubit. The sight of this made me conclude that there is no difficulty so great which by assiduous industry and constant resolution may not be overcome. Cheered with this thought I determined with myself never to faint or give over my most strenuous endeavours to unlock the cabinet of this great minister wherein I knew all the secrets of Europe were laid up. I left no stone unturned to compass my design. I haunted the court daily and followed the cardinal like his shadow. I insinuated with his followers and creatures, flattered the soft and ambitious, presented gifts to the covetous, was merry and frank with some, reserved and grave with others. In fine, I so aimed to comport myself with everyone that I might win all. At length knowing that there was a private agent from Prince Ragotzky [2] come to this court, my zeal for the Grand Signior suggested to me that if I could wind myself into this man's acquaintance, I should be able to unravel some great secret and do an acceptable service to the Ottoman Empire.

Opportunities are seldom wanting to the watchful and diligent. I had acquaintance enough at the court, and appearing often in the retinue of Mazarin, and the cardinal sometimes singling me out and discoursing with me in the presence of the Transylvanian, this stranger took more than ordinary notice of me; which gave me occasion to address myself to him in hopes to accomplish my purpose. But fate had otherwise decreed. The agent remembered my face and told me in the Slavonian tongue that he had seen me in the Grand Signior's seraglio. It is not hard for thee, illustrious Kaimakam, to conceive that disorder I was in at this challenge. But resuming courage I replied that it was possible he might have seen me there, for I had formerly served a German Ambassador at the Ottoman court in quality of secretary. He seemed satisfied with my answer, dissembling his farther thoughts, but as I afterwards perceived, I owe my confinement to this fatal interview. No doubt but he remarked the particular station I was in at the seraglio, when he came thither to negotiate for

[2] Georges Ragotzky reigned as Prince of Transylvania from 1631 to 1648.

Prince Ragotzky in the Sultan Amurath's time. For before I went to bed that night I was sent for to Cardinal Mazarin and strictly examined about my country, my religion, my business at Paris, and other matters, and was sent away prisoner to the Bastille (which was formerly a citadel erected to awe this town but not being found serviceable in that kind is since made a prison). That which most puzzles me is that I was not confronted face to face with this Transylvanian.

My confinement was very close, being denied the use of pen, ink and paper and the access of any of my friends. Indeed, I knew not what use to make of those materials, nor durst I write to anybody lest I should have brought them into the same snare and done myself a greater disservice. All my comfort was that I had left no writings in my lodgings which could discover the affairs of my commission. 'Tis true when I was searched they found the Alcoran in my pocket, which gave a mighty jealousy to the cardinal, but I excused it by saying I kept that book that I might not forget my Arabic, in which the cardinal knew I was well skilled, having formerly seen a translation which I made out of that language for Cardinal Richelieu. Besides, they found in my chamber Plutarch's *Lives,* the *Annals* of Tacitus, Livy's *Roman History,* philosophical treatise of Averroes and a small tract of St. Augustine, one of the Christian fathers; which made it appear as reasonable to conclude me a Pagan of a Christian for having their books by me as a Turk for having the Alcoran.

I still persisted in asserting myself to be Titus of Moldavia and that I was a Christian. (Heaven forgive the perjury!) I had a friar sent to me, who exhorted me to a confession of my sins, thinking this way to pump the mighty secret from me. But this turned to my advantage, for calling to mind a learned and ingenuous friar, with whom I had conversed and contracted some friendship, I signified my resolution to confess myself to him. This is a privilege that could not be denied me, it being lawful for every man to choose his own confessor. The friar was sent for. This being the only time I was like to speak to any of my friends without witnesses, I improved the advantage and to make my confession seem the more sincere, I accused myself of what I ne'er was guilty of, telling him with a well-counterfeited sorrow that the true reason of abandoning Moldavia was because I had murdered a near kinsman there. My confession ended and absolution granted, the friar embraced me and told me that he would do me all the service he could in order to my release. I expressed my gratitude in the best terms I could and begged of him to visit me often, since he was the only person would be allowed to do me that kind of office. I will not detain thee longer, sage Bassa, in expectation of the issue.

This honest friar was as good as his word. He was admitted to see me almost daily without suspicion. I trusted him with Eliachim's acquaintance, which rendered him very serviceable, for he often brought me money from the Jew, when he knew not how otherwise to convey it to me. In a word, between them both they so wrought on the cardinal that after six moons imprisonment I was released and am now in more credit than before.

The great God grant that the malice of the infidels may always turn to the advantage of the true believers, and that from their jealousies occasions may arise to promote the interest of the Ottoman Empire.

Paris, the 24th of the 7th moon of the year 1645.

To the Instructed in All Knowledge, the Venerable Mufti

Volume III, Book I, Letter III

Hail holy interpreter of the sacred law. May the divine light guide thee beyond the errors of human frailty. I am amongst infidels, enemies to truth, who yet seem as certain of being in the right as thou art sure they are in the wrong. They hate us with an inveterate hatred. I must dissemble my resentments whilst with the lowest prostrations to the Unity, I celebrate His glorious mercy, who has sent us such a star to guide our feet into the way of peace.

The Christians scoff at the faithful people as divided into several sects. Would my death could wipe out these reproaches and vindicate the honour of the holy profession. I could retort that error shows itself infinite in them, but I must hold my peace and restrain myself lest my zeal transport me beyond discretion, remembering I am not sent here to dispute but to act secretly for my great master, whose empire be extended over all the habitable world.

These poor wretches boast much of their traditions, their sacred synods and fathers, as if we ever wanted holy men working wonders and penetrating into the profoundest mysteries by only wiping their eyes with the dust on their feet.

They talk much of faith and reason, at which I smile, as knowing it to be only education. Yet as the worst of people have something that is good; so these are not wholly destitute of devotion. They pray often but not so often as the true believers, it being as thou knowest a just exception against a witness amongst us that he prays not six times a day. They pray to men and women deceased, whereas thou knowest there is no deity but one. They fast often but not so strictly as those assisted with the virtue of the Supreme Dispenser of graces. They are charitable, but this hinders 'em not from excluding all from the blest abodes who are not of their belief; whereas thou affirmest (who art the resolver of all the problems of faith) that it will go well at the last day with all honest people, seeing these have all the same object of worship. Their different religions are but as so many different ways, which lead a man to the same place of rest like various roads to the same city.

These Christians whip themselves often with small cords, which humour they say was set on foot by an hermit's preaching and example. Not many countries distant from that where I am, there happened such an odd instance of this extravagant zeal (which was to be heightened, it seems, with the fumes of wine) as plainly justifies our Prophet's wisdom in charging the faithful to avoid it. It was particularly the custom of several people in this place in their processions to whip themselves till the blood streamed down their frocks, which were so made as to cover their faces and leave only their backs bare. One of these zealots distrusting the firmness of his constitution had taken such large draughts of this intoxicating liquor that reeling up and down with his whip in his hand and his head against the walls he was followed by all the boys of the town hooting after him, which so lessened the repute of this sottish religion as made 'em abstain for the future from this pompous usage of it. What low thoughts have these people of the Almighty Lord of all, when allowing Him to be omnipotent yet represent Him to themselves and others as delighting in cruelty! Whereas thou knowest this passion is only to be found amongst the weak and miserable.

That the divine preserver of men may continue thee long for the edification of his elect are the passionate wishes of the meanest of thy servants Mahmut.

Paris, the 4th of the 8th moon of the year 1645.

To Shashim Istham, a Black Eunuch

Volume III, Book I, Letter V

At length thou hast condescended to beg my pardon for the calumnies thy tongue has loaded me with.[1] I am not ill pleased with thy letter. It abounds with elegant expressions of thy sorrow for an offence to which thou hadst no provocation. Thy submission, though late, abates my resentment, and if thou performist thy promise 'tis banished. The first crime so ingenuously acknowledged claims a title to forgiveness; let eternal oblivion seal it. I am not by nature revengeful. I rather blush for shame than grow pale with anger at him that injures me. Yet self-preservation will rouse our choler, which is the most active humour, and precipitates many to violent courses. The effect it has on me is to put me on my guard lest he who has wronged me without any signs of repentance should continue his malice to my destruction. But thou hast dispersed all my suspicions by thy seasonable address, and if I cannot pronounce thee innocent, I will believe thou art not incorrigible. The best advice I can give thee is henceforwards to attend to thy affairs and refrain from those of others, remembering the Arabian proverb: He that peeps in at his neighbour's window may chance to lose his eyes. There is a

[1] The black eunuch and others in the seraglio intrigued to have Mahmut recalled home by impugning his religious orthodoxy and abilities.

great deal of wisdom couched in these short sentences. They are not the product of one man's experience nor of a few, but they are the result of universal observation. And our country has been happy above others in the choice of her proverbs. This that I mention is peculiar to the East, yet I can produce an instance whereby 'twas verified in the West.

There is hardly a night passes in this populous city wherein some murder is not committed in the streets. Two nights ago a man was found dead on the ground, whereupon a tumult was gathered about his bleeding carcass. Among the rest a fellow came crowding in, inquisitive what should be the matter. Those who stood by beholding his clothes bloody, which he was not sensible of himself, seized on him as the murderer. His wild looks increased their jealousy, and the incoherent words with which he endeavoured to excuse himself rendered him guilty in the judgment of the rabble. They carried him before a cadi,[2] by whom he was strictly examined. He stoutly denied the fact, and no proof could be brought against him but his stained clothes. 'Tis the custom here to put to the torture persons suspected of capital crimes in order to draw a confession of the truth. This they did to this poor wretch, and in the extremity of his pains he acknowledged he had killed his wife that evening but was altogether innocent of this poor man's death, who was murdered in the streets. All the torments they inflicted could force no other confession from him save that which his real guilt prompted him to make, for which he was condemned to death according to the laws. Thou seest by this that had he gone about his business without prying into other men's matters, he might have escaped a discovery. But that meddling itch of the imprudent betrayed him (not without the particular direction of fate) to a death, which indeed he merited, but not on the score of the murdered man, whom he went out of his way to see.

Thou wilt say this story is not applicable to thy case, since thou hast never yet embrued thy hands in any man's blood. I tell thee what I have said was not designed as a reflection on thy past offence – let it be forgotten – but as a caution for the future not to engage thyself in matters out of thy sphere. For a busybody is never without trouble.

[2] A judge.

Above all I counsel thee to practise the government of the tongue, which is a great virtue especially in the court of princes. The Arabians say that a wise man's soul reposes at the root of his tongue, but a fool's is ever dancing on the tip.

Thou hast no reason to take in ill part the freedom with which I advise thee for thy good, unless thou thinkest thyself too old to learn. But I have a better opinion of thee than to rank thee among Pythagoras's asses.

I have said enough for a friend, too much for an enemy. It is in thy own choice to make me which thou pleasest. Adieu.

Paris, the 4th of the 8th moon of the year 1645.

To Iksingi Cap' Oglani, Preceptor to the Royal Pages of the Seraglio

Volume III, Book I, Letter X

There is a vast difference between thy letter and that of Shashim Istham. He is eloquent in the acknowledgment of his crime; thou, rhetorical in thy own justification. Thou hast plundered Demosthenes and Cicero and robbed 'em of all the flowers and tropes of oratory to dress up a faint lifeless excuse. Such an artificial apology, instead of cancelling, heightens thy offence. It might have procured thee the applause of the academy, but it comes short of giving me satisfaction for the injuries I have received at thy hands. I have reason to esteem them such, because so designed, although they took no effect. For wrongs of this kind ought to be measured by the intention of the author, not by their success. The ministers of the divan will hardly be prevailed on to suspect Mahmut, who has given substantial proofs of his fidelity.

Tell me in the name of God and Muhammad what was the motive that induced thee to slander me? Wherein have I merited this persecution at thy hands. It could not be revenge, because I never gave thee occasion unless thou still retainest a grudge on the score of my studying in the academies, and that at my return from Palermo thou wert not able to expose me in the presence of the mufti in any point of language or learning. But I had rather charitably believe 'twas thy ambition not thy malice which gave birth to those calumnies thou hast vented against me. Thou enviest me the honour of serving the Grand Signior in this station, thinking thyself capable of discharging this office more successfully than Mahmut. I censure not thy abilities but I think 'tis best for every man to be content with his own condition, since destiny distributes the employments of the world among men by rules into which we cannot penetrate.

Thou art master of the French tongue, but dost thou think that a complete qualification for a man in my post? Art thou fit to converse in the court of a foreign prince, who canst not govern thy tongue in that of thy native sovereign? Thou art yet to learn a courtier's masterpiece, which is to dissemble even the necessary art of dissimulation. That is as the Arabians say, to have a veil upon a veil; or as the Italians, to have a mask with a natural face on the outside. Thou art so far from this that thou canst not yet draw perfectly the first rough strokes of a counterfeit.

To speak plain, hadst thou by an artificial feigning of friendship to me, made way to insinuate thy story into the belief of the grandees, thou mightest have praised me to my ruin. But to go bluntly to work without preventive encomiums discovered at once the weakness of thy judgment and the strength of thy passion, giving the ministers occasion to think there was less of truth than of design in thy accusations.

For the future I advise thee to mind thy books and scholars and meddle not with Mahmut, whose business is to study men. Adieu.

Paris, the 5th of the 10th moon of the year 1645.

To Cara Haly

Volume III, Book I, Letter XXVII

The time of year is now come where the earth turns her inside out, and nature calls forth the hidden virtues of that element to grace the world with an infinite variety of pleasant forms and colours. The eye is lost in such a crowd of different beauties, and every sense is ravished with delightful objects. The young men and virgins throng the fields to behold the resurrection of flowers and herbs, and the old feel new vigours springing in their bodies as though they had been in Medea's cauldron.[1] Even Mahmut himself, who has drooped all the winter, now begins to lift up his head and partake in the common restoration of all things.

If I am capable of guessing at the occasion of my frequent sickness, I believe it may in part be attributed to the want of fresh air in the place where I lodge. There is a vast difference between the streets of Paris and those of Constantinople. I seem to myself to be buried alive in this close city where my chamber window affords me no farther prospect than I can spit; whereas in Constantinople, the gardens are so intermixed with houses that it looks like a city in the midst of a forest, and by the advantage of its situation is always refreshed with breezes from the sea.

Besides the impurity of these infidels, who empty all their filth in the streets so that the dirt of Paris may be smelt some miles off, the uncleanness of their diet contributes in no small measure to my distemper, being forced either to feed on flesh with the blood in it or live on herbs. They laugh at the niceness of the Mussulmans who will eat no meat that was knocked down or strangled. They seem to be greedy of blood, saving it in vessels, and mixing it with flour of wheat, make a certain bread thereof, which they devour without the least squeamishness. A true believer would tremble at the sight of such impiety. I tell thee it is impossible to live among them and not

[1] Medea rejuvenated Aeson, Jason's father, by boiling him with special herbs.

be polluted. They have no methods of purification. They wallow and hug themselves in their uncleanness; they are worse than the beasts.

Now the spring has provided a new banquet wherein there is no impurity, I am resolved to live like a Mussulman and conform to the precepts of our Holy Lawgiver, who when he beholds my zeal and abstinence, will send the angel of health from his paradise to repair my decayed constitution.

The French philosophers are busied in an inquisition after certain kinds of birds, which from the second day of this moon, they say are not to be found in the whole kingdom, though the woods and fields were full of them during the winter. Some are of the opinion that they fly to the moon, asserting that if wings will but carry 'em beyond the magnetic force of the earth, it will be no pain to glide through the upper airy region till they arrive within the attractive energy of that planet, where they will naturally seek rest. Others with more probability say that these birds take their flight to some other region of the earth, whose climate is more agreeable to their natures at this time of year.

I wish I could as easily once a year take my flight to Constantinople, where my heart is, winter and summer. Adieu, dear Haly, and pity Mahmut who counts himself unhappy in nothing so much as in being absent from his friends.

Paris, the 7th of the 4th moon of the year 1646.

To the Aga of the Janissaries[1]

Volume III, Book II, Letter X

I perceive thou hast followed the advice I formerly gave thee to read histories, wherein thy letter speaks thee very conversant. Thou wilt have no reason to repent of a labour that affords so agreeable a diversion, especially to a soldier and a statesman. They open the graves and call forth the dead without disturbing their repose and present to us those heroes living, talking and acting great things, whose bodies have

[1] Commander-in-Chief of that militia.

lain buried in silence and obscurity many ages. They introduce us into the closets of princes revealing their most secret counsels. They make us familiar with the intrigues of politicians and the stratagems of warriors. In fine, there is nothing public or private in the courts or camps of the greatest monarchs to which an historian is a stranger.

I applaud the choice thou hast made of Grecian histories and others of the East, yet I counsel thee not to neglect those of the West. The ancient Roman writers are full of rare examples, and modern France, which emulates all great and glorious undertakings, takes equal care to commit to posterity the lives of illustrious persons. I say not this in contempt of other countries in Europe. The Christians of these parts in general are accurate historians. They are universally learned, in regard there is no kingdom in Europe where they have not schools and academies, where all languages and sciences are taught. The ploughmen in the field speak Latin and Greek, which thou knowest are now grown obsolete and nowhere to be learned but in books. The mechanics are philosophers and every man sets up for an historian or an antiquary. It was not so in former times when the ecclesiastics had engrossed all manner of learning to themselves except some few of the nobility and gentry who had the advantage of patrimonial libraries and leisure to apply themselves to study. For then it was difficult to purchase books, there being but few, and for those they were obliged to the labour of the scribe. Hence it came to pass that only such as had plenty of money and a strong inclination to knowledge, monopolized the choicest manuscripts into their hands and bequeathed them as a legacy to their offspring. But since the invention of printing, books are infinitely multiplied, grown cheap and common. And those histories and sciences, which before were shut up on the Latin, Greek or some of the Oriental languages are now translated into the vulgar speech of every nation, whereby the lowest sort of people who can but read have the privilege to become as knowing as their superiors, and the slave may vie for learning with his sovereign. This makes the Nazarenes upbraid the true faithful with ignorance and barbarism because printing is not suffered throughout the Mussulman empire. They consider not the bad consequences of this art, as well as the good, and that the liberty of the press has filled the world with errors and lies. Besides, they are strangers to the education of the Mussulmans, who are generally taught the Arabic and Persian tongues from their childhood, in which two languages how many famous histories have been writ! There is no point of useful wisdom, which is not comprised in the writings of the Eastern sages. And as for unprofitable treatises and pamphlets with which the Europeans abound, they are superfluous and burdensome, bringing a double loss both to writer and reader, while they rob them of their time and money and commit a rape on their understandings. Add to this the fatal effects which this depraved indulgence of printing has produced in Christendom. What sacrileges, massacres, rebellions and impieties have overflowed most parts of the West in this licentious age? What hatred among Christians, what seditions among subjects, diversities in religion, contempt of all law both divine, natural and those of nations? The vices at which former times would have blushed, nay, at the very naming of which our fathers would have started as at a prodigy, are in these days committed openly without shame, without contradiction; whilst there are authors who dare publicly assert the cause of impiety and patronize all manner of profanations.

But thou who hast the honour to guard the incorruptible seat of justice and virtue, the bright throne of the Osman emperors,[2] who are the shadows of God on earth, hast made such a choice of books as commends thy wisdom and the sincerity of thy morals. Thou wilt not suffer thy imagination to be tainted with those enchanting ideas of evil, which are drawn by the pens of some elegant writers. All that thou seekest in books is to inform thy understanding, rectify thy judgment and enflame thy affections with the love of virtue. To this end serve the divine precepts of our holy doctors and other learned sages, the writings of philosophers and the examples of renowned heroes. From these thou gatherest strength to practise the four maternal virtues and all the good qualities that spring from those roots.

Go on and increase in the graces and accomplishments, which shall render thee worthy to be made the subject of a

[2] Ottoman sultans.

particular history, while the old shall recommend and the young shall covet nothing more passionately than to read the life of Cassim Hali, Janissary Aga.

Mahmut salutes thee with a kiss of affection. Reverence thyself and all men will honour thee: So taught Pythagoras.

Paris, the 17th of the 8th moon of the year 1646.

To Ibrahim Hali Sheik, a Man of the Law

Volume III, Book II, Letter XVI

If it be a sign of a flourishing state when vices are suppressed, one would presage that Paris is in a thriving condition. The governor of this city has newly published an edict forbidding all stews and brothel houses under severe penalties, banishing all harlots and such as by the toleration of the government have hitherto made a profession of whoredom, getting a livelihood by debauching the youth of the city. This appears a great novelty to the French, who in this matter have been permitted all along to live in an unbridled licentiousness. The lewder sort exclaim with open mouths against this unseasonable rigour (as they call it), and those who are ashamed to appear public advocates for harlots, yet privately murmur against their superiors for retrenching a liberty without which they say their lives would be uncomfortable.

They give a very favourable character of a whore, calling her a certain kind creature born to mitigate the labours and soften the cares of human life. They plead that such women are necessary members of a commonwealth, whilst with their caresses they restrain libidinous youth from falling into greater enormities; that the state receives no small profit from the tribute which is levied on these houses of pleasure; and that therefore they have been and are permitted in all countries; that the holy father himself tolerates an infinite number of them in Rome, which nevertheless has acquired the title of the Holy City. That all the princes in Italy have followed his example, there being no other way to prevent adulteries, incests and the vice which ought not to be named; that the state regarded not the morality or immorality of men's actions any farther than they tended to the public welfare; and in fine, that so vast a number of priests and religious served for no other end but to atone by their sacrifices, prayers, alms and fastings for the sins of the people.

These are the discourses of such as patronize the corruption of the government and are unwilling to be weaned from a wickedness established by immemorable custom in the city. But those who cherish an esteem for virtue and an incorrupt life applaud the wisdom and resolution of the magistrate, saying that he deserves a statue to be erected to his memory who first had the courage to check this popular evil and introduce an integrity of manners.

I, who was bred in the profession of purity and the law which admits no pollution, cannot but acquiesce to the sentiments of the latter; our Holy Lawgiver having expressly forbidden the practice of uncleanness and fornication with strangers and women that prostitute themselves to all lovers. It being sufficient that to gratify human passion and to sweeten the toils of life, he has indulged us the use of four wives and as many other females as we can purchase either by the sword or money.

Adieu, sage Sheik, and if I have interrupted thy more important studies with so trivial a subject, believe that it is for want of a proper occasion to signify to thee how much thou art in my thoughts, and that I would not have our friendship die through too long silence.

Paris, the 24th of the 10th moon of the year 1646.

To Mustapha, Bassa of Silistria

Volume III, Book II, Letter XVII

The fortune of war has ravished Asac[1] from the Grand Signior but has not robbed thee of the glory thou acquirest three years ago in the conquest of that city, nor sullied thy

[1] Asac or Azov was a Turkish fortress in the Crimea which was the site of many battles and sieges in the war between Cossacks and Turks in the third and fourth decades of the seventeenth century.

present arms with any marks of disgrace that were of late so vigorously employed to relieve it. Had the Muscovites performed the same part when thou didst encircle that nest of pirates with the Ottoman forces, as they have now done, the Cossacks would not then so tamely have abandoned their native seat and left the characters of their despair imprinted in the ruins of the habitation. The protection of that potent crown has given them new vigour, and 'tis to the valour of those northern savages they owe the liberty they now enjoy to sit by their own fires.

The Muscovites are a fierce and warlike nation, inured to hardships from the womb. The midwives plunge the newborn infants in cold water, and if they outlive not that trial, the mother thinks her child not worth a tear. The women have no partial tendernesses for their babes but cherish all for the service of their country. They teach 'em when young to roll in snow and bathe themselves in ice dissolved to water. They make 'em familiar with the extremities of heat and cold, hunger, thirst and labour, that when they come of age and can bear arms, they may go boldly to the wars and bravely throw their lives away to serve the public good. In this they seem to revive the wisdom of the ancient Spartans, who gloried in nothing so much as in educating their youth hardily and free from the effeminate softnesses of other nations. They esteemed infancy and youth, the springtime of good manners when virtue is in the blossom. If that be nipped or blasted, the fruit must prove abortive and unprofitable. Therefore they took care to season their early years with wholesome instructions and masculine exercises.

Who among the warlike Osmans does not laugh at the unmanly education of the Persian sophis,[2] who being for so many years confined to the company and discipline of females seem fitter to be made overseers of a nursery than to ascend a throne?

But thou wilt say I take large leaps from the north of Europe to one of the most southern tracts in Asia. I was dis-

[2] The Persian princes of the blood. Because there was no clear succession to the Persian throne, all the princes were brought up and educated by women so that no faction could form around a designated heir apparent. The result was that the monarchs finally chosen were untrained and often lacked the wisdom or courage to lead a nation.

coursing of the Muscovites and the assistance they afforded the Cossacks in recovering Asac. I passed from thence to the manner of their education. Permit me now to divert thee with something peculiar and uncommon in the character of the Russian women. I am acquainted with a gentleman in this city who has travelled through all that part of Europe and resided some years at Moscow. He says the Russian wives think themselves not beloved by their husbands unless they beat them every day. They take his correction as a mark of his favour and esteem. If these silly females are angry or peevish, he has no other way to court 'em into a better humour but by stripes. This is the only convincing argument of his sovereignty over them, the demonstration of his manhood, the charm which fastens both their love and obedience.

He highly applauds the absolute resignation which this people show to their great duke, in that they pretend not to possess their estates and lives but through his favour and during his pleasure. He says the succession of the czars or great dukes of Russia was in former times determined after this manner. A great stone was placed in a large field belonging to the city of Moscow. When any czar died, his sons or the next of kin were conducted into this field and placed all at an equal distance from the stone. Then at a certain signal given they all ran together towards it, and he that first reached it so as to stand on the top of it was established in the throne.

The reverence which these people pay to their prince may in part be ascribed to his seldom appearing in person to them, and then surrounded with his boyars or nobles in the most magnificent equipage that can be supposed proper to strike a terror and awe into his subjects and cause them to honour him as little less than a god. The eyes of the vulgar are dazzled with so many splendours of silver, gold and jewels. When the great duke makes his solemn appearance or cavalcade, they are almost ready to think that heaven has descended to earth to do them the honour of a visit. These are the arts of Russian policy by which such an infinite number of people are charmed into an obedience to the sovereign. Doubtless the majesty of a king receives no small lustre from external ornaments, the multitude being captivated with whatsoever is gay and glittering. Yet our glorious sultans scorn to borrow advantage from or owe their grandeur to anything but their exalted blood and sublime innate virtues.

But every nation have their peculiar customs and distinct reasons of state. The constitution of all governments is not alike: the model of Lacedaemonian policy would suit ill with Athens.

Thou, whose education was in the royal seraglio of the Osman emperors, that hast been instructed to imitate the bee, which sucks honey from every flower; thou that knowest how to make a choice of good examples and to reject the ill, practise the valour of one nation, the prudence of another, the frugality of a third, so shalt thou be consummate in virtue and acquit thyself a good general.

Paris, the 15th of the 11th moon of the year 1646.

To Dgnet Oglou

Volume III, Book II, Letter XXVIII

Thou art the man that must participate in all my adventures, and I should be a churl in not letting thee share with me the pleasure I found in a late journey to Orleans, one of the presidiary towns of France. It was by the order of the Vizier Azem I undertook that journey. Somebody had informed him that this town was full of merchant travellers of several nations but especially of Germany, who brought the choicest jewels of the East to vend in this place at ordinary rates. That minister gave me commands to buy certain stones with instructions to treat of another affair, which it is not necessary for thee to know. I accordingly set out from Paris, the third day of the fifth moon, and Eliachim the Jew (of whom thou hast heard) bore me company.

I need not describe to thee the country through which we passed; it exactly resembles the plains of St. Isidore not far from Palermo in Sicily. Thou and I have reason to remember that place of our captivity, carrying the marks of our master's cruel anger yet in our bodies. Those plains, thou knowest, afford a very agreeable prospect, especially at this time of the year, when the verdure of the trees mixed with the brightness of the cornfields and the parti-coloured meadows tempt the eye into a controversy of pleasure, a man neither knowing well how to take it off nor yet where to fix it in such an orderly confusion and medley of charming objects.

Such is the province between Paris and Orleans, which has this advantage of those Sicilian plains that here all the way one rides, innumerable magnificent and beautiful palaces appear, shooting up their glittering turrets above the lofty groves which environ those seats of pleasure. Indeed, this is one of the purest airs and the most fertile soil in all the kingdom, which invites the nobles and gentry to reside here during the summer and occasions much travelling on this road.

About midday we came to a town called Chartres, where we alighted to refresh ourselves. Travellers in these western parts are better accommodated with provisions than they can be in Asia, where they must carry their own beds with them and dress their own victuals or lie on the naked floor fasting. This makes the Nazarenes call the East inhospitable. They consider not at the same time that 'tis the niceness and delicacy of the Muhammadans which occasions this custom. For the Eastern people are fearful of defiling themselves by eating meat prepared by other hands than their own or those of their servants, as also to lie on a bed common to all passengers. But these infidels are like the swine, to whom all meat is welcome and every ditch an acceptable bed. Here are inns all along the roads whereinto when you enter the host provides you both bed and all other necessaries. A man must venture to sleep on the same pillow where perhaps a leper has lain the night before or some person infected with a worse disease. The host examines none but harbours all alike, provided they have money to pay him. And as for victuals, 'tis the custom for all travellers to eat together at one common table, where several dishes of meat are served up and every man is free to eat what and how much he pleases, paying a stated price for his dinner.

Thus no sooner were we coming to our inn at Chartres but the host saluting us after the manner of the country invited us to sit down at the ordinary (for so they call their public dinner in an inn). We were not so scrupulous as to refuse his offer but followed him into the chamber where the dinner was prepared. There were many guests at the table and all busy in feeding themselves. We took such seats as we found vacant, and without much ceremony fell to eating. The Jew trusted to the indulgence of Moses and I to that of Muhammad for eating with the uncircumcized, whose meat is seldom free from the pollutions of blood. We knew that neither God nor his prophets required us to starve.

There was plenty of wine and that so delicious as would have tempted an hogia [1] to taste it without the mufti's dispensation. To avoid singularity I made a show of eating as the rest, but the greatest part of my repast consisted in bread and some fruits with that exhilarating juice of the grape.

The honest Jew swore 'twas a banquet prepared by Cupid to render him the most miserable of all men. For just in the midst of our mirth came in a French gentleman with a lady in his hand who placed themselves at the table exactly opposite to us. I perceived evident symptoms of some disorder in Eliachim, who seemed to read his fate in that fair creature's face, yet had not power to check his wandering eyes or guard 'em from inevitable wounds. He'd almost acted o'er the story of the Egyptian wives whom Joseph's mistress had invited to behold his beauty; they cut their fingers for their meat whilst gazing on the charming youth. So poor Eliachim was all confusion, turned to a statue whilst he looked on this enchanting Gorgon. He had forgot to eat or drink till I began to rouse him from his dream. I told him softly in the ear this lady was but the younger sister of Ixion's mistress. [2] This brought him to his sense again but could not restore his peace. Prudence taught him to dissemble the violent emotion of his soul and not to expose himself in such a company, but nothing could expel the fatal poison from his breast.

When we had sufficiently reposed ourselves we bid adieu to the inn, all joining company and setting forward to Orleans. On the road both Eliachim and I had many opportunities of conversing with this young lady, such familiarity with women being allowed in France. We found her wit sur-

[1] Hogia (or hoggiah, heggiah) means a judicial decision, but the word has been sometimes applied as a title to an ecclesiastical doctor who settles disputes over Islamic law.

[2] This may be an oblique reference to Hera, whom Ixion attempted to seduce and for which he was severely punished.

prising as her beauty, and her mien and conduct such as gave advantage to them both. In a word Eliachim was lost amidst so many perfections.

When we came to our inn at night and were in our chamber together, he vented his passion in these words: 'Mahmut, I've passed these years hitherto without any other sentiments of love, save those which in general I owe to all our race and some more particular regards of friendship and duty. But since I saw this lovely creature, methinks my friends and all that ought to be beloved on earth is now contracted into her. 'Tis not her snowy skin or matchless features are of force to move me – though they are such, thyself being judge, as would have foiled Apelles' art[3] to imitate – but 'tis a lustre which I can't express! Surely 'twas lightning darted from her eyes, those fair avenues of her brighter soul! The subtle flame glanced through my breast and in a moment scorched my reason up! The lovely basilisk shot deaths at every look. Thou sawest how I sat as one transformed, so lifeless and without motion was I, whilst gazing on my ruin! And to this hour a fatal numbness spreads through all my veins as if I'd touched some dire torpedo.'

Thus went he raving on till I interrupted him with laughter and raillery, endeavouring to cure him of his love-sick humour by ridiculing it. I told him my own experience of this foolish passion, rehearsed my former adventures with Daria and how at length I got the victory of this vain fondness by absence and the exercise of my reason. But all that I could say made no impression on the stupid lover. He grew but worse and so I left him to seek repose from sleep.

We came not to Orleans till next day, where we tarried not long, having no other business as it happened but to see the rarities of the town and inform ourselves of those things it is convenient for travellers to know. After which we returned to Paris, I with the same sentiments I had at my first setting out from thence, but, it seems, the world was metamorphosed in poor Eliachim's opinion. To him the trees had now lost all their greenness; the flowers and grass and corn looked withered; the birds blew hoarse unwelcome sounds; and every-

[3] Apelles was a fourth century Greek painter who had painted Aphrodite, among other subjects.

thing in nature seemed to him to droop, because Falante was not there (so was the fair one called, as Eliachim had learned of her) when we parted from Orleans. In this melancholy condition the poor brain-sick Jew has continued ever since. When his cure will commence I know not.

If thou yet retainest thy native liberty and hast not sacrificed it to unhappy love, learn by this misfortune to watch thy senses, which are the first traitors to the soul. Adieu.

Paris, the 1st of the 6th moon of the year 1647.

To Solyman, his Cousin, at Constantinople

Volume IV, Book II, Letter XIX

Thou seest what thy libertinism has brought on thee. For my part I am sick in reading thy letter full of melancholy and the worst kind of enthusiasm. Hadst thou followed my advice or if that be condemned hadst thou but obeyed the precepts of thy father, an honest man and one that went down to the grave in peace, thou wouldst have lived as happily as other men, but now thou art overwhelmed with hypochondriac vapours and dreams of a sickly brain. I counsel thee to purge thyself with hellebore, for thou hast more need of that than of books. In all my life I never heard such religious nonsense from a Mussulman as thy last letter is stuffed with.

I have not patience to make repetitions or answer every particular whimsy of thine. But in God's name what makes thee fright thyself with such a wrong notion of hell? It is a common maxim in nature that nothing violent is permanent. Either, therefore, the pains of the damned are not infinitely intense or else they are not external in their duration. Thou wilt say the Alcoran itself asserts the eternity of those torments. But dost thou understand the figurative manner of speech used in that divine book and in all our Eastern writings? Is it not common to call a very high mountain, the mountain of God? – as if all the mountains and valleys of the earth were not equally his. So to express an uncertain length of time 'tis customary to use the epithet 'eternal'. Thus we in ordinary conversation say in Arabia, 'I love you eternally, I will serve you, fight for, etc. eternally,' and the same of the contrary passions. And yet we all know we shall live but a few years.

But granting that the Alcoran speaks in a literal sense, it does not follow that those pains are without intervals of rest. We read of the tree Zaggum, [1] which grows in the centre of hell, but who will interpret what is understood by this plant?

Cousin, make use of thy reason and practise the best things. As for our condition after this life, trouble not thyself, for no man knows what will become of him when he goes hence. However, we cannot believe the Supremely Merciful delights in cruelty.

There is a path which the eagle has not winged nor the serpent traced though 'tis obvious to both. But their own rashness blinds them and they cannot discern the way of the wise. There are men of towering speculations and others very crafty, yet neither one or the other can grope out the direct road to bliss. If I may advise thee, let nature be thy guide. Do nothing but what humanity prompts thee to. 'Tis this alone distinguishes thee from other animals. Honour the memory of thy deceased parents, love thy friends and be generous to thy enemies. Do justice to all men; observe the purifications and prayers prescribed by the law. But give no credit to the fables of infidels. It is common here among the Christians to paint hell with horrid flames and devils flying up and down with red-hot prongs to toss the damned from fire to fire. And their preachers make long and direful harangues on the same subject, when all the while, neither they nor we know what or where hell is or after what manner the wicked shall be chastised.

Only the illuminated of God have this standard of truth: That both our pains and pleasures after this life shall be exactly proportioned to our virtues and vices. There is no malice or injustice in the good Creator of all things.

Cousin, once again, let thy senses be awake and suffer not thy reason to dream of things which have no existence. For assuredly, God is the most impartial judge of the universe.

Paris, the 22nd of the 10th moon of the year 1651.

[1] The Zaggum tree is mentioned in Suras XXXVII, 60-64; XLIV, 43, 44; LVI, 51-53.

To Abdel Melech Muly Omar, President of the College of Sciences at Fez

Volume IV, Book III, Letter I

Thou hast formerly received a letter from me wherein I mentioned the tenets of a certain French philosopher who maintains that the earth moves like the rest of the planets and the sun stands still being the centre of this our world, for he asserts that there are many more. The name of this sage is Descartes, renowned throughout the world for his learning and knowledge. He lays as a basis of all his philosophy this short position and inference: I think, therefore I am. In this alone he is dogmatical, allowing a lawful scepticism in all the uncertain deductions which may be drawn from it.

Pardon me, oraculous sage, if I expose before thee my infirmities. I am naturally distrustful of all things. The temper puts me upon perpetual thinking. And that very act convinces me of the truth of my being according to the method of this philosopher. But what I am, I know not. Sometimes I fancy myself no more than a dream or idea of all those things which men commonly believe do really exist: a mere imagination of possibilities. And that all which we call the world is but one grand chimera or nothing in masquerade.

At other times when these wild thoughts are vanished, and my spirits, tired in the pursuit of such abstracted whimsies, begin to flag and that my lower sense awaked by some present pain or pleasure, rouses my sleeping appetites. When I am touched with hunger, thirst or cold or heat and find experimentally I am something that cannot be a mere thought or dream but of a composition which stands in need of meat, drink, garments and other necessaries, then rather than fret myself with vain and endless scrutinies, I tamely conclude I am that which they call a man; I lay the sceptic aside and without any farther scruples or doubts fall roundly to eating, drinking or any other refreshments my nature craves for.

But no sooner have I tasted these delights when my old

distemper returns again. I then consider myself as a being, capable of happiness or misery in some degree, as I shall possess or want those very delights I just before enjoyed. This is a sufficient damp to a thinking man when he knows that he stands in need of anything out of himself. But 'tis far greater when he will take the pains to number all the train of his particular necessities, which he is not sure he shall always be able to supply.

This makes me presently conclude that as I am indebted to other creatures for my sensible happiness, so I owe my very being to something beside myself. I examine my original and find I am born of men and women who were in the same indigent circumstances as myself. And that it is not only so with my particular family but with all mankind, our whole human race being born natural mendicants from the womb. As soon as we breathe the vital air, we cry, and with those inarticulate prayers beg for help and protection from others without whose generous aid we could not subsist a moment. So poor and beggarly a thing is man from his birth. This is the condition of all; neither is a king any more exempt from this common character of mortals than the slave who sweeps the streets.

If I could have rested in this thought, I should have been happy, for it would have had this influence on me, either to convince me that I ought to be content with the condition to which I was born or to rid myself out of so despicable a state by death.

But alas, one thought produces another, and from the contemplation of our present misery in this life, I fall to thinking what will become of us after death. For as we know not what or where we were before we came into this world, so there is no human certainty whither we shall go or in what condition we shall be when we leave it. And therefore it would be an unpardonable madness to throw myself headlong into a state of which I have no account, and to avoid the little miseries of this life, which must have an end one time or another, cast myself down a precipice (for ought I know) of intolerable torments which has no bottom.

I hear the philosophers talk of immortality, the poets of Elysium, the Christian priests of heaven, hell and purgatory, the Indian Brahmans of transmigration. But I know not what or which I have reason to believe of all these. I speak after the manner of philosophers, for if we come to faith the case is altered. Think not, I beseech thee, that I call in question the sacred oracles, the revelations of the sent of God. But I only acquaint thee how my natural reason batters me with doubts.

I see men everywhere professing some religion or other, paying divine honours to some superior being or beings, according as they have been educated, which many times tempts me to think that religion is nothing but the effect of education.

Then I wonder how men, when they come to years of discretion and their reason is able to distinguish between things probable and mere romances, can still retain the errors of their infancy. 'Tis natural for children to be wheedled or awed into a belief of what their parents, nurses or tutors teach them. But when they come of age they soon rectify their misled understandings in all things, save the affairs of religion. In this they are children still, tenacious of the sacred fables of their priests and obstinate in maintaining them, sometimes even to death.

It puzzles me to find out the cause of so strange an effect that men otherwise endued with mature judgment and an extraordinary sagacity in all things else should yet be fools in matters of religion and believe things inconsistent with the common sense and reason of mankind. I could never give credit to the histories of the ancient pagans, which acquaint us with the devout adoration they paid to the creatures of the painter or carver. Did not I see the same practised among the Christians? Or that those wise men of old could swallow the forgeries of their priests concerning their gods and goddesses, were I not an eye witness how bigoted the modern Nazarenes are to the legends of their saints and the Jews to those more ridiculous figments of the Talmud.

It perplexes me to see mankind generally labouring under so great a darkness, not so much the effect of ignorance as of superstition; to behold men well versed in sciences and all kinds of human learning, yet zealous asserters of manifest contradictions in matters of divinity rather than oppose or so much as examine the traditions of their fathers.

When I behold mankind divided into so many innumerable

different religions in the world, all vigorously propagating their own genius, either by subtilty or violence, yet few or none seeming by their practise to believe what they with so much ardour profess, I could almost think that these various ways of worship were first invented by politicians, each accommodating his model to the inclinations of the people whom he designed to circumvent.

But when on the other side I consider, there appears something so natural and undisguised in the furious zeal and unconquerable obstinacy of the greatest part, I am as ready to join with Cardan[1] and conclude that all this variety of religions depends on the different influence of the stars. This was a famous philosopher in Europe, who held that the religion of the Jews owed its original to the force of Saturn, that of the Christians to Jupiter and ours to Mars. As for the pagans, he assigns to them many constellations and aspects.

Thus there is so equal an appearance of truth and falsehood in every religion that I should not know how in human reason to fix on any. Superstition renders a man a fool and scepticism is enough to make him mad. To believe all things is above reason; to give credit to nothing is below it. I will keep the middle path and direct my faith by my reason.

That faculty tells me that if I were inclined to adore the sun, moon and stars for their beauty and influence, I might on the same ground worship my own eyes without which I could not behold their tempting splendours. Or I might as well pay divine honour to that more intimate sense, my feeling, or any of my other senses, which only render me capable to know the virtue of these luminaries. The same may be said of the elements and of all visible beings.

What then shall I adore or to whom shall I return thanks for all the blessings I enjoy (for even in this miserable life I taste some happiness)? To what being, I say, shall I address my vows and supplications for all the good that I possess and want? Is it to any thing that I have seen or can see, or that I can represent to myself under a figure? Is it to any part of the universe or no? No. To the whole complex together? No. I

[1] Girolamo Cardan (1501-76), an Italian mathematician, physician and astrologer, achieved great celebrity in his lifetime for his treatises on nature and astrology.

have a thousand kind thoughts for the sun, moon and stars, for the elements and many other compound creatures. My soul and that of the world are unisons. [2] But 'tis the profound depth of eternity, the infinite and immortal, who is the diapason and makes perfect harmony.

To that being which has no resemblance, neither is divided into parts nor circumscribed with limits, whose centre is everywhere, circumference nowhere, who hath neither beginning nor end; to the only Omnipotent, from Whom all other things flow and to Whom they all return, to Him I owe all that I have and will pay what I can. And something by His determination I am indebted and will discharge it to thee, orient light of the Moresque Mussulmans; that is the duty of an humble slave in begging pardon for this presumption.

Paris, the 14th of the 2nd moon of the year 1652.

To Cara Haly

Volume IV, Book III, Letter IV

The Christians seem to have too proud an opinion of themselves and set a greater value on human nature than suits with reason. They assert that all things were made for man and style him lord of his fellow creatures, as if God had given him an absolute dominion over the rest of His works, especially over the animal generations; and that all the birds of the air, beasts of the earth and fish of the sea were created only to serve his appetite and other necessities of life. I remember a letter I formerly sent to thee wherein I discoursed of the Cartesian philosophers and their contempt of the beasts in denying them souls or the use of reason. [1]

Give me leave to entertain thee now and divert myself with some farther remarks on this subject. 'Tis a refuge from melancholy when I can thus freely discover my thoughts to a friend who I know will not be partial to the truth.

I have been long an advocate for thy brutes and have en-

[2] His soul and the world are in harmony.

[1] See above pp. 51-53.

deavoured both to abstain from injuring them myself and to inculcate this fundamental point of justice to others. This is owing to the example and philosophy of Muhammad, the eremite in Arabia, that light and glory of religious men. And were it not that my honour is to be doubtful in all things, the influence of his conversation would make me a professed Pythagorean, a disciple of the Indian Brahmans, a champion for the transmigration of souls.

The last letter save one I writ to that solitary was upon this subject; such an one as would divert him in his cave. It contained an account of the primitive manner of life practised by the ancients, a narrative of the golden age, a history of human innocence and the steps which men first took to use violence and cruelty to their fellow creatures.[2] Now I will present thee with some additional observations, some remnants of antiquated truth, gleaned from philosophers and historians and winnowed from the chaff of error and superstition.

Who would not believe the beasts to be endued with reason when he beholds them perform all the actions of rational creatures with more caution, though less pride than men? They are more provident than we and much more subtle in avoiding any affliction or danger. Witness the Thales's philosopher mule, which he often employed to carry salt to a certain market, but the cunning beast finding herself overloaded when she was passing through a river lay down, whereby the water penetrating into the sacks of salt melted it away and lightened her burden. And this was her constant practise, till the philosopher, perceiving himself thus outwitted by his beast, was resolved to circumvent her another way. Wherefore, instead of salt he loaded her with wool. But the wary mule, sensible of the difference of her burden, would couch no more in the water but seeing no other remedy, went forward on her journey.

Who will not admire the wisdom of the fox in cold countries, which the inhabitants use as a guide when they would pass over any frozen lake or river. For this creature going before them lays her ears close down to ice and listens to try if she can hear any motion or noise of the water running under-

[2] Not included in this selection, the letter is in Volume IV, Book I, Letter V.

neath, which if she does, she will not venture on the ice; but if all be still, then by a logical deduction she concludes the ice is thick enough to bear passengers, and so she leads the way whilst the men follow.

When a dog is hunting in the thick woods and by chance comes to a place where three paths meet, he first scents the one then the other, and perceiving that the game is not gone by any of those two ways, he throws himself swiftly forward in the third, without such a particular application of his nose, which is evident argument that he makes use of the like choice we ourselves should do.

And now I have mentioned this creature, I cannot forbear celebrating their virtue and fidelity, whereof we have daily experience; and there are many pleasant examples recorded by grave historians. Such is that of Hircanus, a dog belonging to Lysimachus,[3] who would never depart from the body of his dead master, but following it to the funeral pile, leapt into the fire and was burned for company.

But the gratitude of a lion to a certain slave in Rome is beyond all parallel.[4] This slave was one of those who were appointed to combat with wild beasts in the amphitheatre according to the custom of the ancient Romans in the public shows which were exhibited to the people. As soon as the lion was let loose in the pavement, he ran furiously at the slave but coming nearer, he stopped on a sudden as one astonished. Then he came gently towards the slave, fawning upon him and licking his hand, which caused all the people to give a shout. The emperor being present and taking notice of the seeming friendship and acquaintance that was between the slave and the lion, sent for the slave and enquired the occasion of so strange an accident. To whom the slave made the following relation: 'My name,' said he, 'is Androcles, and I am slave to a certain proconsul, who having determined to kill me, I made my escape and hid myself in a cave, where I had not lain long before this lion, which you now see, came in, being very lame of one foot. As soon as he spied me, he came limping to-

[3] Lysimachus was one of Alexander's generals, who after the death of Alexander became King of Thrace. He died in 281 B.C.

[4] Here is recounted the familiar story of Androcles and the lion, the source of which is Aulus Gellius, Book V, Chapter 14.

wards me and stretched forth the paw that was wounded as though he begged of me to ease him. Affrighted as I was, I took his paw in my hand and pulled out a great ragged thorn, which stuck fast in it. Then I washed the wound with my own water, whilst he lay very patiently till I thoroughly dressed it. The ease he found by my application made him fall asleep, and when he awaked, he licked my hands and showed other signs of affection and gratitude. I lived with him thus three years in that cave and every day he brought me a share of his prey, on which I sustained myself. But at length tired with this manner of life, I took my opportunity when he was gone abroad to make my escape. I wandered up and down three days when a company of soldiers meeting with me and knowing to whom I belonged took me and brought me hither to my old master, who had condemned me to this cruel death. But it seems, fortune so ordered it that this lion should be taken about the same time and appointed to be my executioner this day. Yet you see he refuses to perform his office out of gratitude to me for my former kindness.'

The emperor, astonished and pleased at this passage, gave the slave his life and freedom, bestowing also the lion on him, which brought him in a constant livelihood by showing him to all people, who having heard of this wonderful accident were desirous to see both the lion and his tenant, for so they styled the slave, and some called him the lion's physician.

I should think I had said enough already to tire thy patience and make thee forswear reading my letters for the future, were I not well acquainted with thy genius and know that thou delightest in relations of this nature, being no enemy to the harmless brutes.

Whatever thy sentiments are towards these I dare be sure thou art my friend and wilt bear with my importunity when I strive to convince all men and confirm myself in this truth: that the wild beasts are not void of reason and moral virtue.

Paris, the 20th of the 7th moon of the year 1652.

To Cara Haly

Volume IV, Book IV, Letter III

Since what I wrote last in behalf of the brute animals is so acceptable to thee, I will comply with thy request in continuing that discourse.

'Tis certain the ancients had another opinion of the beasts than these French philosophers, who deny 'em the use of reason. Socrates used to swear by the animal generations and so did Rhadamanthus before him. The Egyptians formed the images of their gods in the similitude of beasts or birds or fishes. So the Grecians fixed the horns of a ram on the head of Jupiter's statue and those of a bull on the image of Bacchus. They compounded the image of Pan of a man and a goat and painted muses and graces with wings. And the poet Pindar makes all the gods winged and disguises them in the shapes of several beasts, when in his hymns he introduces them chased by Tryphon. Thou knowest also that our holy doctors affirm the angel Gabriel to have wings with one of which he once gave a mark to the moon.

When the poets bring in Jupiter courting Pasiphae, he appears in the form of a bull. And in his amours, if we may believe them, he changed himself sometimes into a swan, then into an eagle. They report also that he was suckled by a goat.

For these and other reasons, the ancients not only forbore to injure their fellow animals but entertained them with singular affection and friendship. A dove was the darling of Semiramis. A dog was the joy of Cyrus. Philip, King of Macedon, made a swan his companion. And our Holy Lawgiver was often wont to sport himself with a cat. He loved this creature for its cleanliness and activity, and therefore we Mussulmans generally have a cat in great esteem and veneration.

That favourite of God understood the language of beasts and conversed as familiarly with them as with men. So it is famed of Melampus and Tiresias of old, as also of Apollonius Tyanaeus, who affirmed to his friend sitting by him that a sparrow, which he heard chirping to his fellows, told them of an ass which he had seen fall down with his load a little way off from that place.[1] It is also recorded of a boy who understood all the voices of birds and by that means could foretell things to come that his mother by pouring urine into his ears when he was asleep deprived him of this incomparable gift for fear he should be taken from her and presented to the king. There is no question but several nations have certain knowledge of the speech of some animals. My countrymen by a peculiar gift bestowed on our fathers and their posterity forever understand the language of crows and eagles. And the ancients were so well versed in this knowledge that when they conversed with the birds or at least when they heard them in their language utter presages of what should shortly happen on earth, they persuaded themselves that those birds were the messengers of the gods. Therefore the eagle was supposed to be the messenger of Jupiter, the crow and hawk of Apollo, the stork of Juno, the owl of Minerva and so of others.

It is evident that our common huntsmen understand the different voices of their dogs, when at a distance they signify by one kind of cry that they are questing after the hare; by another that they have found her; by a third that they have taken her or that she is turned to the right hand or to the left. So those who look after cattle know by the voice of the bull when he is hungry, thirsty or weary or when he is stung with lust. So by the roaring of the lion, the howling of wolves, the baaing of sheep, men are made sensible of the various wants, inclinations and passions of those creatures.

Nor are these animals ignorant of our language, but by our voice and words they know when we are angry or pleased, when we call them to us or drive them from us. And our domestic animals obey accordingly with as much promptness and alacrity as a man or maid servant. All which could not be if they were not endued with faculties comformable to ours.

[1] Philostratus in his life of Apollonius of Tyana reports (Book IV, Chapter 3) that it was a boy carrying barley who slipped, and the sparrow informed his fellows that a rich repast of scattered barley was to be had, which intelligence Apollonius overheard.

They also teach their young ones to sing artificially.[2] In a litter of dogs, huntsmen choose the best by this experiment. They take all the whelps from the bitch and carry them to some place a little distant; then they observe which she first carries back again, and those always prove the best dogs. What is this distinguishing faculty in the bitch but reason or something like it?

We see apparently that every living creature knows its own weakness or strength and knows how to use most dextrously those weapons with which nature has furnished it for its own defence. They are also sensible what places are most convenient for them to dwell in and which not. Thus the weakest creatures, as dogs and cats, live altogether in houses and cities with men, whilst the lions, tigers and such fierce animals dwell in the desert. Thus sparrows and swallows make themselves almost domestic with men, whilst eagles, hawks, vultures and other birds of prey build their nests in woods or rocks remote from human society. Some birds change their habitations at certain seasons of the year as best suits with their convenience. Others always remain in the same place. The same is observed in fishes. And in all living creatures it is easy to trace the footsteps of prudence and forecast in order to their own preservation. Let men call this what they please, instinct or nature or sense; it is evident that there is an exact conformity and resemblance beween these faculties in brutes and what we call reason, wisdom and prudence in men. And we have no more ground to conclude them void of reason because they do not enjoy it in that perfection as ourselves than we have to conclude ourselves blind or deaf because we see not so clearly and hear not so readily as the brutes; and that we have no legs because we run not so swiftly as some of them do.

Doubtless, the brutes are endued with a faculty of reason as well as we, but this faculty in them is weak and imperfect for want of discipline and art, which polish all things. This is manifest from those creatures which are taught to dance and play a thousand tricks, to tell money, to shoot off guns, to find out hidden things and bring them some miles to their masters,

[2] That is, the young are taught by artifice to sing, which by nature they would not ordinarily do.

as well educated spaniels will do. What can be a greater argument of the proficiency they make in reason and knowledge? Are not elephants taught all the arts of war and placed in the very front of the battle? Do not the Indian princes repose as much trust in their carriage and conduct as in the service of their stoutest and wisest commanders? This creature is as tractable and prompt to learn anything when young as a boy at school, which cannot be done without the use of reason.

To conclude, I have omitted five hundred arguments, which might be brought to prove the brute animals to have souls as well as we, to have faculties and affections conform to ours. And therefore, it is little less injustice to kill and eat them because they cannot speak and converse with us than it would be for a cannibal to murder and devour thee or me because we understood not his language nor he ours.

God, who locketh up the winds during the time the halcyon hatcheth her young, thereby showing that this bird is his favourite, will assuredly grant us perpetual tranquillity if we abstain from injuring our fellow animals.

Paris, the 2nd of the 1st moon of the year 1654.

To Murat, Bassa

Volume IV, Book IV, Letter IX

It seems the devils have been lately loose in these western parts, if we may give credit to the deposition of such as have accused certain supposed witches.

In Bretagne, a province of this kingdom, above forty old women have been seized and imprisoned for holding correspondence with infernal powers. And above half of them condemned to death, God knows with what justice. Some of them are accused of enchanting the persons of their neighbours, others for bewitching their cattle and a third sort for dissolving the mischievous charms of the first and second; all of them for assembling in the night-time and using certain diabolical ceremonies, which they say begin and end in kissing the posteriors of a goat or the devil in that form.

I know not how for these poor superannuated figures of mortality may be wronged. 'Tis a question whether their judges are always in the right. A shrivelled meagre face, a hollow eye, joined with irrecoverable poverty are many times the chief grounds of suspicion, which improved by superstition, mistakes and malice have often prevailed on those who ought to administer justice to condemn poor wretches more innocent than themselves as guilty of witchcraft.

Yet it cannot be denied but that there have been both men and women versed in magical arts, as they are commonly called, which I take to be only the more mysterious science of nature. Such was Zoroaster, the great-grandchild of Noah and king of that part of Asia which was then called Bactria.[1] Such was Apollonius Tyanaeus, Philistides Syracusanus[2] and many others of ancient date. These understood the hidden force of the elements, the influence of the stars, the specific operation of metals, minerals and other subterranean bodies with the virtues of all vegetables. They knew exactly how to frame astral images and talismans by the help of which they were able to effect wonders. And all this perhaps without once dreaming of infernal spirits or having the least society with devils.

Yet I believe Lucian, an ancient writer, who never spoke seriously of anything, scarce believed himself when he related the story of Pancrates,[3] a famous magician of Egypt, who by these talismans was able to transform inanimate things into the appearance at least of living creatures. Thus he would turn a stick or piece of wood into a seeming man who should walk, discourse and perform all the actions of a rational being.

A certain stranger travelling with him once to Memphis and lying with him in the same caravansera, as soon as they were alighted from their camels, Pancrates took a plank of oak, and having touched it with his talisman and pronounced two or three syllables, incontinently the stock moved, stood

[1] Modern northern Afghanistan and Russian Tadzhikistan.

[2] This may refer to Philistus of Syracuse, a fifth-century B.C. historian.

[3] In the dialogue 'The Lover of Lies' in *Lucian*, trans. A. M. Harmon, Loeb Classics, III, 371-377.

upright, walked, and taking the camels by the bridle, led them to the stables, after which this wooden man came in and prepared their pillow, went of whatsoever errands Pancrates sent him. And when they departed, the magician using a certain private ceremony, this officious servant returned to a plank again. This was his practise all along the road.

One day his fellow traveller being resolved to try the experiment, took advantage of the magician's absence who was gone to the temple and left his talisman behind him. The curious traveller having been often an eyewitness of this trick, takes a piece of wood and touches it with Pancrate's talisman, repeating the syllables he had heard him utter. Immediately the inanimate timber became a man asking his pleasure. The traveller astonished at the event, commanded his new servant to bring him a bucket of water. The enchanted spark obeys. The traveller told him it was enough and bid him return to a piece of wood again, but instead of that he continued drawing of water and bringing it in till the house was full. The traveller fearing the anger of Pancrates thought to dissolve the enchantment by cleaving the wooden animal in two. But this augmented his trouble, for each piece taking a bucket fell to drawing of water so that of one servant he had made two. This continued till the magician came to his rescue, who having sternly rebuked the traveller's rashness at a word turned the two busy drudges to their primitive logishness and inactivity again.

I do not tell this story as if I would have thee believe it or that I give credit to it myself. Let us imitate the author of it, who laughs at all that delight in such fables. But the Christians, who believe a piece of bread is transformed to flesh and blood and becomes an immortal God at the pronouncing of four words by the priest, may be excused if they put confidence in the figments of poets and orators.

I have in my custody the journal of Carcoa, who formerly resided at Vienna, a private agent for the ever happy Porte Some of his letters speak of the superstition and credulity of the Germans in this kind. Yet in a letter to the mufti he acknowledges himself overcome by the unquestionable testimonies of such as had been eyewitnesses of the life and death of one Faustus, a German magician who played a thousand infernal pranks (as he calls them) even before the emperor himself.

He tells also of another magician called Zyto, who lived in the days of the Emperor Charles IV.[4] And when the emperor's son, to whom Zyto belonged, was to marry the Duke of Bavaria's daughter, the duke to oblige his son-in-law, who was much taken with magical tricks as were all the Germans, sent for a great many sorcerers to the wedding. Among the rest, while one was performing a rare exploit, on a sudden Zyto, the prince's conjurer, came up to him with a mouth seeming as wide as that of an old crocodile and swallows him up at a morsel. When he thus had done, he retires and voids him again in a bath and brings him thus drenched into the company, challenging any of the other magicians to do a feat like that, but they were all silent.

I hear of no such tricks done by those French witches who cause so much discourse at present. The worst they are accused of is bewitching their neighbour's hogs to madness, which thou knowest may be only a natural malady.

I pray heaven defend us from the enchantments of a deluded fancy, that domestic incubus of every mortal, and we need fear neither witch nor wizard.

Paris, the 20th of the 5th moon of the year 1654.

To Dgnet Oglou

Volume IV, Book IV, Letter XIV

Hitherto I have been in a wilderness or at least I shall suppose it, wandering up and down lost and confounded in the dark without sun, star, landmark or any faithful guide to direct me. What shall I do in this case? I am tired with perpetual rambling, and rest I dare not, neither can I; such is my uneasiness even in the only circumstance which gives to other men repose.

Thus I discourse with myself when I am alone and con-

[4] Holy Roman Emperor who reigned from 1349-78.

sider my present state as a mortal. The miseries of this life are the themes of my first contemplation, and 'tis but reason it should be so, because we feel 'em every moment. They touch our sense nearly and afflict us with sharp pains. Yet they are but like the sting of a wasp, violent for a time but last not long.

This thought carries me farther and puts me upon an endless meditation what will befall me after I'm dead. When I have contemplated all that I can, run over a thousand paths of fancy and tracked all the footsteps of the wise or of such as were esteemed so, still I find myself in a desert, more entangled than a traveller lost in the forest of Hyrcania, which extends from the most northerly part of Muscovy to some provinces in the German Empire and is reputed five hundred leagues in length.

In this bewildered condition I meet with many pretended guides, one telling me this is the way, another that. But because they do not agree in their advice, I know not which to trust and am inclined to suspect some for cheats and the rest for fools, as much at a loss, if not more than myself.

Permit me to discourse with freedom, my dear Dgnet, and let us unmask like friends. What signifies all that the imams and mullas[1] can say of paradise and hell, since none of 'em have been there to make an experiment? Why should we suffer ourselves to be amused with notions of things, which for aught we know, have no other existence but in the harangues of the preachers and the fancies of the credulous?

Think not that I am going to persuade thee to the heresy of the Mutazila,[2] who deny the being of a God. I tell thee I am no atheist. From everything I behold my thought soon flies up to a first cause, and there 'tis dashed into a thousand queries. This I lay as a solid foundation: all things were not always in the same state as they are now. (My experience demonstrates to the contrary.) But how much longer they have been otherwise than my own remembrance, I cannot be

[1] An imam is a religious leader, analogous to a priest; a mulla is a scholar.

[2] The Mutazila is a sect of Islam which denies the physical attributes of God, but believes in the perception of God through reason. Mahmut's supposition of the atheism of the Mutazila is not justified. He may be echoing (for satiric reasons) the conventional Muslim reaction towards this sect, which bears an affinity to European deism.

assured but by the confidence which I repose in people that are older than myself and the faith I give to books. Both which agree in this, that they are guilty of contradictions without number.

Those that were born before me and lived in the days of Sultan Muhammad III tell me many passages of his reign, quite different from the relations of others who also lived in those times and remarked the transactions of their age.

A like disagreement I find among authors who have committed to writing the histories of former times. 'Tis difficult to encounter with two men of the same opinion even as to matters of fact. Some take a pride in disguising the truth, whilst others have not skill to take off the mask. There are a sort of persons in the world, men of supine and easy judgments, credulous and not daring to call in question what has been transmitted to them from the authority of such and such a writer. They superstitiously revere as an oracle the manuscripts and mistakes. And all this only because they have been taught to do so from their infancy. So forcible is the influence of education. Thus the Hebrews believe the records of their nation to be of divine original, though they want not verbal contradictions and abound with logical and philosophical inconsistencies. But that which is of greatest moment is that neither they nor any other nation, no not even the Assyrian or Egyptian records come near the immense chronologies of the Chinese and Indians. So that amidst such a variety of accounts, a man knows not where to fix his belief. But whether the world be only five or six thousand years old or of a more indefinite antiquity, this is a sure maxim that something is eternal. Even the Jews and Christians, who deny the eternity of matter and assert the creation of the world out of nothing in a determined period of time, must of necessity own there was an eternal and infinite emptiness or vacuity which is the same as Moses calls by the name of nothing; which will sound as harsh in philosophy as the eternity of matter does in their divinity. Nay, if I mistake not, 'tis of a worse consequence even in the doctrine of religion to assert an infinite privation or want of existence to be coeternal with the substantial God, who is omnipotent, living and strong, than to affirm matter itself to be coeternal with Him, since this is an actual substance and may with reason be supposed as a necessary emanation of his power and goodness; whereas the other is a mere naked potentiality, a nonentity, as the western philosophers call it, and therefore can not be conceived to flow from the divine nature, which is essential life and being. Yet in these nice and remote speculations I am timorous and dare not be positive, lest I should profane the honour of that sovereignly good, who is the breath of our nostrils. To speak the truth I am wavering in all things but this: That there is an eternal mind everywhere present, the root and basis of all things visible and invisible, whom we call Allah, the support of infinite ages, the rock and stay of the universe.

Let thou and I, dear friend, persevere in adoring that superlative essence of essences, with eternal and profound devotion. Let our thoughts be pure, our words few and those full of innocent and grateful flames. For assuredly God delights not in the babbling of the tongue.

As for the rest, let us live according to our nature and reason as we are men. For we may believe that the indulgent Father of all things will accept us if we square our actions according to this rule without aiming at the perfection of angels. In a word, let us love all of the human race and show justice and mercy to the brutes. For in so doing we shall not be unkind to ourselves.

Paris, the 13th of the 7th moon of the year 1654.

To Adonai, a Jew, Prisoner in the Tower of Nona at Rome

Volume V, Book I, Letter XI

This comes to thee by the hand of a trusty friend: give entire credence to his instructions. To say I'm sorry to hear of thy misfortune would but faintly express my passion; 'tis not easily described in words. I am as melancholy as an antelope when the sun's in conjunction with Saturn. This is a sad sort of a beast that will neither eat, drink nor sleep during that dull aspect.

In God's name, how camest thou to be so free with thy tongue among the Romans? Or what tempted thee to meddle with their religion and laws? Was it not enough that thou and all the Jews in that city had liberty to frequent your synagogues and there curse the Christians in antiquated Hebrew? Must you needs rail at them in plain Italian too? And that over your cups when men ought to be good-natured to all the world? Of what import is it to you whether they be idolators or no, so long as they give you leave to adore one God, Creator of the worlds? Or what signifies it if they are guilty of ten thousand injustices and follies among themselves, whilst you live quietly under their protection and government? Adonai, I am ashamed of the immorality of those of thy nation; I blush for your ingratitude, pride and malice. Surely if the Nazarenes did really believe what they profess, they would sacrifice you all to the ghost of their Messiah, whom they say you crucified. They would not leave a Jew living in Christendom but do their utmost to exterminate you from the earth. I speak not this as my wish but only to upbraid your impertinence and vanity in thus foolishly provoking those with whose permission it is that you live and enjoy the elements.

The prophet Moses, your lawgiver, left you another rule, a lesson of civility when he said, 'Ye shall not blaspheme the gods of the people.' Had thou and thy companions obeyed this precept, ye might have been at liberty, but 'tis bad falling into the hands of the inquisition. However, I am glad to hear that you are not transported to the castle of St. Angelo; that would have been a tragical remove at this juncture. But now, as I'm informed, not one of you is in danger, for they say that all the prisoners in Rome are by custom released upon the death of the Pope except those who are in that fatal fortress. And 'tis generally supposed the good old caliph is no long-lived man. For they never used to remove the prisoners designed for death till the physicians are past all hopes of the holy father's life.

However, in regard there is no certainty in human affairs but a perpetual change and circulation of events. Lest some unhappy turn of fortune should either now continue thy restraint or hereafter bereave thee of thy liberty, I send thee here enclosed a receipt of a chemical liquor, which may be of some service to thee in all the strongest prison on earth. 'Twas revealed to me by my mother, who learned it of an Egyptian artist at Cairo. Despise it not, because it comes from a woman's hand, for I have made an experiment of it and find it effectual. 'Twill render iron as brittle as glass. 'Tis more powerful than the water of the river Styx, which no vessel could hold but the hoof of a mule. After an hour's application, thou mayest make the thickest bars, chains and bolts fly in a thousand pieces as if they were made of porcelain.

Thou wilt not wonder at this when thou considerest the innumerable strange inventions of men prying into the secrets of nature and fortunate in their searches. Above all, chemistry has brought to light the greatest prodigies of art and knowledge. This mysterious science was the peculiar boast of the primitive Egyptians from whence all other nations learned it. And had not Moses himself been instructed from his youth in all the learning of Egypt, perhaps he would have been at a loss when he calcined the golden calf and gave dust to the Israelites to be mixed in their drink as the only expiation of their idolatry. Doubtless this secret among others was transmitted down to those times from Philemon, the good priest who was in the number of them who escaped the flood in Noah's ark and whose grandson, Masar, was the first king in Egypt after the deluge.

Philemon, the better to establish the state of his offspring, revealed to them many hidden things, taught them the hieroglyphics of the Dgebel Pharan or the pyramids with all the mysteries of the talismans and the chemical preparations of moncatom, the forcible waters and essences, powders and other ingredients by which they made marble as pliable as wax or clay. These things he had learned of those who perished in the flood. He retained the wisdom of the ancients, his coevals and predecessors, leaving the rudiments of so profound a knowledge to his posterity as an invaluable treasure of which they could never be robbed. Thus science became hereditary to the Coptim, the son of Masar, the first king of Egypt since the rainbow appeared in the clouds. And 'twas from one of that race my mother learned that admirable secret.[1]

Trust not to words but try the experiment. The receipt will give thee all necessary directions. Yet I counsel thee not to be big with it like him who having found out the art of making glass malleable or fit to be beat by the hammer into any shape or figure, as the silversmiths work their metal, must needs go and discover his secret to the prince expecting a great reward; when on the contrary he lost his head on the spot. The prince thinking it great injustice that so many thousand people as got their bread by making of common glass should be all ruined to promote one man's profit and advantage.

In fine, use this secret to serve thyself or the cause thou art engaged in; but trust it not to another unless on the same equal terms as I commit it to thee, wherein the greater hazard is thine in divulging it.

Paris, the 15th of the 1st moon of the year 1655.

To Kerker Hassan, Bassa

Volume V, Book I, Letter XIII

Thou mayest report it to the divan for a certain truth that the chief mufti of the Christians is dead, which puts all the courts in Europe upon new strains of policy.

He was called Innocent X after his assumption to the papacy, for his true name was Pamphilio. But some say it has been a custom for the Popes to change their names ever since a certain priest was lifted to that dignity, who was called

[1] The genealogy of Philemon, Masar and Coptim, who were founders of Egypt and the Coptic people, is a typical example of Arabic artificial genealogy, created to explain the origin of Egypt. Masar is a corruption of Misr (or in Hebrew Mizraim), who in Genesis X is called the son of Ham. By tradition this Misr was the founder of Egypt; the name Misr is often used to denote Egypt and also the city of Cairo. The origin of Philemon, which is obviously a Greek name, has not been determined.

Coptim is the founder of the Copts, who are associated with the scientific knowledge which flourished in Egypt of the ancient world. According to tradition the Copts retained the ancient knowledge and secrets of Egyptian science.

Bocca de Porco or Hog's Face. He, ashamed of this ignominious name as soon as he sat in the chair of Peter, assumed the name of Sergius. [1] Yet all his successors have not observed that rule.

These popes have an authority greater than our principal mufti, for they are obeyed by kings and emperors. And being esteemed little less than gods on earth, they are solemnly adored on the day of their coronation by all the cardinals, princes, prelates and foreign ambassadors at that time in Rome. And for that end they are seated on the altar, which the Nazarenes call the tabernacle and habitation of their God.

If I mistake not in my observation, these Roman caliphs aspire at a sovereignty over all kings and princes; they would make that which they call the hierarchy, a superlative independent monarchy to which all the governments in the world should pay homage and be subject.

This puts me in mind of a certain preacher at Naples who some years ago, when Adonai, the Jew, was in that city and happened to be present in the Church, the preacher having made a very elaborate speech to persuade the people that the priests were superior to kings, at length he broke out into this passionate exclamation: 'O ye princes of Christendom, ye are pharoahs and we priests are your gods. O ye pharoahs, obey your gods. Ye can only command the creature, but we make the Creator Himself come down on the altars at our pleasure.'

This relation I had from the Jew in his travels through Italy. And it is asserted by some of their doctors that the Pope has not only power to excommunicate the greatest prince on the earth but also to pull a saint out of paradise and send him to hell. If they could persuade the Nazarene princes and people to believe they have such an exorbitant power, perhaps in time they might reduce them to as blind a superstition as the ancient kings of Egypt were guilty of, who were so besotted to their priests that when he whom they call the cater or master of the celestial influences, commanded the king to kill himself, for that it was the will of heaven; the poor

[1] Sergius I, Pope 687-701, son of Tiberius and native of Antioch. Sergius, however was not the first to adopt a pseudonym; the custom had long been established by the seventh century.

bigoted monarch durst not dispute the orders he had received but in simple obedience became his own murderer.

Those Egyptian priests indeed were masters of great science, profound astrologers, excellent mathematicians and perfectly skilled in the secrets of natural magic. They performed things transcending the more common and obvious works of nature, by which it was easy to strike terror into the hearts of ignorant mortals. But as for these Nazarene priests all that they can boast of is that they have read the histories of former times and are able to discourse in philosophy and other sciences without having the power to work any prodigies. Unless thou wilt count it one to keep so many warlike nations in a servile awe of their authority with the bare pretence of turning a piece of bread into a god.

Yet for all this there are many poor prelates and other ecclesiastics who are invested with empty titles, having little or no revenues: among which the poverty of some is so remarkable as to become a proverb. Thus 'tis common in the mouths of the Romans to say, 'The Pope's mule fares better than the bishop of Orvieto.'

Illustrious Bassa, live thou in the faith of a Mussulman and the favour of the Grand Signior, for in that state thou mayest despise the greatest of these ecclesiastic infidels.

Paris, the 13th of the 2nd moon of the year 1655.

To Asis, Bassa

Volume V, Book II, Letter II

I know not whether thou wilt praise or condemn the sentence which the Elector of Saxony announced not long ago on a poor fellow for killing a deer. Yet because there is something very singular in it, I will relate the whole passage as I received it from Nathan Ben Saddi, the Jew at Vienna.

In the moon of Shawwal, [1] a certain citizen of Württemberg was accused before the elector for hunting in his forest and killing one of his deer. The duke in a rage commanded him

[1] The tenth month of the Moslem year.

to be set upon a stag, his hands chained to the horns and his feet under the belly of the beast, ordering that the stag with this burden should be let loose to run whither he would. The poor frightened stag not being accustomed to such a load and terrified with the rattling of the chains, ran away full speed over hills and dales, through thickets of briars and thorns, never stopping till he had measured above three and thirty German leagues, and then tired with so vast a race he fell down. At which instant a caravan was coming by that place out of Silesia.

The poor wretch on the back of the stag, almost dead with the pains he had undergone in so continued and violent a motion, being also sorely bruised and his flesh torn and mangled by the boughs of trees as the stag rushed through thick woods, cried aloud to the caravan, begging that some of them would in mercy dispatch him out of his torments. But they, either for fear of the duke's displeasure or for other reasons, refused him this kindness. So that after the stag had rested a while and recovered new spirits, he began a fresh career and never ceased running till he arrived at a certain monastery or convent of religious, where he beat against the gate with his horns till some of the dervishes opened it and let him in. They, astonished to see a man thus pinioned to a stag, his face, arms, legs and all his body covered with blood and himself ready to expire, immediately brought him cordials and other refreshments, whilst some were employed in loosing his chains. But being informed by his own mouth how he came into this condition, they began to think of turning him loose again for fear of the duke's anger. However, suffering themselves to be overcome by the importunity of the miserable man and relying on their ecclesiastic privileges (for here in the West the convents are generally allowed sanctuaries for all sorts of offenders), they took him into their protection; but he expired that night.

It is hard to determine whether the duke or these dervishes were in the right or wrong. The French who of late have by a fashion learned to grow obdurate, justify the proceedings of this prince, saying that pity is a passion fit only for women, children and fools. They esteem it a mark of a great spirit, a mind capable of empire not to be moved with the sighs or tears of the miserable, but to frown or laugh at misfortunes of others. This, they say, is the only method to harden men for war, conquest and plunder, where the victors are to cut their way to honour and riches through the hearts of the vanquished, to quench the ardent thirst of glory with human blood and to celebrate their triumphs only in the midst of horrid massacres and funerals.

'Tis true, these principles and actions are allowable in men of the sword when they fight the battles of their king and country in heat of blood. But clemency and compassion are virtues becoming the greatest prince or most valiant general when their enemies are reduced by the fortune of war to kiss the dust of their feet and beg for mercy, or when in time of peace their subjects fall into a crime which may admit indulgence. Certainly these western infidels have wrong notions of humanity in asserting that cruelty is either a sign of a noble nature or a step to true happiness, since the most hard-hearted tyrant, one time or other, will have need of compassion himself, especially in sickness and the agonies of death, which perhaps prove more tormenting to him than to the merciful and generous. It is recorded of Al Hejai Eb'n Hesha'm[2] a famous Arabian captain, that when in a malignant fever he called for water to drink, and it was denied him by the physicians who had care of his health.

'It is enough,' he said, 'Rueno'd Daula, once my lieutenant, to whom I forgave three treasons and who died a natural death, has refreshed me at this minute with a liquor unknown: sure 'tis the wine of paradise.'

And from that moment he began to recover his health after which he lived many years, often rehearsing this passage among his familiar friends of his last day.

But the infidels are either ignorant of these examples or if they know 'em, pride will not suffer 'em to learn morality and justice. They are destined the greatest part to be incredulous to the day of judgment. How many prophets has God sent into all nations to teach them the right way and not the way of such with whom he is displeased! Yet they will not be converted; they look on the apostles and messengers of the eternal with eyes of swine; they grunt under the burden

[2] This may be Hadjdjadj (661-714), an Omayyad statesman and general.

of their sensuality and like those filthy animals return to their mire again. Yet that superlatively Merciful winks at their frailties and visits them with His graces every morning. But they put their fingers in their ears and turn away in disdain, as from a beggar. They reject the King of all things as a fugitive and vagabond on earth.

From that delectable essence, the odour of whose sweetness is diffused through the elements and refreshes the minds of the true faithful, let us by continual devotion and virtue attract divine tinctures till our hearts be all transformed into incense and in this aromatic pile our souls expire like the phoenix to revive again in the joys of paradise, in amours which know no end.

Paris, the 8th of the 5th moon of the year 1655.

To Solyman, his cousin, at Scutari [1]

Volume V, Book II, Letter XVI

I see thou art given over to a spirit of discontent. Nothing can please thee. Thou murmurest at providence and castest obloquies on the ways of God, as if the order of all things and the established economy of the universe must be changed to gratify thy humour.

Formerly thou wert troubled with dull melancholy thoughts about religion. Now thou art angry with thy trade and pinest that thou wert not educated in the academy. A mechanic life, thou sayest, is tedious and irksome; besides that, it is beneath one of thy blood to be always employed in making of turbans. Thou wishest rather to have been a courtier, soldier or anything, save what thou art.

Cousin, let not pride and ambition corrupt thy manners. Dost thou not consider that all true believers are obliged to exercise some manual occupation, and that the sultan himself is not exempted from this duty? Did not the Prophet himself practise it and enjoin it to all his followers? Hast thou ate anything sweeter in this world than what is acquired by his

[1] A suburb of Constantinople across the straits of the Bosphorus.

own labour? Doubtless all the prophets and holy men have gained their bread by their lawful employments. Adam was a gardener, Abel a shepherd, Seth a weaver, Enoch a tailor, Noah a shipwright, Moses, Saguib [2] and Muhammad were shepherds; Jesus, the son of Mary, a carpenter, Abu Bakr, Omar, Gali Gabdorachaman [3] and Othman were merchants.

Dost thou esteem thyself of better blood than Adam from whom thou receivedest thine? For shame, prefer not thyself to Noah, the restorer of mankind, to Jesus the Messiah, to Muhammad our Holy Lawgiver and to the rest of those excellent persons who thought it no contempt to work at their several trades and eat the bread of their own labours.

Besides, dost thou consider the dangerous intrigues of a prince's court? Art thou sufficiently armed with wit and dexterity to secure thy station against the wily trains of designing men? I do not reproach thy abilities, yet I think thou wilt do better in the post allotted thee by destiny; that is in thy proper calling than in the perilous condition of those who stand or fall at the pleasure of others. Whereas thou art now thy own man and needest fear no tempests of state or frowns of thy price so long as thou pursuest none but thy private affairs. Many sovereign monarchs have envied such as thee when they have seen how cheerfully and quietly they pass away their time under the umbrella of an obscure and private life; whereas at the court there is nothing but intriguing, plotting and treachery; one undermining another to make way for their own advance. The court is a perfect theatre of fraud, dissimulation, envy, malice and a thousand vices, which there act their various parts under the habit and disguises of seeming virtues. There a man must flatter the great and speak against his own sense and the truth to procure the favour of some dignified fool, which nothing is more ignoble and base.

This puts me in mind of a pleasant repartee which Diogenes, the philosopher, gave to a courtier. The spark, passing by Diogenes as he sat in a tub eating of turnips, put this scoff upon him:

[2] Probably the Prophet Shuaib mentioned in the Koran in Suras VII, 83-91; XI, 85-98; XXVI, 176-189; XXIX, 35 sq.

[3] This may refer to Abd al-Rahman, a general in the Prophet Muhammad's army. He is reported to have become immensely wealthy from trade.

'Diogenes,' said he, 'if thou wouldst but learn the art of flattery, thou needest not sit here in a tub, scranching of roots.'

To whom the philosopher replied:

'And thou vainglorious man, if thou wouldst but learn to live contented with my homely fare thou needest not condescend to the fawning of a spaniel.'

But cousin, let not this passage cause thee to emulate the philosopher's manner of life for he had his vices as well as other men. If he was no flatterer, yet he was proud and opiniative; he laid trains for the applause of men in all his actions and so taught others to become flatterers, though he was none himself. All his pretended humility, mortification and rigour were but so many decoys for fame. Of this Plato was sensible, who was a far more excellent philosopher than he. As this sage was one day walking with some of his friends in the fields, they showed him Diogenes standing up to the chin in water whose superficies was frozen over, saving one hole that Diogenes had made for himself.

'Pooh,' says Plato, 'don't regard him, and he'll soon be out, for had he not seen us coming this way he would not have put himself to this pain.'

Another time this philosopher came to Plato's house and as he walked on the rich carpets with which the floor of the hall was covered:

'See,' said Diogenes, 'how I trample on Plato's pride.'

'Yes,' said Plato, 'but with greater pride.'[4]

Certainly, the greatest philosophers, doctors and even saints themselves have their errors and failings. Do not therefore affect to change thy calling for the life of a student or a contemplative man. For the same discontent will still haunt thee in that state which makes thee so uneasy now. Thou art a perfect stranger to the intolerable anguish of mind which afflicts thinking men and such as apply themselves to the study of the sciences. They labour under a perpetual thirst of knowledge, and the more they learn the greater and more ardent is their desire of farther discoveries. So that the most accomplished sages are no more satisfied with their own

[4] The source of the anecdotes is Diogenes Laertius's account of Diogenes, the fifth century B.C. cynic philosopher, in *Lives of Eminent Philosophers*, trans. R. D. Hicks, Loeb Classics, Volume II, Book VI.

acquisitions than he who has never meddled with books. Then as to their bodies they are always vexed with one malady or other, proceeding from the vident agitation of their spirits, the intenseness of their thoughts, perpetual poring upon books, and their sedentary life.

In all that I have said I do not dissuade thee from seeking after knowledge, I rather counsel thee to read books, and I gave thee the same advice in a former letter. But do it with moderation. Let not thy studies intrench on the affairs of thy calling. Read histories or other tracts according to thy fancy when thou hast nothing else to do. But do not follow it so close as if thou aspirest to the character of a complete historian or philosopher. Still remember that thou art a turban maker and that by the decrees of fate thou art born for this business. Follow it with alacrity and mirth. When thou art at thy work, 'twill be pleasant meditating on what thou hast read at thy spare hours. Thou wilt find thyself much more happy in thus mixing studies with the necessary offices of thy trade than in abandoning thyself wholly to a contemplative life. And in the midst of thy disgusts thou mayest comfort thyself with this reflection that thou art of none of the most despicable callings which serve the necessities of man's body. Had thy employment been only to make *papouches* or sandals which cover the feet, it might have been an argument of discontent to thee in regard the foot is the most contemptible member in the body. But now thou passest thy time in making ornaments for the head, which is the noblest part and commander of all the rest; thou hast no reason to repine.

If after all thou resolvest to change thy course of life, I advise thee to turn soldier, for then thou must be contented and patient perforce.

Paris, the 13th of the 4th moon of the year 1656.

To Sedree al-Giraw'n, Chief Treasurer to the Grand Signior

Volume V, Book II, Letter XIX

The troubles of the sublime Porte touched me so nearly and embarked my soul in such a tempest of solicitous thoughts and anxieties for the honour and safety of the Osman Empire that I had no leisure to think of my own particular hazards whilst I was writing the other letter. Yet I have been engulfed in abundance of vexatious circumstances and perilous accidents. It generally happens that when one misfortune befalls a man it brings a train along with it. So that at some seasons we seem to be besieged with evils or at least so closely blocked up by an army of calamities that there is no passage left open either for relief or intelligence.

So has it fared with me of late and with thousands of others, I doubt not, in this populous city. The rebellion of the prince of Condé is the occasion of all this. For the king, having some reasons to apprehend a secret conspiracy of the prince's friends and well-wishers in Paris and other places, has caused a very severe scrutiny to be made of all strangers and sojourners. The *soubashis* or officers go to every house within their precinct, taking down the names of all the inhabitants in writing, and seizing the persons of those whom they suspect. The prisons are filled with people of all ranks, and the nobles are sent to the castle in the wood Vincennes. 'Tis said the king has a list of many thousands of Condé's party in Paris, who designed on a prefixed day to take up arms for that prince and that their example would have been followed all over the kingdom.

God knows what is in the hearts of these infidels; I am sure Mahmut is wholly a stranger to their plots, though last year I received certain instructions from the Vizier Azem, commanding me to act secretly in the Prince of Condé's behalf to abet the faction and use all the endeavours and art I could to raise a new party for him among the courtiers. But I waived so dangerous an employment by proposing to him the vast expenses it would require and the necessity of sending some extraordinary embassy to this court to countenance the business. To tell thee the truth I esteemed it a thing impracticable and a mere caprice of that active bassa, who had a natural kindness for rebels and delighted to have a hand in difficult undertakings whether there was any likelihood of success or not.

But he is dead and let that atone for all his rebellions when he had the command of Aleppo. I love not to load the departed souls with accusations. What I have to say is in my own vindication, who could not approve his politic chimera. In regard, had it succeeded, no profit or advantage would from thence arise to the Ottoman Empire. And had it been discovered, not only I and all the secrets of my commission would have lain open to the infidels, but also it would have been an eternal dishonour and blemish to the high resplendent Porte to be found guilty of violating in so notorious a manner the faith it had given to the most ancient and puissant monarchy among the Nazarenes.

Besides, I know not but this minister had a private grudge against me for accusing him formerly to the divan when he held conference with the Venetians. And that he studied this way to be revenged by employing me in an affair which must needs be my ruin. However, I think I had reason to be cautious and apprehensive of the worst. This made me dispatch to him a letter full of specious umbrages, seeming to approve his design but entangling it with such difficulties as would divert him from farther thoughts of it.

Yet after all, I have been really brought into danger on the bare suspicion of being concerned on the Prince of Condé's side, by which thou mayest guess at the consequence had I hearkened to the vizier's advice.

One morning early the officers appointed for this purpose entered my chamber, and having demanded my name, business and quality, I answered, 'My name was Titus Durlach Nieski, but that for shortness and to denote my country, I was commonly called Titus the Moldavian, and that by this name I was well known to Cardinal Mazarin, as I had been to his predecessor Richelieu and other courtiers of great quality.'

I told them likewise that I was a clerk who understood some foreign languages and therefore had been often employed by those cardinals in translating books out of Greek and Arabic into Latin and French. For which reason, being recommended by Cardinal Richelieu I had been introduced into the acquaintance of several nobles, whose children I taught those languages, and that some of them had promised to make me curate of St. Stephen's church as soon as it was vacant.

They seemed to be very well satisfied with what I said but told me moreover they had a commission to search my lodgings for arms and treasonable papers.

It is impossible to express the horror I was in when I saw them go roundly to work, prying into every corner and searching my trunks, coffers and even my bed itself. Not that I had any guilt upon me of concealing either arms or papers relating to this conspiracy, but my concern was for my box of letters to the ministers of the Porte. As for arms they found no other but an old sword, which I told them I travelled with out of my own country and a brace of pistols for the same use to defend me from robbers, assassins and other injuries.

These fellows seemed mightily pleased with the curious workmanship of my weapons, surveyed them all over, and having drawn my sword out of the scabbard and made a pass or two with it against the wall after the French mode of fencing, they put it up again telling me they had no authority to take these arms from me, since they were necessary for my defence. But when they came to my box of letters and saw them written in a strange character, which none of them could read, they began to look on one another and change their countenance, as if there were some dangerous matter contained in these papers and therefore writ in ciphers.

They went aside to one end of the chamber whispering together, and nodding their heads with all the symptoms of jealousy. At length I interrupting them said:

'You need not, gentlemen, be concerned about these papers; they were left with me by a merchant Jew of my acquaintance, and they are letters of correspondence between him and some of his brethren at Rome, Venice, Amsterdam and other places in Europe. 'Tis therefore they are written in a character which to you appears strange, it being Hebrew, the national language of the Jews. They contain only matters of traffic, being letters of mart and exchange; for you know the Jews are the greatest merchants, brokers and bankers in the world.'

These words with some gold which I gave them dispersed all their suspicions, cleared up their cloudy brows and turned their frowns into smiles and complimental addresses. They told me I was a very honest man, and they would do me what service they could. So bid I adieu.

By this thou mayest see the mighty power of that charming metal which commands all things. For whatever I could have said without that had been insignificant. But these idolators melted into an indifference at the first sight of glistering pistoles, and when I had once rendered them thus ductile, 'twas easy to frame them to the most devout appearance of respect and friendship. They promised and swore no hurt should be done me.

But I knew the fickleness of human fidelity better than to repose any great confidence in these men's words. As soon as they were gone I conveyed my letters to Eliachim, who could easily conceal them in any private corner of his house, desiring him to furnish me with some letters of indifferent concerns written in Hebrew, that if these searchers should come again and demand a second view of my box, perhaps with design to carry it to some minister of state, I might have those Hebrew dispatches ready to show, which being put in the same box, would not be known from the other by such ignorant fellows to whom Hebrew, Arabic and Chinese were all alike; and so I should be acquitted from all future trouble of this nature.

And this event answered my expectation. For within three days the same men came again with others in their company, pretending they had fresh warrants and were sworn to be impartial. Wherefore I was forced to attend them, whilst they carried both me and my box before a cadi or judge who having examined very strictly concerning my name, country, religion and other matters and seeming well satisfied with all my answers, at last sent for a priest well versed in the Hebrew tongue, ordering him to peruse the letters, which when he had done, he assured the cadi that there was not a word in any of them relating to the state, being purely matters of private contracts and bargains between merchant correspondents with bills of lading, etc. So I had my box of sham letters restored to me again and was honourably dismissed.

Yet though this storm was soon blown over, I was very near running on rocks and sands through the persecution of thy predecessor Kienan Bassa and Kisur Dramelec with many others in the seraglio, the first keeping from me the pension allowed by the Grand Signior, the second either sending me no intelligence or else baffling me with trifling news nothing to the purpose; the rest aspersing me to the ministers of the divan.

I desire thee to send me the arrears that are behind for the space of nineteen moons as thou wilt find in the register of the hazne.[1] Had it not been for Eliachim, that honest Jew, I should have been ruined in this place for want of money.

I need not say more to thee who knowest that gold is the grand talisman, which works all the miracles in the world.

Paris, the 22nd of the 7th moon of the year 1656.

To Dgnet Oglou

Volume V, Book III, Letter I

Who can penetrate into the mysterious conduct of destiny? – whether God governs this world by the influence of the stars or by the ministry of spirits or by his own immediate powers. Or whether all things did not proceed from chance and are still ruled by the same? Be it how it will, there remains something adorable. Even that chance itself, supposing Epicurus'

[1] Treasury.

opinion true, is worthy of supreme honours and sacrifices, which has with such exquisite luck performed all the parts of infinite wisdom and forecast in forming and preserving the universe. Were I a disciple of that philosopher, every morning when I beheld the rising sun and at midday when I saw him climb the meridian and in the evening when he takes his *congé* of this upper world to visit our antipodes, would I with profoundest veneration cry out:

'O eternal chance! O omnipotent causality! O incomprehensible blindness! I adore thee, I burn incense to thee and do all things which the duller sort of mortals think are only due to an all wise, all good and all mighty God.'

Thus would I address to that infinite pell-mell of atoms, could I believe with Epicurus that from such an inconceivable hurly-burly proceeded all this admirable beauty and order which we behold.

Thou wilt perceive by this that I am religiously disposed and rather than not adore some supreme being, I would make a deity of that which to others is the fountain of atheism. And I think there is reason on my side. For let this world be produced how it will, whether by the casual concourse of atoms or by the deliberate act of an eternal mind, whether it be eternally self-existent, according to the stoics or by the genuine result of the divine ideas, as the Platonists say; it is but just that we should pay the most devout and grateful acknowledgments to the source of so many immense prodigies and wonders.

But then what shall we say for all the evil that appears in the world? That there is such a thing as evil scattered up and down through all the ranks of being, and as it were blended and riveted in their very essences, is manifest at first view; and every man has his share of this epidemical contagion. But whence it proceeds, who can inform me? I am not the first that have asked the question. Many years ago the inquisitive world was busy in searching out the root of evil, and there were almost as many opinions about it as there were nations on earth.

Some asserted that all evil came out of the north, others derive it from the south, as if the two poles were the centres and native seats of this malady of the world. But these seem to be men of short discourse and shallow reason, supinely credulous and willing to take up with anything rather than to be at the pains of attentive contemplation.

Yet this opinion has so far prevailed in these western parts that the Nazarene priests when they celebrate their mass stand on the north side of the altar at the reading of the gospel, turning their back to that quarter of the world. And the reason they give for this ceremony is because in the written law it is said, out of the north comes all evil. I have heard them seriously maintain this argument. But God knows whether there be any such place in the written law or no; or if there be, whether it must be taken in this sense. Yet I must confess the Romans have some reason to believe it, having experimentally felt a great deal of evil from the northern Goths and Vandals who in former ages rushed out of their frozen regions and came down like a torrent upon Italy and other parts of Europe, making havoc of all things civil and sacred. And if this be the ground of their ceremony, they have greater reason now to change their station and turn their backs to the southeast, having been much more fatally handled by the victorious Mussulmans.

The ancient Parthians held that there were two principles or sources of all things, viz. good and evil, and that there has been an eternal quarrel between them, but in the end they say the good shall get the victory and exterminate the evil. This opinion was embraced by a sect of Christians whom they call Manichees. The founder of that sect was a Persian by birth; his name was Manes, a very learned man as records of the East testify, yet the Christians rank him among the most pernicious heretics. He taught that wine was the blood of devils and therefore forbad it to his followers. He also prohibited the flesh of animals. This he learned from the priests of Egypt, where he resided a considerable time.

But to return to the sentiments of men concerning the origin of evil. There are some who affirm God is the author of it, which is not far from blasphemy. Others say that when the devils were exterminated from the earth, they in revenge sowed the seeds of evil in the universe. But that of the stoics seems the most plausible to me, for they asserted that nothing is evil of itself, but that the contrariety which we behold in the world is very good and concludes to establish the order and economy of all things.

My dear Dgnet, do not esteem me an atheist because of the liberty I take in discoursing of these mysterious things. There are a sort of people here in the West whom they call deists, that is men professing the belief of a God, creator of the world, but sceptics in all things else. They have no implicit faith in historical religion but think it the part of men as they are endued with reason to call in question the writings of mortals like themselves, though they had the character of the greatest prophets. Thus they think it no sin to canvass the books of Moses and the Hebrew prophets, the gospel of Jesus, the son of Mary and the Alcoran of Muhammad, our Holy Lawgiver, choosing what is agreeable to reason and rejecting the rest as fabulous inserted either by the craft of men or the interloping of the devil.

I protest; there appears to me no reason to call these men atheists or infidels. They rather seem to deserve the title of philosophers or lovers of wisdom and truth. And 'tis from them I have learned this unwillingness to be imposed on in matters of religion. I find them in all things men of great morality and goodness far exceeding the zealots of the age in true virtue and pious actions. But they make no noise of what they do, and whilst only their human frailties are conspicuous to all, their benefactions lie concealed under the veil of an unparalleled modesty.

Such of old were the associates of Zaid ibn Rifaa, my countryman. This was a person of an ardent spirit and prodigious understanding, educated in the Mussulman law, but when he came to those years wherein men usually examine the grounds of their religion, he sought the most learned men and such as are versed in all sciences. After he had conversed some time with them and found them to be persons of integrity as well as men of sense, he proposed to them the convenience of frequent clubs among themselves where they might with an unrestrained freedom discourse of all things, and being united in an inviolable friendship might improve one another's knowledge and virtue without regarding the legends and harangues of the mullas. This society composed fifty books of so many several kinds of science that they called them

Ikhwan al-Safa [1] or the writings of the sincere fraternity, concealing their names. They treated of human and divine matters without reserve or caution, asserting that the Mussulman religion was corrupted and alienated from its first institution, having imbibed many errors, and that there was no way to restore it to its primitive purity but by joining to it the philosophy of the ancients. In a word, they endeavoured to reform whatever was amiss in the doctrines and manners of the faithful by reducing both to the standard of reason.

I know not whether thou wilt approve or dislike their enterprise. But I am sure thou art sensible, as well as I, that there are bigots among the followers of the Prophet, and that those deserve correction. The devil will set his foot in the temple of God, but do not thou follow his steps. If thou do, he that made the devil fetch thee back again.

Paris, the 30th of the 7th moon of the year 1656.

To Abdel Melec Muly Omar, President of the College of Sciences at Fez

Volume V, Book IV, Letter IX

I received the packet of venerable import containing sacred counsels and acceptable intelligence, replenished with noble memoirs and illustrious remarks, sage precepts and refined improvements in philosophy and the mysterious sciences of nature.

With abundance of affection and joy I read the character of Musu Abu'l Yahyan [1] and the encomium of his wisdom

[1] The Ikhwan al-Safa was an association of religious and political thinkers who flourished in the latter half of the tenth century; their headquarters were in Basra. Zaid ibn Rifaa was only one of the contributors to the writings of the group, which consists of fifty-two treatises, seemingly an encyclopaedia of the sciences. Like earlier Moslem philosophers they attempted to reconcile the older Greek philosophy with Islamic traditions. They emphasized the mystical Greek philosophers, and their doctrines have a decided neo-Platonic bias. Mahmut's attempt to make the group appear as deists must be regarded with suspicion.

[1] A professor of philosophy at Fez; many years later Mahmut corresponds with him. See below pp. 164-67.

and virtues. May a constellation of such lights always adorn that renowned college and from thence disperse their learned influence and rays not only through Africa but over all the earth that Fez may be numbered among the cities whose fame is sweet; that it may be ranked with Jerusalem the holy, Masre[2] the ancient, Medinat Alnabi[3] the chaste and the salutiferous Babylon, acquiring a peculiar title of honour, an attribute worthy of respect when men shall everywhere call it Fez, the mother of sciences.

My soul has been very inquisite and restless for many years and I think this is owing to my captivity in Palermo. For before that, whilst I lived at ease in the seraglio basking under the warmer influence of royal majesty, the sacred presence of the Grand Signior, who like the sun gives motion, heat and life to all things, I never regarded books or once applied my mind to study anything but to acquit myself in my station and strengthen my interest at the court, esteeming all other learning as barbarous which conduced not to this end.

Foreign histories and languages were equally contemptible to me. I thought it beneath a Mussulman courtier to give his tongue and mind the fatigue of any other dialect, save the Persian, Arabic and Turkish, or to load his memory with the records of other nations, designing to be the slaves of true believers.

As to the speculative sciences, I was naturally desirous enough of knowledge. But I either had not leisure or wanted books and other advantages of study. So that all the knowledge I could then boast of consisted only in some loose notions of logic and metaphysics, which I had got by reading an old Arabic manuscript. And I thought myself historian enough after I had perused the annals of the Ottoman Empire and now and then cast an eye on the Turkish translation of Herodotus and Plutarch.

'Tis true, indeed, by conversing frequently with the Greeks I soon learned their vulgar dialect, but this is far from the polite language of the ancient Grecians. And a page of the treasury taught me the rudiments of Slavonian,[4] which afterwards I learned more perfectly, hoping it would be of some

[2] Cairo. [3] Medina in Arabia. [4] The Slavic language.

service to me one time or other.

All these were very superficial accomplishments; yet I thought myself happy enough without searching any farther. The pleasures and gaieties of a courtly life took from me the edge and gust with which I have since pursued more solid studies and looked into the wisdom of the ancients.

But when once misfortune had changed the scene of my life and instead of the honourable post I had in the Grand Signior's service, fate had rendered me a miserable abject slave in Sicily, I began to grow very thoughtful and pensive. The continual drudgery and labour I underwent soon mortified my former passions and weaned me from all hopes of worldly honour. And the cruel stripes I daily received from that barbarous infidel, my master, so broke my spirits that servitude became familiar to me, and despairing to be happy in this world, I was only ambitious to be wise.

I grew very contemplative, and having acquainted myself with an honest carpenter in the town where we lived, who had a great many books in his custody, he lent me several choice treatises, and I borrowed all the hours I could from sleep to peruse them with attention and profit. That carpenter pitied my condition and did me many good offices of friendship without other hopes of reward, save what he expected from God. By his means I contracted a familiarity with two or three learned men, who spared no pains to instruct me in the Roman and ancient Greek languages as also in the principles of philosophy. My master often beat me for this, attributing the neglect of his business to my bookishness (as he called it) and keeping the priests company. But all his severity could not abate my ardent thirst after knowledge. I still continued studying at certain seasons till the happy hour of my redemption, and then I frequented the academies. Ever since which time I have neglected no opportunities of improving my reason, yet find myself at this day much in the dark.

There appears no certainty in any science but the mathematics; all the rest are entangled with a thousand controversies and riddles, which has made me turn sceptic in most things. Only I retain an inviolable faith for the Alcoran and the book of prophetic doctrines and traditions. Next to these

I pay a profound respect to the writings of Porphyry, the philosopher, who seems to approach nearest to reason of all the ancient sages. His true name was the same as thine (Melech), which thou knowest in the Syriac signifies king. Whence his tutor, Longinus, taking occasion from the usual colour of royal robes, called his Porphyrius, which in the Greek signifies one clad in purple. He was born at Tyre, the metropolis of the ancient Phoenicians. His pedigree was noble and his education generous. Nature had also formed him for a sage, and fortune favoured him with advantages enough. For besides his first tutor, whom I have already mentioned (who was the greatest grammarian and orator of his time) Porphyry went to Rome where he gained the friendship of Plotinus; and that philosopher accomplished him in the perfection of all science: so that he had power over the demons and expelled the genius Atan, which infested certain baths in Rome. In a word, his doctrines appeared divine and his actions more than human. Yet he himself before his death published a reverse of his former writings, which is a sufficient argument that there is no stability in the thoughts of mortals.

Therefore, since the wisest of men contradict themselves and turn sceptics, tell me, O oracle of the age, why may not I?

Paris, the 29th of the 8th moon of the year 1658.

To Pesteli Haly, his Brother, Master of the Grand Signior's Customs at Constantinople

Volume V, Book IV, Letter XIII

I have received a dispatch from our cousin Isouf. He has been in a cold region within the Arctic Circle but now is at Stockholm in Sweden. The parts he has visited are the farthermost tracts of our continent to the north. They may be called the territories of night and darkness, for they have but one day in a whole year. The sun appears but once above their horizon during his annual progress through the Zodiac. Yet he makes them amends by the long continued light he affords them at that season, for that one day is without the miracle of Joshua prolonged the space of four, five or six moons according to the proportionate distance of each country from the pole.

Isouf relates strange things of those dark countries and such as seem almost to surpass credit were they not confirmed by many grave and learned writers. He says that in some parts of Norway no tree is to be seen by reason of the violent force of the winds which blow down all before them, carrying away even the roofs of houses and scattering them at a great distance. So that the inhabitants are forced to dwell in dens and caves and burn the bones of fishes for want of better fuel, since it is impossible for any plant to grow in those parts. Neither can men travel safely on horses or foot at certain tempestuous seasons, for the wind will either throw down horse and man to the ground or catch them up into the air.

But when he describes the horrible coldness of those regions, the very idea of it is enough to make one quake. He says cold is an active quality and reigns under the North Pole as in its proper kingdom or centre, from whence it darts its freezing rays through the earth. Yet others are of opinion that cold is only a privation of heat, a bare passive disposition of the elements and therefore more sensibly felt in those climates that are farthest from the warm influence of the sun, whose beams give life and vigour to all things. Be it how it will, its effects are very remarkable in these northern regions.

All rivers, lakes and seas there are frozen up during the winter. Men, horses, wagons, coaches and even whole armies pass as commonly over the ice as before ships sailed there or as we travel over the firm land. And last winter the Baltic sea was the road of ice over which the king of Sweden marched with his army of horse and foot into Zealand [1] to prosecute the war in those parts. They also raise strong forts of snow able to sustain the battery of bullets and engines of war with all the violence of the fiercest assaults. They build caravansaries on the frozen seas and lakes for the convenience of travellers and set up branches of firs or juniper as marks to distinguish the holes and fissures of the ice from that which is solid and secure, for there are highways on those congealed waters and

[1] Zealand or Sjaeland is the island which forms the eastern portion of Denmark.

officers appointed to survey them and take all necessary orders for the security of travellers, and sometimes they fight pitched battles on the frozen element.

Our kinsman also has made curious remarks on the triumphas, obelisks and funeral monuments of ancient heroes among the Goths and Swedes, for these nations boast of giants and famous warriors. These monuments, though of stone and exquisitely shaped, yet were never cut by the hand of man but are so many splinters of rocks and mountains torn from the main body by the violence of earthquakes, thunders or the like motions of nature, and falling down in the forms of pyramids and other artificial figures were of old set up by graves of giants and other renowned persons; having also inscriptions on them, signifying the particular hero who there lies buried, such as these:

> I, Uffro, fighting in defence of my country with my own hand killed thirty-two giants, and at last being killed by the giant Rolvo, my body lies here.

and

> I, Ingolvas, that subdued all oppressors and defended the poor and weak, now grown old, poor and weak myself, yet having my sword girt to my thigh, am forced to yield to death (who conquers all things) and to go down to this sepulchre, which I prepared for my last retreat.

It seems there are infinite numbers of these tombs all over the deserts, mountains and valleys of the North, which is an argument that however contemptible these people may seem to the true believers, yet they have not been wanting in valiant men and heroes. Doubtless God has dispensed His virtues and graces to men of all nations; He is not partial in his gifts. We ought to praise Him in the beginning and end of all our actions. And if we contemplate His honour in the middle of our affairs, we shall not do amiss, since as He is first and the last of the universe, so He is the centre of everything.

I had not these relations from Isouf but out of the historians themselves who write of these countries; yet our kinsman informs me of some things which are omitted by those authors. Every traveller is singular in his observations, for all men have not the same genius. And thy journal of the East abounds with remarks which are not common with other writers.

Brother, if I may advise thee, it shall be to do nothing by imitation but pursue the dictates of thy own sense and the peculiar bent of thy soul! For whatever is forced and affected is nauseous.

Paris, the 19th of the 12th moon of the year 1658.

To the Kaimakam

Volume V, Book IV, Letter XV

It rejoices me to hear that Adonai's place is supplied by a Mussulman, in whom the sublime Porte may put more confidence than in any of the Jewish race. 'Twill be encouragement to the true faithful and a precedent of good import. For no nation loves to see their prince bestow offices of trust on strangers when his own people are as capable of employment as they. 'Tis generally taken as an affront and contempt of their abilities or their virtue and has often produced ill consequences.

I deny not but there are many honest and wise men among the Hebrews, persons of merit and honour from whence the sultan receives no small services, but this ought not to diminish the reputation of those who are of the same faith with their sovereign. Doubtless Arabia and Turkey are not barren of good soldiers, prudent statesmen and dextrous ministers.

I know not the character of Zeidy Alamanzi, whether he be a natural-born Turk, a tributary son of a Christian or a voluntary renegade. However, the choice that is made of him convinces me that the unerring divan esteem him a man fit for the business committed to his charge.

He ought to be perfectly skilled in Italian or at least in some other language of the Nazarenes that so he may pass the better unsuspected among the people where he resides, who are more jealous of strangers than any other nation in Europe. 'Tis a crime thought worthy of imprisonment for a Venetian to converse with a foreigner too frequently and in private, for they are afraid lest by that means a dangerous correspondence should be established betwixt some ill-affected subjects of that commonwealth and its enemies, whereby their secrets may be betrayed and measures taken to ruin them.

For this reason also they have forbid false hair or perukes to be worn by any in their dominions lest this might serve as a disguise for villains and traitors. Yet nothing is more common in France and other countries of Europe than for men to wear on their heads ornaments of women's hair instead of their own.

As to religion I believe they will not much trouble him, being no zealots themselves. And provided he does but profess himself a Christian and a Catholic, they'll make no farther inquisition.

The Italians in general are much like the ancient Romans in their humour: men of grave aspect and carriage and much composed in both than the French, who appear ridiculous through the levity of their discourse and actions. The former abound in sage precepts of morality and politic aphorisms, which serve as a rule whereby to square the course of their lives; the latter only affect some flashy improvements of wit and conversation, studying rather how to please women than men, coveting to be perfect in external accomplishments and the graces of the body, whilst they slight the more valuable endowments of the mind. In a word they are mere apes and mimics. On the contrary the Italians are men of an awful and majestic behaviour, solid judgment and deep reach. If you see them smile you shall seldom or never hear 'em laugh, whereas the motion of a feather will set the French abraying like asses. These will contract a warm friendship with any man at first interview, heighten it with a thousand compliments, make him their confessor and unbosom all their secrets. Yet a second encounter shall extinguish this passion and a third shall revive it again, whereas those (Italians) are cautious and slow in the choice of their friends, and when once that knot is dissolved, 'tis never to be fastened there again. They are irreconcilable in their hatred and revenge.

But there are men to be excepted in both nations who fall not under these general characters. France affords many wise and learned persons and Italy not a few fools and idiots.

Virtues and vices are strangely mixed in all people. War, commerce and travel with other human occurrences alter men's natural dispositions and give the lie to the exactest observations that can be made. Besides, time changes all things, and the qualities which this age remarks in the Italians may in the next be transferred to the French. For there is no constancy in anything under the moon.

Zeidy will find great examples of frugality among the Venetians in the necessary expenses of their persons and families, yet abundance of magnificence in whatever relates to the public, which the subjects of that commonwealth serve with open purses and free hearts. Indeed they are not so remarkable for their temperance as some other parts of Italy. Libertinism and voluptuousness reign uncontrolled in Venice. Women and wine are there almost as common as the elements. Yet 'tis observed that strangers generally debauch more with both than the natives. God preserve Zeidy from their temptations.

If it be his fortune or duty to visit Padua, he ought not to make too long an abode in that nest of philosophers and physicians, lest they first anatomize his soul and discover the secrets of his commission and then turn his body to a skeleton, as they once served a Moor whom they dissected alive to make experiment perhaps whether a Muhammadan's blood circullated the same way as a Christian's.

Those Italian physicians are very cruel and think it no sin to try poisons and other fatal tricks on the poor that so they may be the better able to keep the rich on the rack at their pleasure and make their market of them.

I know not Zeidy's appointed station or what cities he is to see, but wherever he goes, 'twill be necessary for him to use abundance of caution, for the Italians are the closest, slyest and most judicious people in the world.

But I forget that he is chosen by the divan for this employment, to whom the characters of all nations are known, and who penetrates into the most interior recesses of men's spirits.

Therefore I lay my hand upon my mouth in profound submission and acquiesce to my superiors, still praying that the Grand Signior may have faithful and wise ministers at home and no novices for his agents abroad.

Paris, the 3rd of the 2nd moon of the year 1659.

To Dgnet Oglou

Volume VI, Book I, Letter I

It makes me smile sometimes when I reflect how often I was put to it for an address suitable to the manners of the Nazarenes and the particular mode of Paris when I first arrived at this city. For thou knowest we had other employments than to learn fashions and *congés* at Palermo. The mind of a slave is dejected under the circumstances of his captivity, so that he has not leisure to regard anything but how to accomplish his daily task and to please his patron. All his study and care is bent upon this and there's no room left for generous thoughts, neither has he means or courage to venture on projects or improve the present occurrences in order to assure his future happiness. Nay, he hardly dares think of ever being happy again. This was my case and I believe 'twas not much better with thee.

Yet notwithstanding all the rigorous usage I had – the bastinadoes, kicks, bruises, cuts and wounds I received from the hands of that barbarous giafer,[1] my master, which made me sometimes incapable of doing him any service by day or taking any rest myself by night – I was resolved to find some spare time for books. I rose early and went late to sleep, neglecting no moment wherein I could apply myself to study. The acquaintance I had with that Sicilian carpenter, our friend, was of singular advantage to me in this kind; for thou mayest remember he was well stocked with many ancient and learned treatises. He furnished me with Plutarch, Polybius, Strabo, Pliny and other histories. All which and many more I devoured with greediness, for I had a strong appetite to knowledge. And after my redemption I passed away some time in the academies, where I learned the knotty tricks of logic, how to split moods and figures and chain one impertinent syllogism to the tail of another to eternity. I also ran

[1] Giafer is probably a corruption of ghiaour, which means idolator and infidel. The Turks apply it to those who do not profess the Islamic faith.

through a course of philosophy and other sciences. Neither was I altogether ignorant of men; for the reading of histories fits a man the better to make practical experiments in the affairs of the world. To which also philosophy is not a little helpful in directing out observations on the various tempers of people, the personal dispositions and singularities with the humours and customs peculiar to this or that nation. For these things depend many times on the difference of the climate, the nature of the soil, the qualities of the air and the manner of their diet.

But neither history, logic or philosophy were able to efface the impressions of my early years or unteach me the manners in which I had been educated from my infancy. I brought Arabia and Constantinople along with me even to Paris. And because I had not been used to dissemble the profession and carriage of a Mussulman during my thraldom in Sicily, I was at a loss in my deportment when I came first hither.

How often have I been like to discover myself by pronouncing the sacred Basmala, either when I sat down to eat or put a glass of water to my lips or when I began any other action of importance. So likewise the Hamdala[2] after a repast or when anything happened which prompted me to praise God.

When I met any of my acquaintance in the streets, I was apt to forget I had a hat on. And instead of putting off that, according to the fashion of the Franks, I laid my hand on my breast and sometimes bowed so low that my hat fell off from my head before I was sensible of my error.

If I had occasion to address myself to a person of quality, I was ready to take up the bottom of his cloak, gown or robe and to kiss it in token of reverence as is the custom in the East when we salute the Grandees. Nay, sometimes I could not forbear falling on my knee or prostrate on the ground before Cardinal Richelieu and those of his high dignity. All which, nevertheless, passed only for clownishness and want of courtly education, which teaches the nice punctilios of address. They took me for a kind of Moldavian rustic without any farther jealousy. Or perhaps they smiled at all this as some singular caprice or humour like that of the philosopher

[2] The Basmala and the Hamdala are two formulaic prayers used in Islamic worship.

Pasicles,[3] who coming to salute a great captain, and the ceremony of those times requiring him to touch the captain's knee, he laid his hand on the captain's genitals. At which the captain being affronted and thrusts his hand away with scornful words.

'What!' says the philosopher, 'does not that part belong to you as well as your knees?'

It often diverts my melancholy to consider how many errors of this kind I have committed not through ignorance or any cynical humour but only in pure oversight and forgetfulness.

It was a long time ere I could frame my fingers to handle a knife and fork at meals as is the custom in these western parts; whereas thou knowest we make use of no other instruments in eating but our fingers and teeth. Whence it was that I could not sometimes forbear thrusting my hand into a whole dish of meat, which is counted a great indecency in France. And after I was reconciled to those nicer instruments of voluptuousness so as to carve my meat *à la mode*; yet when once I had it on my own plate, I laid aside those tools as useless and tore it asunder with my fingers and teeth, feeding *à la turquesque* as the French call it, that is like a Mussulman.

Nevertheless nobody suspected me, but all these miscarriages passed for Moldavian barbarisms, the savage customs of that my supposed country. I tell thee that though the manner of eating among the French seems to have something more of neatness and delicacy in it, yet it appears full of softness and luxury, and I cannot in reason prefer it to the more natural and simple method of diet used in the East. Neither would the French themselves condemn us for savages in this point, as they commonly do, did they but consider that this negligence very well becomes men of the sword, and that in

[3] The basis of this anecdote is Diogenes Laertius' biography of Crates (Book IV, 88), but the account above is a free embellishment of the incident. There are two persons named Pasicles mentioned by Diogenes, one the son of Crates and the other a brother of Crates; but neither of these two was involved in this anecdote.

It seems that Crates, making a request of the master of the gymnasium, laid hold of the master's hips. The master pushed him off; to which Crates replied, 'What, are not these hip-joints yours as much as your knees?' (Hicks's translation, Loeb Classics).

their campaigns their own generals are ambitious to appear careless in everything relating to their body.

Doubtless the ancient Romans, who brought the greatest part of the world under their power, shunned all finesse in diet and apparel till such time as their manners were debauched and their empire in its decline. Our annals record that when Sultan Selim[4] lay down with his army before a certain place and the governor of the town sent commissioners to treat with him about a surrender, they found him at dinner which consisted only of two or three onions, a little salt and bread.

Histories also relate of the faithful Omar, successor of the Prophet, that when he was with his army not far from Jerusalem, the Nazarene prince who governed that city sent a spy into the host of the Mussulmans to observe their discipline and bring him a lively character of their general. The spy went according to his master's orders and having tarried some time in the Arabian camp, returned again and thus spoke to the governor:

'It will not be needful to recount everything I observed among these soldiers, since by what I shall say of their leader, thou mayest comprehend the manners of them all, for they obey him and follow his example in everything with exquisite silence and modesty. I saw Omar their prince at the head of his army, sitting on a camel, his face tawny and scorched by the sun, in a vest of Persian cotton girded about with a belt of leather at which hung a scimitar and dagger with a knapsack tied behind him like the meanest soldier. I saw him take out from thence hard crusts of bread, shaking off the husks of millet which stuck to them, and saying, "In the name of God," he ate heartily of the same. Then he drank water out of a leathern bottle hanging by his side, and when he had done, he said, "Praise be to God." All his army made their repast at the same time and in the same manner with admirable temperance and such an order and modesty as I never saw before, neither can I express.'

When the prince heard this he stood still a considerable time, musing as one astonished. Then turning to the seniors

[4] Selim I, reigned from 1512-20 and was responsible for the enlargement of the empire.

and chief of the people who were present, he said:

'It is necessary that we surrender our city to these people, for they have the smiles of heaven. Their Prophet and their law oblige 'em to temperance, frugality, obedience and a modest deportment. These virtues are certain steps to victory and empire. Besides, I have received a tradition from my ancestors that a people shall come out of Arabia with a new law and religion, which shall abolish all that went before it. They shall subdue Palestine and Egypt and shall build mosques wherein their prayers shall sound like the humming of bees. Their empire shall extend from east to west and to the extremities of the earth. This is what I have learned from my forefathers and which I believe is now coming to pass. Therefore it will be in vain to resist these men, for they are invincible by a decree from above.'

Those that were about him did not approve the counsel of this wise Nazarene. However, he sent to Omar and obtained favour for himself and his family.

Thou wilt say I'm got wide of the mark of my first discourse, which related to myself and not to any of the primitive caliphs, but 'tis impossible to restrain our thought from roving. Some say they hang together like the links of a chain, and that one idea being fastened to another in our memory, we muster them in rank and file according to their proper order when we think or make reflections. God knows how 'tis. This I am sure of, that when I write to my friends I study not to make an elaborate speech on't, as if I were penning an oration, but pursuing my first intention at random, I run on, letting one thought and word beget another.

But I was telling thee how great a bungler I was at first in all the ceremonies and manners of the Franks which differ from those of the East. I was as much to seek in my address as an ass would be to play on a lute, according to the Roman proverb. Yet time and practise rendered all these things familiar and easy. Now, methinks, I'm a thorough-paced Nazarene as to my exterior. I go to the court and temples with as much seeming formality as the Christians, whilst, God knows, my heart is somewhere else. All my actions are out of their natural bias so long as I am absent from the society of true believers.

In a word, I'm forced to imitate the fox, which creature when it is environed with the huntsmen and dogs, counterfeits a barking like the latter and so passes undiscovered for one of their company.

Paris, the 3rd of the 9th moon of the year 1659.

To the Reis Effendi

Volume VI, Book I, Letter II

I am at this time possessed with more apprehensions and jealousies than an old infidel usurer. My lodging affects me with greater melancholy than would a prison. And my uneasiness the same when I go out of doors. Everybody that meets me looks either as my accuser or my judge. And some appear as terrible as executioners. By day my imagination torments me like a fury and by night I am affrighted with melancholy visions. I dream of nothing but racks, wheels, saws, gibbets and such like instruments of human cruelty. Or that I am in some dark dungeon, condemned to more unsufferable tortures by order of the state with Cardinal Mazarin sitting by me like a Spanish inquisitor and in the most tyrannical manner threatening me with pains to which the damned themselves are wholly strangers if I will not confess what I am and reveal the secrets with which I am entrusted.

The occasion of these terrors which harass me night and day is this: I have for four or five days together found myself dogged up and down Paris by a man whose face I never saw before in my life. Let me go where I will he's always some distance from me. If I stand still, so does he, or if I turn back, he's quickly at my heels. I have endeavoured by all the prudent methods I could take to drop him in the crowd of people or in the churches. But all in vain, for still I encounter with the same face. He pursues me like my shadow. Neither coach nor boat, land or water, house or alley can rescue me from the fellow's eyes, who is more quick-sighted than Argus and nimbler than Mercury. He is very cunning also in this business and as dextrous as a juggler, conveying himself when he pleases out of my sight; yet presently after he's in view again. And if I chance to lose him in the dark, I am sure to find him not far away from my lodgings next morning.

This it is which gives me so much disturbance and pierces me with a thousand anxieties, for I know not what to conjecture of this fellow's design. Sometimes I think he is employed by Cardinal Mazarin to watch my motions, observe me in all my appointments. And I am the more confirmed in this suspicion when I reflect on my former imprisonment in this city and the occasion of it. Besides, when I went yesterday to see Eliachim the Jew, this spark followed me near to the door, and though I tarried there two full hours, yet when I came out I had not walked a hundred paces before I saw him again footing it after me in a careless manner with his arms folded and his eyes fixed on the ground, as if he knew nothing of the matter. These are convincing circumstances that he is set at work by the cardinal or somebody else to discover my business.

But when on the other side I consider that if the cardinal suspected me he might go a nearer way to work and seize me in my chamber where my letters would betray me, this thought vanishes and I am at loss what to think.

Then comes into my mind the encounter I had once with my Sicilian master, who strove to set the rabble upon me in the streets of Paris, but my better stars delivered me out of his and their hands, whilst for aught I know he drew upon himself the mischief he designed for me. However, when I reflect on that passage, I am apt to think he may be now in Paris and having by some accident seen me go in or out at my lodgings, contrives how to revenge himself on me, and uses this fellow's assistance in compassing his ends. Perhaps, think I, he will cause me to be stabbed or pistolled at some convenient season, or he will find out some other way less noisy and more malicious to dispatch me. It may be he seeks to entrap me and render me obnoxious to the state. I have a thousand imaginations about it and know not what to conclude. I value not myself, nor am I careful to prolong a miserable life for my own sake. All that I can hope to enjoy in this world would come far short of tempting me to screen myself from the stroke of death by an action unworthy of a philosopher and a man. But the duty and affection I owe to the Grand Signior's service makes me willing to live till I have acquitted myself of my province with perfect success that so I may return to Constantinople with honour. And then I care not how soon I post to that unknown world where all the generations of mortals take up their eternal rest, for in this there's nothing but labour and grief.

In the meantime I know not what conduct to use in this emergency, whether I'd best to speak to this fellow or dissemble my suspicion; whether it will be safe to trust this event to the general providence or to sacrifice him that gives me so much disquiet and so secure my peace. I could easily have him dispatched without any farther noise. But then my conscience would trouble me with afterclaps, lest I should have murdered a man without reason, which is expressly forbid by the Alcoran. Besides, I should always stand in fear of some discovery. I protest I am at a loss for want of ample instructions in such cases as these. And I am weary of mentioning what I have so often intimated already to the ministers of the Porte without any direct answer. However, I will do what my reason suggests and leave the event to destiny.

Happy minister! The affairs of this world are full of dark windings and meanders, and we have all need of a guide or a clue to conduct us through them. May that Omnipresent assist us, whether we are catched in a knot or lost in a labyrinth of difficulties.

Paris, the 25th of the 9th moon of the year 1659.

To Dgnet Oglou

Volume VI, Book II, Letter VII

My business in this place obliges me to keep company with all sorts of people; hence I indifferently associate myself with statesmen, soldiers, courtiers, priests, fiddlers, mechanics, seamen or persons of any profession from whom I can hope for any improvement. For there is hardly so despicable a fellow in the world who may not teach an inquisitive mind something to which it was a stranger before.

Sometimes I converse with painters, whom I generally find to be men of wit and sense but very lewd and dissolute. However, they serve to divert my melancholy, to which thou knowest I am much inclined. For they are the merriest sparks in the world, abounding with smart repartees, jests and comical stories, besides a hundred mimical tricks of good buffoonery to make one laugh, that it is almost impossible to be sad in their company.

They are most of them bred in the academy or in colleges and schools where the sciences are professed, it being in a manner necessary that all men of this trade should have a smack of all sorts of learning and especially that they should be indifferent good historians; they being many times desired to represent pieces of antique and modern history without a pattern. They have a very facetious way also of telling a story to the life as well as of drawing it so in a picture. They would dissolve the most stiff and morose hogia into laughter and jollity to hear how gracefully they will ridicule the most serious matters and turn everything into burlesque, for they are admirable satirists by nature. Yet these are not all alike but differ in their tempers like other men. Some of them are proud and stately, others fawning and abject, and all of them great humourists.

It was an old whim of Martin Heemskerk, a famous painter that was born at a village of the same name. He died in the year of the Christian's hejira 1574. This man had amassed together in his lifetime a vast quantity of money and having no wife or children nor other relations of his own to leave it to, he was resolved to do something for which he might be talked of after his death. I have heard of many dying men that have had one caprice or another in making their last will and testament, but thou wilt say this of Martin was singular. For on his deathbed he bequeathed all his wealth to be distributed into equal dowries or portions wherewith to marry a certain number of maids of Heemskerk, his birthplace, yearly on this condition: that the newly-married couple with all the wedding guests should dance on his grave.

It is necessary for thee to know that since his death there

has been a great alteration of religion in those parts. The inhabitants, which in his time were Roman Catholics, are now all Protestants. And at the time of this change or Reformation, as they call it, it was the general practise of the Protestants to demolish all images and crosses wherever they found 'em. Now, it was the custom of the Roman Catholics to set up a cross at the end of every sepulchre of the dead. Yet so great a veneration have the Heemskerkers for the memory of this painter that whereas there is not a cross to be seen standing in all the country besides, yet his being of brass remains untouched as the only title their daughters can show to his legacy.

'Twas a more cruel and inhuman caprice of an Italian painter (I think his name was Giotto [1]), designing to draw a crucifix to the life, wheedled a poor man to suffer himself to be bound to a cross for an hour, at the end of which he should be released again and receive a considerable gratuity for his pains. But instead of this, as soon as he had him fast on the cross, he stabbed him dead and then fell to drawing. He was esteemed the greatest master in all Italy at that time. And having this advantage of a dead man hanging on a cross before him, there's no question but he made a matchless piece of work on it.

As soon as he had finished his picture, he carried it to the Pope, who was astonished as at a prodigy of art, highly extolling the exquisiteness of the features and limbs, the languishing, pale deadness of the face, the unaffected sinking of the head. In a word he had drawn to life not only that privation of sense and motion, which we call death but also the very want of the least vital symptom.

This is better understood than expressed. Everybody knows that it is a masterpiece to represent a passion of a thought well and naturally. Much greater is it to describe the total absence of these interior faculties so as to distinguish the figure of a dead man from one that is only asleep.

Yet all this and much more could the Pope discern in the admirable draught which Giotto presented him. And he liked it so well that he resolved to place it over the altar of his own chapel. For thou knowest this is the practise of the Nazarenes

[1] This apocryphal story is not reported in Vasari's account of Giotto.

to adore pictures and images. Giotto told him since he liked the copy so well, the painter would show him the original if he pleased.

'What dost thou mean by the original?' said the Pope. 'Wilt thou show me Jesus Christ on the cross in his own person?'

'No,' replied Giotto, 'but I'll show your holiness the original from whence I drew this, if you will absolve me from all punishment.'

The good old father suspecting something extraordinary by the painter's thus capitulating with him promised on his word to pardon him. Which Giotto believing, immediately told him where it was and attending him to the place, as soon as they entered, he drew a curtain back which hung before the dead man on the cross and told the Pope what he had done.

The holy father, extremely troubled at so inhuman and barbarous an action, repealed his promise and told the painter he should surely be put to an exemplary death. Giotto, seemingly resigned to the sentence pronounced upon him, only begged leave to finish the picture before he died, which was granted him. In the meanwhile a guard was set upon him to prevent his escape. As soon as the Pope had caused the picture to be delivered into his hands, he takes a brush and dipping it into a sort of stuff he had ready for that purpose, daubs the picture all over with it, so that nothing could now be seen of the crucifix, but it was quite effaced in all outward appearance.

This made the Pope stark mad. He stamped, foamed and raved like one in a frenzy. He swore the painter should suffer the most cruel death that could be invented unless he drew another full as good as the former, for if but the least grace was missing, he would not pardon him. But if he could produce an exact parallel, he would not only give him his life but an ample reward in money.

The painter, as he had reason, desired this under the Pope's signet that he might not be in danger of a second repeal, which was granted him. And then he took a wet sponge and wiped off all the varnish he had daubed on the picture. And the crucifix appeared the same in all respects as it was before.

The Pope, who looked upon this as a great secret, being ignorant of the arts which painters use, was ravaged at the strange metamorphosis. And to reward the painter's treble ingenuity, he absolved him from all his sins and the punishments due to them, ordering moreover his steward to cover the picture all over with gold as a farther gratuity for the painter. And they say this crucifix is the original by which the most famous crucifixes in Europe are drawn.

I need make no other reflection on this than that as the supposed murder of Jesus, the son of Mary, is the source of all the Christians' devotion, so the real homicide which this painter committed has made it more intense and fervent, by how much the crucifixes drawn after this pattern excel all that were seen before them in the tragical portraiture of the martyred messiah.

And for this reason it is that painters are in so great esteem among the Italians, because they form the gods which those infidels adore. It is no wonder therefore that the chief head of their church should so easily absolve murder in a painter as a venial sin, especially when it is done in *ordine ad Deum,* as the Jesuits say; that is, to promote God's glory as the Pope easily persuaded himself this was, since idolatry is the main engine which supports the state and grandeur of the Roman court. And all the world knows that holy city is a type of heaven, or so the crafty priests would fain represent it so.

My friend, thou and I have seen enough of their tricks and holy frauds in Sicily. Praise be to God they had no power to pervert us. Our faith remains inviolate; we still possess the integrity of Mussulmans, the native attach we owe to the Prophet, who was sent to exterminate idols. In a word, we adore none but one God, Creator of the worlds. May that Incomprehensible forever keep us in the same faith and practise till the release of our souls.

Paris, the 13th of the 9th moon of the year 1661.

To Cara Haly

Volume VI, Book II, Letter X

The court of France in all things endeavours to imitate the ancient grandeur of the Roman emperors and their policy. As they had their amphitheatres whereon were exhibited all sorts of shows and spectacles to divert the people in time of peace, so have these their theatres whereon according to the more acceptable mode of the present age are represented the various kinds of virtue and vice, men's follies and perfections, modern humours and the ancient morality, intrigues of love and of state, surprising actions of war and the subtle overtures of peace, the tyranny of sovereigns and rebellion of subjects. In fine, whatsoever is treated of in books is here acted to the life on the stage and with so much advantage of scenes, interludes, music, dances, language, wit, humour and the like charming circumstances that a man at some hours cannot better pass away his time than in being present at these entertainments, where all that he has read either in ancient or modern history deserving remark shall be successively presented to his view as efficaciously as if the persons were now living and in presence, whose actions each play describes.

There you shall be introduced as it were into the court and camp of the Grand Cyrus. You shall accompany Alexander the Great in his expeditions through Asia; you shall see him die of poison at Babylon, and the Macedonian empire cantonized among his officers. You shall behold all the Roman Caesars in their rise and fall with whatsoever particularities were observable in this or any other renowned monarchy on earth, not excluding the last and most universal empire of the Ottomans. For these infidels presume to act o'er again the part of Tamburlaine and lead about in dramatic triumph the enraged yet still invincible Bajazet. In habits, [1] which only become the destined conquerors of the world, these slaves dare personate the glorious Solyman, Muhammad the Great,

[1] That is, dressed in costumes.

the victorious Selim and even Amurat himself, the stoutest emperor that ever reigned; I mean the uncle of our present sovereign.[2]

Besides true history thus represented, the spectators are sometimes diverted with fabulous entries of gods, nymphs, fauns, satyrs, muses, graces, monsters and whatsoever we find in the ancient poets. There you shall see Prometheus fetching fire from heaven to give life to his man of clay; Lycaon transformed into a wolf for his inhospitable carriage to Jupiter; Ganymede snatched up into heaven by an eagle and made Jupiter's cupbearer for his singular beauty. It is pleasant also to see Phrixus with his sister Helle swimming o'er the Hellespont on the back of a ram with golden fleece, whilst she for fear falls off and is drowned. And from her name (Helle) that sea is supposed to be so called. In the meanwhile Phrixus swims forward and arrives at Colchis, where he sacrifices the ram and hangs the golden fleece up in the temple, which was afterwards stolen away by Jason and his argonauts. It is equally diverting to see the artifice of the scenes and machines which represent Jupiter transforming himself into a shower of gold and so descending into Danae's lap when he begets Perseus on her, who subdued the Gorgons and with Medusa's head turned the Cephen nobles into statues. In a word all the ingenious fictions of Orpheus, Homer, Hesiod, Ovid and the rest of the Greek and Roman poets are here translated, not so much from one language to another as from words to action and from dead inanimate characters to living figures of the things themselves. For these sort of plays are acted by men, women and children, culled out and educated for that purpose; and the managers are at a vast charge for variety of proper scenes and dresses for every occasion, each actor being exactly apparelled according to the different quality of persons represented and the mode of the age and country wherein they lived.

These sorts of divertissements are very agreeable both to the court and city. The king takes great delight in them, especially in ballets and pastorals, which consists chiefly of good songs and dances mixed with bold and uncouth entries

[2] Mahmut refers to the following Turkish emperors respectively: Solyman I, Muhammad II, Selim I and Murad IV.

of antiques, representing monsters and devils, as the Christians usually describe 'em.

But there was lately a check given to their sport by an accident which has surprised all people that heard of it and has puzzled the most intelligent heads to give an account of so strange an occurrence. On the nineteenth of this moon the king and the whole court were present at a ballet, representing the grandeur of the French monarchy. About the middle of the entertainment there was an antique dance performed by twelve masqueraders in the supposed forms of demons. But before they had advanced far into their dance, they found an interloper amongst 'em, who by increasing the number to thirteen put them quite out of their measures, for they practise every step and motion beforehand till they are perfect. Being abashed therefore at the unavoidable blunders the thirteenth antique made 'em commit, they stood still like fools gazing at one another, none daring to unmask or speak a word, for that would have put all the spectators into a disorder and confusion. Cardinal Mazarin (who was the chief contriver of the entertainments to divert the king from more serious thoughts) stood close by the young monarch with the scheme of the ballet in his hand. Knowing therefore that this dance was to consist but of twelve antiques and taking notice that there were actually thirteen, at first imputed it to some mistake. But afterwards when he perceived the confusion of the dancers and that they could not proceed, he made a more narrow enquiry into the cause of this disorder. To be brief, they convinced the cardinal that it could be no error of theirs by a kind of demonstration in that they had but twelve antique dresses of that sort, which were made on purpose for this particular ballet, whereas the thirteenth dancer was disguised after the same manner. Therefore, they concluded that either the devil or somebody else had put a trick on them. That which made it seem the greater mystery was that when they came behind the scenes to uncase and examine the matter, they found but twelve antiques, whereas on the stage there were thirteen.

The preciser sort of bigots gave it out for certain that the devil was amongst them, whilst others more probably say 'twas only some envious or ambitious dancing master, who was either resolved to be revenged for not being one of the twelve, or designed to show his parts incognito against another opportunity, and in the interim set the court a wondering at his singular skill and dexterity; for it was observed that one of the thirteen far surpassed all the rest and did things to a miracle.

Be it how it will, it has brought to memory a passage that happened on the like occasion at a town not far from Paris about eighteen years ago, yet 'twas not half so much talked of then as 'tis now, which was the reason I took no notice of it in any of my letters. But now they are big with it; 'tis the general discourse of all companies who make comparisons of that event with this. Perhaps 'twill not be unpleasant to thee to know it.

In the year 1644 towards the latter end, a company of stage players were at a place called Vitry entertaining the people with comedies, but there happened something really tragical to one of the actors. This man was to perform the part of one dead and then he was to revive again by magic. He acted his part too truly and baffled the necromancer's art. For when he touched him with his talisman as the rules of the play required in order to his resurrection, the inanimate trunk could not obey. The man was dead indeed.

Whether he overstrained himself in imitating the silent, still and irrecoverable privations of that passive state and gave his slippery soul a strong temptation with a fair opportunity to escape its bonds or whether heaven had a particular hand in so remarkable a catastrophe, I will not presume to divine. But this and the other occurrence has put the people out of conceit with plays.

Sage Haly, remember the Arabian proverb which says, 'Tis not good to jest with God, death or the devil. For the first neither can nor will be mocked; the second mocks all men one time or another; and the third puts an eternal sarcasm on those that are too familiar with him.

Paris, the 30th of the 1st moon of the year 1662.

To Ibrahim Eli Zeid, Hogia, Preacher to the Seraglio

Volume VI, Book II, Letter XII

They have a proverb here in the West which says, All is not gold that glisters. And 'tis frequently verified in their own priests, who are generally the greatest hypocrites in the world.

I had not been long in this city before I sent a letter to Bedredin, Superior of the Dervishes of Cogni in Anatolia,[1] whose soul is now with God; wherein I gave him an account of the converse I once had with a Jesuit. For, pretending to be a student and retainer to the clergy, I could not avoid the company of ecclesiastics. Besides, it was my interest to insinuate into their acquaintance, and to tell the truth I have made it a great part of my business to gain a familiarity with priests and dervishes ever since I came hither.

There was abundance of reason for this on several accounts. For I improved myself much by the society of those amongst them that are learned, and I am edified not a little by the very ignorance and follies of others. From some I squeezed out secrets of state and the designs of cabals. By others I penetrated into the mysterious vices of their own order. In a word all of them taught me something or other which I knew not before, and I never had occasion to repent of keeping them company.

I contracted a particular friendship with an honest friar or two in this city who were persons of candour and learning, but now they are dead. Besides, I have had no small intimacy with Cardinal Richelieu and his successor Mazarin. I tell thee even if I had not coveted the friendship of these princely priests, yet it had been impossible to escape their knowledge, as obscure a figure as I make. For it was their constant practise thus to seek out all the strangers and travellers in this city under the pretence of that great regard they had for men of merit but in reality to pump out of them foreign secrets.

[1] See the letter to Bedredin, pp. 8-13.

Cardinal Richelieu professed a great kindness to me because I had been at Constantinople and in other parts of the Grand Signior's dominions. He seemed also to value me not a little for my skill in interpreting Greek, Slavonic and other languages of the East. What he thought of me in his heart I cannot divine but I have reason to think he suspects me for a Mussulman. And yet I wonder he never searched for the main proof, the mark of circumcision. Perhaps 'twas an effect of his good nature as being loath to ruin me irrecoverably. But I had rather ascribe it to providence, which would not suffer him, it may be, to make so fatal a reflection. Yet by his order some years ago I was imprisoned for six moons. What the meaning on it was I could never dive into. But I had a shrewd jealousy of a certain Transylvanian resident at this court who perhaps might do me some ill offices. The world is like a lottery wherein we must expect to meet with many unlucky chances.

By what I have said thou wilt easily perceive that although the priests make a fair semblance of piety, mortification and other religious virtues, yet they are great busybodies and wholly taken up in secular affairs.

If this were the worst character they deserve they might pass for very good men and necessary instruments of the public welfare, because they have the tutelage and guardianship of all men's consciences; they have many advantages of studying the politics of all men's consciences; they have many advantages of studying the politics more than other men, as being all educated in the academies, where if they be not very dull they cannot fail of becoming good historians and indifferent statesmen. For their libraries abound with all manner of ancient and modern writers, and their conversation is generally refined and pregnant in intrigues.

But they corrupt their learning with false maxims which they borrow from an intolerable pride and sensuality, persuading themselves that they are so far above other men, that is, the laity, as those are above the beasts; that God has bestowed on them a dignity superior to that of the greatest temporal monarchs; and in fine, that this earth is a paradise and themselves the gods and lords of it.

When I speak at this rate of the Nazarene priests, understand me not without restriction. There are some good and holy men amongst them, persons of unblemished manners and incorrupt sincerity. But these are very rare, and the French priests are esteemed the most sincere of any within the pale of the Roman church.

As for the Italian clergy they are mere libertines, the most debauched and profligate fellows in the world. Adonai the Jew, a late private agent of the Grand Signior, who had travelled up and down through all Italy and resided a considerable time in the chief cities and towns of note, made many curious observations and remarks on the lives of the priests, which he set down in his journal. This I have by me now, it being sent me, according to my desire, after his death by Zeidy Alamanzi, his successor in that station, who is at present at Venice.

I have perused this relation myself with no small pleasure and believe 'twill not be unwelcome to thee to give thee an abstract of what he says. It is possible he may exaggerate some things and deliver himself too partially in others out of the natural and inherent aversion the Jews have for Christians. But thou wilt find that in the main he insists only on such reflections as it becomes any man to make who has the least spark of common morality and reason.

In the first place he finds fault with the ecclesiastics in that they abstain from marriage themselves yet recommend that state to the laity as a very holy sacrament and mystery of religion, whilst they indulge themselves at the same time in all manner of lasciviousness, wallowing in fornication, adultery, incest and sodomy itself. He says there is hardly one priest in ten who does not keep two or three harlots, and the most recluse dervishes are either pimps to other men's lusts or they indulge their own with the most infamous courtesans and catamites. These pretenders to perfection and sanctity are often found masquerading and revelling about the streets in the time of the carnival with a company of whores for their attendants. Nay, all the year round their monasteries are no other than stews or brothel houses. They introduce women into their cells in a monastic habit and so they pass for men who come to visit them as friends, relations or travellers. These ladies of pleasure lie thus concealed for many days and nights together. And the superior of the convent winks at this for a little money, being most commonly as bad as any of them.

These holy fathers go marching and slouching along the streets in the most mortified manner imaginable. You would take 'em for perfect santons[2] and idiots. Yet this is all but mummery, whilst they are the most glozing hypocrites in the world, mere devils in a city and abounding in wicked thoughts and practices.

Adonai tells a pleasant story of a young monastic of St. Dominic's order at Rome. This monk was of noble extraction and his parents were very rich and powerful in the city. On which account he was indulged many liberties denied to the rest of his religious brethren. He was permitted to carry good quantities of gold and silver about him for his personal expenses and to wear a secular habit suitable to his birth and quality. But this liberty had like to have proved fatal to him one night during the carnival.

It was late and very dark when this religious bully was beating the streets upon the hunt for whores, and walking under certain piazzas near the river Tiber, he was accosted by a woman masked and in a very good dress who spoke to him frankly, asking him the way to Il Rotundo. This is the name of a church in Rome dedicated to all the saints; in the time of the gentiles 'twas called Pantheon or the temple of all the gods. The monk being in one of his rambling equipages and his inclination equally bent on pleasure, having also a hundred florins about him, presently made answer. He would conduct her to the place she enquired for. She after some counterfeit essays of a modest repulse at length accepted his offer, and by the way he persuaded her into a tavern. The cunning nymph managed her business so well that the monk overheated with wine and other costly entertainments, grew so in love with her that he forgot she was to go to the Pantheon and offered to wait on her home. She accepted the motion and telling him her house was seated on the banks of the Tiber, they returned the same way as they came.

When they arrived at the piazza where they first met, three persons appeared muffled up in cloaks, two of which suddenly

[2] Moslem monks.

seized the monk, holding their poniards at his breast, whilst the third disclosing the hidden light of a dark lantern, which he held in his hands, fastened on the lady and made her unmask. As soon as he saw her face, he stamped and raved, menaced and swore he would be the death of that villain who had debauched his wife. All this was but a forelaid design. In a word, after all the parts of an abused incensed revengeful husband acted to the life, at last, through the intercession of the two other ruffians and the monk's penitent and submissive address, it was concluded to spare his life and only strip him naked, leaving him in that condition to seek his fortune among the watch.

This was soon put in execution, and the freebooters with all their prey securely marched off. The poor monk thus miserably abandoned without garments, money or anything to comfort him in this calamity or to bribe the watch gave himself over to melancholy and despair in regard this accident would bring an eternal infamy on him, and he should be no longer able to show his face in Rome, the seat of his nativity, nor among any of his kindred and friends. Sometimes he thought to drown himself in the Tiber or else to counterfeit a frenzy and so run brawling, drivelling and talking nonsense through the streets, hoping the rest would never be divulged.

Whilst he was in these pensive thoughts irresolute what to do, the watch, walking their rounds, bolted upon him on a sudden and seeing a naked man at that time of night in such a solitary place, at first were startled as though they had met a ghost but recollecting themselves better, they boldly seized his person and examined how he came in that condition.

It was in vain for him to beg, entreat and promise anything, if they would not expose him to open shame. This did but increase their curiosity and suspicion. In a word, the place of their rendezvous being very near the same tavern where this unfortunate monk had regaled his strumpet, they led him thither and kept him prisoner till the morning. He that kept the house remembered his face again and knowing that the governor of Rome had a secret enmity against the monk and all his race, sent him private intelligence of this adventure, encouraging him to take his opportunity of revenge, hinting withal that he need not take notice that he knew the monk but only punish him as an ordinary fellow breaking the laws of the city.

The governor, being glad of this occasion, when the monk was brought before him, ordered him to be whipped through the very street where his monastery stood. This was done accordingly, and as he passed by the gate his brethren, seeing him in that condition, rushed out and rescued him from the executioner's hands, breathing revenge against the governor and all that were concerned in putting this dishonour on their house and the whole order.

I must be forced to break off before I have informed thee of half their tricks lest I should tire thee with the length of my letters. Besides, it is necessary for me to conclude unless I would miss my opportunity, for the post tarries for no man.

Venerable hogia, live thou to enjoy the serene pleasures of virtue and innocence and pray for Mahmut that he may never be stained with the corruptions and vices of infidels among whom he resides.

Paris, the 18th of the 5th moon of the year 1662.

To the Kaimakam

Volume VI, Book II, Letter XIX

Here is a man come to this city, a Calabrian by birth and of all countries by education, for he has been a traveller from his infancy, if what he relates of himself be true. He speaks all or most of the languages of Europe very fluently and is resorted to by people of divers countries under the character of a fortune teller and physician. He performs both parts to the admiration of all that have been with him.

The princes and nobles of France visit him daily and so do persons of meaner birth. They discover to him their secret maladies and this Apollo seldom fails of success in curing them. He bestows ten hours a day in freely conversing with people of all ranks and qualities, healing the diseases of some and telling to others their future destinies.

I went to his chamber one day to learn my fate (for I have

little faith in modern prophets or astrologers; nor to be cured of my distemper, having no esteem for quacks and empirics; besides, I was in good health at that time), but curiosity was the only motive which led me thither that I might improve myself in other respects by this stranger's company and learn something which I knew not before of foreign courts, whereby I might become more serviceable to the Grand Signior in this station and farther unravel the secrets of Christian princes. For so it often falls out that one man reaps some considerable advantage from the society of travellers and men of experience. And I had good reason to hope for some profit by this man's acquaintance, who is thought worthy to be courted by the grandees of France.

Wherefore I addressed myself to him with abundance of ceremony and regard, using also as much dissimulation as I thought necessary to conceal myself and the design I had in coveting his friendship. I seemed a great admirer of judicial astrology, and told him I was very ambitious to learn the rudiments of that science from him, having heard his skill highly commended not only by vulgar fame but by the mouths of men of sense and quality, who gave him a fair character. I said a great deal more to insinuate myself into his good opinion. But there being company with him, he returned my compliments with much civility and desired me to come to him at a more convenient season, and to leave my name that he might order his servants to give me a kind reception at any time if he himself should be out of the way, because it was common to send many from the door without introducing 'em. I told him my name was Titus of Moldavia and that my business at Paris was to study in the academy in order to my preferment in the church. When he had taken down this in writing, with the hour and minute of the day, after the manner of astrologers, he begged one to excuse the necessity he was under of returning to his company; and so I took my leave.

Not many days after, I went to him again, full of hopes that I should benefit much by his company. But as soon as he saw me, he surprised me with this language:

'Sir, you have ventured much in coming to me, for now 'tis in my power to discover you and your business in this city. But if I should betray any man, my gift would be taken from me. I am neither a follower of Moses, Jesus or Muhammad, nor of any sect that is now extant on earth. But I adore the spirit and soul of the universe, which is eternal and infinite. Therefore I hate no man for his religion, let it be what it will. And you that are not what you seem to be, shall receive no more hurt from me in this place than the coadjutor of Paris. For I am of no party or faction. All men are equally my friends who do me no wrong, and every place is my home.'

Thou mayest imagine that I was in no small astonishment at this discourse. But recollecting my spirits and considering it had always been my opinion that these fortune tellers deal by confederacy, and suspecting that my name being known to him so long before, it was not difficult for him to inform himself something of me; or that somebody of his acquaintance who knew me had seen me go in and out from him and so told him some of my circumstances; I made a show of going away dissatisfied, saying, 'It will be but lost time to hearken any longer to you. For I perceive you know nothing of me in telling me I'm not the man I seem to be.'

'No,' replied he, with an obliging kind of earnestness, 'you are an Arabian and serve some Eastern prince incognito.'

Then he went on and told me in a few words some former passages of my life. He hinted at the dangers I had been in during my residence at Paris, mentioned my captivity at Palermo and the re-encounter I had with my old Sicilian master. To be brief, he told me so many other things which I knew to be true of myself that I grew very uneasy in his company and yet durst not depart from him on a sudden or show any discontent. But mustering together all the dissimulation and artifice I could, I turned the discourse to other subjects. Seeming very importunate to learn astrology of him and promising him a large gratuity if he would teach me, I fairly took leave resolving, if possible, never to see him more.

Never was a man in greater anxiety than I was when I came home to my chamber and pondered what had passed between this stranger and me. I am not credulous of miracles, prophesies or pretended revelations. Yet I protest solemnly, I could not forbear thinking he was endued with an extraordinary faculty of divining, or at least that he was an excellent astrologer. Nay, to this day I know not well what to conclude of him. He may, for aught I know, be a demon incarnate, or perhaps he is a magician. Sometimes I think one thing, and sometimes another. If he performs these prophetic parts by confederacy, still I'm at a loss how he should come to know so much of me, who always thought myself the privatest man in Paris and have neglected no methods that were proper to render me such in truth. Then I suspect my old Sicilian master is one of this man's correspondents and has told him some of my circumstances. For I have no reason to be jealous of Eliachim the Jew. It must be some such way, or else he is more than a man that can thus readily penetrate into the secrets of a stranger.

Sage Kaimakam, I pray God defend thee from the snares of counterfeits and false pretenders.

Paris, the 13th of the 10th moon of the year 1663.

To the Captain Bassa

Volume VI, Book II, Letter XX

What I am going to relate would seem incredible to myself, and for that reason I would not give it any room in a letter to all the discerning ministers of the Port, were it not confirmed by letters from several merchants in the north parts of Holland to their correspondents in this city. And they all agree that on the 9th day of the moon of November, a strange man was seen to float on the sea near the shore, being supported by a piece of timber on which he sat with a bottle of strong waters in his hand. Those who first beheld this spectacle were fishing in a small boat, and judging him to be the relic of some shipwreck (for there had been violent tempests in those seas about that time), made up to him and took him into their skiff. He expressed his gratitude for this kindness in the best manner he could (for nobody understood his language). And when he was come ashore, he fell on his knees; and having lifted up his eyes and hands to heaven, he prostrated himself and kissed the earth. His garments were made of the skins of fishes, the hair of his head of a flaxen colour, and he seemed not to be faint for want of sustenance; which made everyone conclude that he had kept up his spirits with that chemical liquor in the bottle, which was near half emptied.

As soon as he saw the rising moon, he fell on his face and muttered certain barbarous words, knocking his forehead against the ground. Then he rose and danced after a wild manner, singing pretty natural airs; and at every stop with his right hand extended, pointed to that planet, expressing both in tone and actions much devotion and love.

Many learned men were sent for to consider of this stranger, and if possible by signs or other means to discover from whence he came, and what fate or accidents had thus abandoned him to the fury of the winds and waves, to the extremity of hunger, cold and watching, and to the devouring jaws of sea monsters. But all their efforts were unsuccessful. They spoke to him in several languages; he answered them, but still in a dialect different from any of theirs and altogether unknown. He seemed to utter his words in a tone between whistling and singing, which made some conclude he was a Chinese, because that people pronounce many of their letters after the same manner. So do the inhabitants of Tonkin and Malabar with other kingdoms in the east of Asia; and letters with them are as significant as words with the Europeans. They showed him globes and maps of the world done by several hands and in various languages, with particular charts of all the maritime regions on earth. But to no other purpose than to excite his devotion afresh to the moon, whose resemblance he saw on some of those papers. He would smile at that sight, kiss his forefinger, and with a religious complaisance touch the figure of that planet. Then seeming to be in a wonderful good humour, he would turn around and fall adancing, with his arms stretched and turned in the same posture as those who use castanets or cymbals, singing all the while a sort of inarticulate sounds, but surprisingly musical and sweet, so that nobody knew what to make of him.

He appeared very temperate, modest and resigned, refusing no meats or drinks that were offered him, yet neither ate nor drank to excess. Neither was he discontented at his lodging or any other usage, though they tried to vex him several ways that they might see how he would vent his passion. But he smiled at all, and submitted patiently to everything they imposed on him.

One thing was observable that wherever he saw any water he would run to it immediately and wash himself as well as he could in those circumstances, never forgetting to sprinkle some towards that part of heaven where the moon was visible. And when they led him into the fields or gardens, he would crop the grass and flowers and with a composed look would throw them up in the air, adding such religious gestures as convinced everyone that he did it in honour of some power above. Various were the conjectures of men about him; some were of one opinion and others of a quite different. Nobody could positively conclude anything. Neither is it possible, as I'm informed, for the wisest men in those parts to find out this mystery.

Perhaps he is such another as Imam Rapibabet,[1] a Persian writer, mentions, who in the year of the hejira 502[2] was taken up by a merchant ship of India in the straits of Bab el Mandeb pretending to be dumb but capable of hearing, writing and expressing himself several other ways, if anybody could have understood his language. At last he was found to be an Ethiopian slave run away from his master, an ingenious fellow, and one that spoke all the languages of those parts; and therefore that he might be admired, would be sure to write in a character of his own invention, which the greatest sages could not read.

Mighty bassa, thou encounterest on that element with strange monsters and creatures under no name or predicament that is known; yet none so terrible and dangerous as cheats and impostors, from which I pray heaven defend thee and me, for they infest both the sea and land.

Paris, the 17th of the 2nd moon of the year 1663.

[1] This writer has not been identified.

[2] 1108 A.D.

To Kerker Hassan, Bassa

Volume VI, Book III, Letter VII

May God multiply his blessings on thee and cause thy heart to sparkle with fresh lights and new joys like the sky rockets on a Donanma [1] or royal holiday. Accept also a small present not worth an inventory (consisting only of a few pictures, looking-glasses, watches and other manufactures of France) from the hands of Mahmut, thy countryman, son of thy father's neighbour and a voluntary slave of those who serve thee, if I had the honour of an opportunity. . . .[2]

I have often complained of the malicious calumnies thrown on me by Ikingi Cap' Oglani and his associates. [3] And the ministers were pleased to receive my apologies. But now I suspect greater treachery. I sent an account to the Reis Effendi some years ago [4] how I was dogged up and down the streets of Paris by a fellow whom I knew not, and what apprehensions that put me upon. I will acquaint thee farther that being afraid of an assassin in the dark I armed my breast with a quire of paper, which is known to be dagger proof. I was not at all mistaken in my guess, for the last night, as I was returning home to my lodging between the hour of nine and ten, I received a stab in my aforesaid breastplate right against my heart. It was not so dark but I could perceive the person who gave me this blow, and self-preservation taught me immediately to seize on him and grapple as close as I could, extending his arms with mine at a good distance from our bodies. I am but little and short, yet I have a strong spring with my body when I am once roused, as thou wilt imagine I was now. Besides, I have generally a certain presence of mind

[1] A Donanma is a Turkish secular festival.
[2] Eight paragraphs of this letter have been omitted because they repeat what Mahmut has related so often elsewhere; *viz.*, his mission spying on the French and the difficulties of remaining incognito in Paris.
[3] See his letter to Ikingi Cap' Oglani, pp. 73-74.
[4] See above, pp. 140-42.

in time of danger, which fails not to prompt me with the readiest and most proper course to escape. In a word I wrestled the poniard out of the ruffian's hand and stabbed him dead with it, not thinking it safe to make a noise but choosing rather to die if my strength failed me than by crying out for help and run the risk of worse consequences. For I had long expected some such attempt as this upon my life from my enemies at the Porte. And concluding this fellow to be one employed by them for that purpose, I thought it no prudence to have him seized by the watch and punished by the law, lest he should in revenge discover me and my business to these infidels. Therefore I played the executioner myself and sent him out of hand to another world to prevent his telling tales in this. Thou wilt say there was no injustice in this since it was in my own defence and to save the honour of my sovereign. As he fell he uttered these words in a faint broken tone:

'Mahmut, my death will be revenged before long, and you cannot escape the trap that is laid for you.'

Then he expired.

This made me presently conclude that he was employed by somebody at the Porte, for how else should he know my true name? But upon second thoughts I cannot be certain but that he was set at work by my old Sicilian master, since he knew my name also. However, I have great reason to suspect the former because it is not probable that the infidel would take so chargeable and troublesome a method to murder me. Neither had he provocation enough. Besides, for aught I know he may be dead. God only is acquainted with the truth. However, to prevent future assaults of this nature and a great many other inconveniences, I have removed myself to a new lodging in the most obscure corner of the city and very remote from the place where I lived before, being resolved also not to frequent the court nor any public places, as I have done formerly but to take other measures for intelligence.

What I desire of thee is to represent my case favourably to the divan that they may approve of my conduct. Do also whatever else thou judgest the part of a countryman and a friend.

As for the event, I patiently wait for the appointments of destiny. For 'tis vain to be too solicitous.

Adieu, high born Kerker and forget not Mahmut in his distress. For that is the time wherein true friendship is tried.

Paris, the 17th of the 5th moon of the year 1664.

To Musu Abu'l Yahyan, Alfaqui, Professor of Philosophy at Fez

Volume VI, Book III, Letter XIV

By the faith and obedience I owe to Muhammad, our Holy Lawgiver, by the Alcoran and all that is esteemed sacred among the Mussulmans, I swear thy long silence made me conclude my first letter was unwelcome to thee. But now I'm convinced to the contrary. Thy generous answer has removed my apprehensions and filled me with complacency. Henceforth I shall rest assured and confident of thy friendship, promising myself vast improvements from so learned a conversation, though only by letters at many hundred leagues distance.

As to what thou requirest of me concerning the various languages of Europe, I will inform thee the best I can, according to the observations I have made and the intelligence I have received from men of letters and from books, which are the pictures of learned souls, mirrors wherein they may behold their own perfections whilst they are on earth; and after their departure to the invisibles, other men may see the interior beauties of their mind represented to the life. For words are the perfect sculpture of the intellect or at least its mezzotint. They are the express portraiture of divine and human reason. Thus the Alcoran is called by some of our holy doctors the true image of original increased wisdom.

Now of all the words and languages on earth thou knowest the preeminence has been forever given to those of the East, and among them to the Arabian both in regard of its purity and of its antiquity, from whence it is styled the virgin mother of languages, the dialect of the blessed above.

Thou knowest that for this reason the true faithful covet no species of learning more ardently than to be perfectly skilled in so divine a speech, wherein the volume of celestial majesty was penned in heaven before the hand of Gabriel, prince of the messengers who fly on the errands of the Omnipotent. It was sent I say to the Prophet, who could neither write or read, that the world might be convinced of its divine original. Yet the incredulous will not believe, though it is manifest to any man of impartial sense, that a person altogether ignorant of letters could not possibly compose a book, the most elegant that ever was penned in the world and wherein not the least blemish or contradiction can be found from the chapter of the preface to the last versicle which winds up the whole volume. Oh! obdurate hearts of infidels; Oh! wilfully blind that shut their eyes against the splendours of eternal light; Oh! resolvedly deaf that stop their ears against the voices of God and His Prophet, neither will they listen to the soft whispers which are wafted from paradise.

Such are the Nazarenes, who for the sake of the Greek and Roman tongues, of which they are passionately enamoured, educate their children in a fair way to believe all the monstrous fictions of the ancient poets or at least all the lying tales and legends of their own priests, which are ten times more fabulous than the former and more inconsistent with reason. And this they do rather than to be at the pains of learning Arabic, which would instruct them in truths as clear and serene as the Orient sun.

I shall say little of those two ancient languages of Greece and Rome, in regard they being now grown obsolete are only to be learned in schools. Thou no doubt are versed in them *ad unguem* [1] as the Latins phrase it.

That which seems properest for me to inform thee is that the Roman or Latin tongue appears like an old antiquated mother thrust out of doors by her four ungrateful daughters, Italian, French, Spanish and Portuguese. These are her natural offspring begot during the Roman conquests in the West and degenerating after that empire was in its decline. So that now they are taken for no better than mongrels and bastards. In Spanish there is a great mixture of Gothish and Moresco words [2]; the French retain many of their old Gaulish

[1] To a nicety, perfectly.
[2] A mixture of Gothic and Moorish words.

idioms. The Italian is corrupted with a hodge-podge of words left by the Vandals, Huns and Lombards. Yet that fault is recompensed by the abundance of Greek etymologies. As for the Portuguese, 'tis but a dialect of Spanish and lies under the same imperfections.

The only pure maternal languages now current among the common people in any part of Europe are the Teutonic, Slavonic and British. The first is spoken in Germany to perfection but corruptly in Sweden, Denmark and the United Provinces.[3] The second is common to the Hungarians, Moldavians, Poles, Russians and many other nations. The last is confined to the Welsh, a people inhabiting a corner of Great Britain, driven thither by the victorious Saxons, their conquerors, above a thousand years ago. As for the rest, they are only mixed dialects and so not worth taking notice of excepting one mountainous part of Spain where the inhabitants are said to speak pure Arabic at this day. They are supposed to be a remnant of the Moors.[4]

The critics here in the West used to give these following rules in reference to languages. If you would address to God, speak in Greek or Latin because of their antiquity, purity and majestic loftiness; if to kings speak in Spanish in regard of its slow pronunciation and gravity; if to men use Italian, to women French, to dogs Welsh. But if you would affright an enemy or the devil himself, speak High Dutch.[5]

They relate a story of a German ambassador at the French court who delivered his message in Teutonic, which when a certain grandee heard and took notice of its harsh and strong emphasis, he swore 'twas his opinion that this was the language wherein God cursed Adam, Eve and the Serpent. The German turning to him answered briskly, "Tis possible, Monsieur, it may be so, but then I hope you'll grant that French was the occasion of this curse when the devil chose to tempt Eve in that language for its effeminacy, wheedling her *à la mode de Paris* to eat the forbidden fruit.

Renowned Musu, do me the honour of frequent letters;

[3] The Low Countries.

[4] The Morescoes, who remained in Spain in Granada and the Sierra Nevada mountains until the seventeenth century, when they were finally expelled.

[5] By High Dutch Mahmut probably means *Hochdeutsch* or standard German.

instruct me in things whereof I'm ignorant; make me familiar with the remarkable of the country where thou residest. Transport Fez with the other parts of Africa which are known to thee; transport them I say successively to Paris every moon on a piece of paper, and I will send thee all Christendom by way of exchange; for thus it becomes the lovers of wisdom to barter for knowledge.

Paris, the 10th of the 11th moon of the year 1664.

To Mirmadolin, Santon of the Vale of Sidon [1]

Volume VI, Book III, Letter XVIII

What is this world that on all sides invades our senses? This earth under our feet, those clouds whirling over our heads, these winds shaking the trees, that azure sky with all its glittering ornaments? What is all this but an eternal dream, a mere shadow of God Almighty's thoughts? 'Tis pleasant living in it; 'tis also painful. In His sense this universe is perfectly good; in ours 'tis mixed with evil. He made it for His own diversion and our scrutiny. 'Tis to us a field of riddles and contradictions. In summer we curse the heat and in winter blaspheme the cold. Yet we bless both the one and the other when we feel 'em in due measure and season. One hour this colour pleases the eye, another that; and perhaps in the next 'tis disgusted at them both. We never find rest or content in anything. The softest music at sometimes grates our ears like the croaking of toads. The most agreeable odours are as the smell of a sepulchre, loathsome and abominable. The most delectable wines and savoury meats at such seasons are unpalatable as the beverage and diet of hell. Neither can the more insinuating charms of women put us in a better humour. All the whole system of nature joined together is not sufficient to afford us ease. Nothing but a ray from the omnipotent can alleviate our melancholy or give us a taste of ourselves. For

[1] Sidon is a small city on the Syrian coast, which in the seventeenth century was part of the Ottoman Empire; it was formerly the principal city of Phoenicia.

we are the very Deity in scattered fragments, or we are separated drops of the divine essence, volatile spirits of eternity, by fate or chance fixed in proper vehicles of time and matter. O Santon! this whole corporeal universe is but a web spun from the bowels of an infinite God and wrought with inimitable artifice to catch immaterial forms, ideas and souls in, which are the genuine offspring of the eternal mind. We mortals of human race are but so many parcels of the divinity in disguise, trepanned into bodies by certain hidden baits, magnets and charms lurking in embryos, with which we have some sympathy. We are all gods in masquerade. So are the beasts of the fields, the birds of the air and fish of the sea.

Let us not therefore condemn the antique ceremonies of gentile religion which taught men to adore the sun, moon and stars, the elements and all that is within their circumference, especially the souls of departed heroes, demi-gods, nymphs and the rest of those beings which are the eldest progeny of eternal nature. For in so doing they did but build altars to the original fountain of the universe. Since God is in the winds, in the rain, in the thunder, lightning, hail and other meteors; in the heavens and air, sun, moon and stars; in the fire, earth and water; in plants and animals; finally since He is in the elements and everything compounded of them, He is not only in them but is these very things by an ineffable production of Himself. And when the final consummation shall come, it will be but a withdrawing all the extended lines of His infinity into their centre, where thou and I and every divided atom in nature shall meet, be united and swallowed up in eternal beatitude. Amen! Amen! Oh thou Lord and Father of all things, inexhaustible abyss of miracles which know no end.

Paris, the 6th of the 1st moon of the year 1665.

To the Same

Volume VI, Book III, Letter XIX

Supposing it were otherwise than I have said; grant the doctrine of Epicurus true. Believe that we and all things were produced by the fortuitous concourse of atoms; yet still we have the same or greater reason to value ourselves as diminutive gods, since in this sense we must of necessity be eternal, every atom being so, of which we are compounded. In the opinion of these philosophers there is no such thing as an origin or beginning of the universe. Each particle of matter with them is as old as the divinity. We have all ranged eternally from one form and world to another, danced to the measures of fate, been parts of the orbs above and the caverns below, strayed through the heavens and all the elements, taken on universal career through infinite and endless spaces and are now (as fixed as we seem in these solid hulks of flesh) in the same hurly-burly as ever.

These bodies which we carry about us are not compounded of the same atoms as they were seven years ago. There is a perpetual flux and reflux of particles. We die as fast as we live. Every moment subtracts from our duration on earth as much as it adds to it. We move, breathe and do all things by paradox. Our very essence is a riddle. With an open heart, therefore, I applaud thy religious negligence of human affairs in that thou art divinely careless of thyself and everything else, save only to conserve thy innocence.

What signifies it whether we believe the written law or the Alcoran, whether we are disciples of Moses, Jesus or Muhammad, followers of Aristotle, Plato, Pythagoras, Epicurus or Ilch Rend Hu, the Indian Brahman? Or what import is it whether we kneel before images or in a naked mosque? It will be all one in the winding up. We are but the machines of chance. As we live so shall we die, and God knows what will become of us afterwards; neither is it worth our while to be solicitous, since we can be certain of nothing. Perhaps every atom of which we are made may be scattered from the rest; we may be transported piecemeal into ten hundred thousand million of worlds, and sevenfold as many years may expire before two of the minutest particles of our frame meet together again. We need not to be troubled at all this. Nothing can hinder us from being immortal and eternal, though it be but in fragments.

Go on then, sacred vagabond, pious rambler, holy fugitive; go on to assert in the course of thy life this great truth: that all things depend on everlasting chance or destiny. Thy actions shall reprove the hypocrites of the age who abound in specious words. And thy divine indifference shall condemn the hellish zeal of furious bigots who think to please God and atone for their sins by sacrificing human blood and massacring all that are not of their faith.

God or chance or fate shall transport thee after death to happy regions, immarcessible[1] joys and an endless succession of bliss. Every atom shall find its paradise. Thou shalt mount by degrees to full, infinite and eternal felicity. Adieu for a time.

Paris, the 20th of the 1st moon of the year 1665.

To Nathan Ben Saddi, a Jew at Vienna

Volume VI, Book IV, Letter IV

The interruption which made me so suddenly conclude my other letter[2] lasted not long; so that I have time enough to perform my promise by the same post. I was about to relate what the Wandering Jew told me of the religion of those remote Hebrews in Asia, which take as follows.

[1] Imperishable.

[2] In his last letter (VI, iv, 3) in which Mahmut impugns the Talmud and other Jewish commentaries, the subject of the Wandering Jew again arises. The Wandering Jew had told Mahmut about the true law of Moses, which is kept by the ten lost tribes, who live now in a distant place in Asia. This letter then is the promised description of their government, religion and customs. The letter may also be regarded as an example of the genre of utopian writing, which was so popular in the seventeenth century.

He says they are a nation of philosophers bound by their laws to study the liberal arts and sciences. They have none but iron money current among them, the use of gold and silver coins being expressly forbidden by their laws to prevent the temptations of avarice and theft; for who would steal or covet a metal, which for its bulk was not easy to be hid, nor for its beauty very desirable, being everywhere common in the veins of the earth and served only as a method of barter and commerce among themselves where the inequality of merchandises entangled their traffic and would not admit of a ready exchange.

This took from them the occasion of many unnecessary arts at home, and they had no temptation to travel abroad, the chief design of their lawgiver being to oblige them to spend most of their time in religious and philosophical exercises, and the rest in preparing necessaries for human sustenance. They had no need to buy any thing of foreign countries or to build ships for that end, who were bound to live content with the natural product of their own fertile country. For luxury has not as yet set footing in that happy region, if we may believe this traveller. He says they feed altogether on the fruits of the earth, not admitting any art or employment which tends to superfluity but only such as serve the necessary uses of life wherein they show an admirable dexterity and skill.

When they travel from one town to another, which is very frequent, they never carry anything to defray their charges by the way or when they arrive at their journey's end, all entertainment of this nature being free and reciprocal. Such is the custom of the country.

They have no lawyers among them but if any contention arise, 'tis presently determined by the arbitration of the next neighbour, to whose sentence all submit, every man being willing to lose something of his right, rather than disturb the public amity and peace.

As to the manner of their worship, they are strict observers of purity in washing, anointing and shaving their bodies. They have temples also where they assemble every seventh day, and having offered up the first fruits of the earth, they sit down in the courts and banquet together with joy, whilst the priests entertain them with excellent music and songs in praise of God and his works. To this end the courts of their temples are made very large that they may contain so many distinct families, and stately pavilions are set up, adorned with the boughs of green trees with all manner of flowers carelessly intermixed. But amidst all their feasting they are not permitted to taste of flesh; they eat only the fruits of the earth with milk, honey and oil. And their common drink is water and wine.

At the age of sixteen years every man is bound to take the following oath:

> I swear that I will adore but one God, who brought our fathers out of Egypt and has conducted us by a mysterious path to this land of promise. I will religiously serve him all my life, for that he has vouchsafed to plant me in the family of his elect and not either of the two tribes who were left behind in the land of delusions. I will do justly to all men; neither will I voluntarily hurt or kill any living creature unless it be in my own defence. I will not taste of the flesh of any animal but in all things observe the abstinence commanded by Allah[2] to Moses on the Mount. I will religiously obey my Prince to my last breath and rather be torn in pieces by wild beasts than betray him or consent to betray him to another, for he is the viceroy of God. I will never conceal my knowledge of any conspiracy against him or my country; neither will I discover his secrets to any if it should ever be my honour to know them. I will observe the traditions of my fathers and teach the same and no other to my posterity. In fine, I will in all things obey the laws of this sacred kingdom, this region of peace, this garden of bliss. All this I solemnly swear by the first father of light and by nothing, the profound womb of darkness and by silence, the companion of that death which no created being can fathom; which is the same as if I should wish myself annihilated, if I violate this oath in the least point.

These are all the terms of the oath that I can distinctly re-

[2] The use of Allah is certainly a lapse on the part of the author. While Moslems usually refer to God as Allah, there is no reason for Jews to use it.

member, which I here insert to show thee what opinion these people have of the law which was given to Moses on the Mount, and how they reject the two tribes that were left in Palestine and esteemed of that country but as the land of delusions as counting their own country the region of promise and themselves the elect of God.

One would think that these were the posterity of the ten tribes that were carried away captives by Shalmaneser, King of Assyria. And this was also the opinion of that wayfarer, who told me that both their Pentateuch was different from yours and the language wherein it is written. For he said it was rather a dialect of Arabic, in which language thou knowest God wrote the Ten Commandments on the two tables: among which one is, 'Thou shalt not kill.' This prohibition they say extends to all living creatures, though your doctors interpret it as only reaching to men and so do the Christians. But the Mussulmans interpret it thus: Thou shalt neither kill man or beast without reason. By which clause the beasts are privileged from the wanton cruelty of men, who otherwise would murder them only to make sport; yet wicked men are not exempted from a violent death as a punishment of their crimes.

This traveller says also that the people of that country are so healthy that they generally live till they are a hundred and twenty years old, which is almost twice the age of other mortals. This he ascribes to their exquisite temperance and moderation in all things, as also to the dryness of the soil and to the force of certain winds, which continually sweep the air of this delectable region and purge it of all hurtful qualities.

If ever it be thy fortune to see this person, he will acquaint thee with a great many more delightful passages, which it would be too tedious for me to insert in a letter; besides my memory is treacherous and I often forget those things at one time which I remember at another. But if thou art solicitous to hear more, I will oblige thee with all that I can call to mind of this traveller in another letter.

In the meantime make a right use of these hints and weigh one thing with another; examine all things without prejudice or partiality. Trust no man's reason but thy own in matters of a disputable nature, since thou hast as much right to decide the controversy as any man. And thus thou wilt never become a bankrupt in religion.

Paris, the 4th of the 1st moon of the year 1666.

To Kerker Hassan, Bassa

Volume VI, Book IV, Letter XVII

The blessings of God and His Prophet cheer thy heart, as thou hast exhilarated mine by thy last letter, wherein thou encouragest me with the hopes of being removed from this disagreeable post to one more delightful and happy; even to a sweet country retirement, either in Arabia or any other part of the Grand Signior's dominions, which is the very mark of all my wishes.

I have a natural aversion for great and populous cities. They seem to be so many magnificent sepulchres of the living, where men are shut up, imprisoned and buried from all commerce with the elements; or they are like hospitals and pest-houses, where people crowd, infect and stink one another to death with a thousand pollutions. They hive together like bees and build their apartments in darkness. Like nests of pismires they trudge up and down all the summer of their youth to heap up treasures that they may spend the winter of their old age in loathsome ease and benumbed stupidity, not daring to venture out of the purlieu of their nasty smoky habitations, and yet they are ready to be stifled with their own breath.

'Tis with pleasure I contemplate the fact of the infant earth before it was deformed by the unnecessary arts of the carpenter, smith and mason. When men had no other houses save what they made themselves, everyone for his family of the branches and boughs of trees, interwoven with osiers, reeds and ivy and covered thick with leaves and grass to shelter them from wind, hail, rain and other injuries of weather. Or perhaps some had found out a den or cave in the earth or the hollow of a rock for a sanctuary in such cases, where they reposed in perfect tranquillity without fear of snares or violence, without apprehensions of robbers or any tragical surprise. They went out and in, slept and waked, laboured and rested in safety and quiet. Avarice, envy and injustice had not as yet corrupted the minds of mortals. The earth brought forth corn, herbage and fruits without the husbandman's or gardener's labour. All places abounded with plenty of innocent refreshments and those primitive inhabitants coveted no more. The cattle and bees afforded them milk and honey and the fountain waters were generous as wine. This globe was a complete paradise, and no mistaken zeal had taught men religiously to invade another's rights and in a pious fury to murder their neighbours in hopes of meriting heaven hereafter. There was no such thing as bigotry or superstition to be found among any of human race. The law of nature was in universal force; every man pursued the dictates of reason without hearkening after religious sophistry, sacred fables.

But when once the lucre of gold had corrupted men's manners, and they, not contented with the riches and sweets which they cropped from the surface of the earth, had found a way to descend into her bowels, stung with an insatiable desire of hidden treasures; then began injustice, oppression and cruelty to take place. Men made enclosures to themselves and encompassed a certain portion of land with hedges, ditches and pales to fence them from the invasions of others, for the guilt of their own vicious inclinations filled them with fears and made them jealous of one another. They built themselves strongholds, fortresses, castles and cities. And their terrors increasing with their criminal possessions, they persuaded themselves that the very elements would prove their enemies if not pacified by bribes and presents. Hence sprang the first invention of altars and sacrifices, and from these vain panic fears of mortals the gods derived their pedigree. For one built a temple to the sun, another to the moon, a third to Jupiter, Mars or the rest of the planets. Some adored the fire, others the water or wind. Everyone set up to himself such a God as he fancied would be propitious to him. Thus error being equally propagated with human nature, they created an infinite rabble of imaginary deities paying to those idols the supreme and incommunicable honours due only to the eternal essences, father and source of all things.

Besides, they lived in intolerable pride and luxury, in constant wars and strife, in darkness, ignorance and confusion. I speak of such as dwelt in cities and were incorporated together by one common interest. For still there remained some who obeyed the original laws of nature and the traditions of primitive humanity.

These dwelt in tents or other moveable habitations as our countrymen the Arabs do at this day with the Tartars, their brethren. They scorned to fasten themselves to the earth by possessing any part of it in propriety. Every field and wood, hill and valley, river and well were with them in common. They straggled whither they pleased.

This is the life so emulated by me, or instead of that, at least a retirement from cities, that I may breathe out my last hours in a free air, remote from the stifling company and contagion of mortals. I long to range at liberty through unfrequented paths of desert ground o'er wild unpolished heaths, from thence insensibly to fall into some venerable solitude where the dry, mossy barks of trees in silent characters proclaim the antiquity of the place; and gentle whispers of the wind instruct the methods of platonic love, inspire strange passions, which we never felt before and teach us to converse with satyrs, nymphs and other harmless tenants of the shades. How great is the pleasure to be thus surprised with some harmonious, warbling stream or silent, soft, deep crystal river; to speak incognito with dryads, hamadryads and the sporting echoes; to lie dissolved in loose yet innocent enjoyments on the banks, to talk with nature with immortal substances and with eternity itself. Oh God! is not this ravishing?

'Tis difficult to say whether it would be pleasant or painful to return from these ineffable parades of the soul to our domestic felicities, though even in a rural life, which I acknowledge to be the happiest on earth. Yet there to trace the herds and flocks, to walk amidst the high-grown corn and grass, to pluck the bearded ears of barley, to let our eyes roll o'er the various figures of the wind-blown wheat and millet; our noses to suck the fragrant airs of marjoram, thyme, oranges and lemons with innumerable spices; our ears to hear the inimitable melody of birds and every sense to be transported, snatched away and lost in sacred ecstasies must needs be ranked among the highest kind of earthly pleasures.

But to descend from those enjoyments to the meanest and most common diversions of a country life, methinks there is something peculiarly charming in the very situation of the houses, whether it be on the brow of a hill or the bottom of a valley in the midst of a wood or the opening of a heath, on the side of a road or in some obscure corner of the country. 'Tis agreeable when walking in the morning to hear the bleating of sheep, lowing of oxen, screaming, quacking and crowing of geese, ducks, cocks and other home-bred animals; to hear the louder winds, threatening to tear up trees by the roots, demolish houses and remove the globe itself, if possible, from off its basis. This would be better music to me for a change than a concert of dulcimers, theorbos,[1] timbrels and viols. Human nature delights in variety, and there is a certain audacious curiosity in the soul which loves to venture on extremes. The rain, the dirt, the stink of hogs, camels, dromedaries and other necessary rural beasts would please me better than the constant tedious ease and fulsome sweets of courts or city. I sweat whilst thus shut up within these walls. It cloys me to be daily walking in a circle, to trample always o'er the same ground in a vast labyrinth of houses, where my senses meet no new refreshing objects but my ears are hourly nauseated, vexed and tired with the rattling din of coaches, carts, artificers and the harsh voices of such as sell flesh, fish and other things about the streets. My eyes can find no grateful prospects but dashed with surly rugged looks of proud and wealthy infidels or with the sly satiric smiles of well-shaped people who condemn me for any bandy legs and crooked back.

In a word, my dear bassa, I long to feel the gentle breezes of the East purifying my soul and cleansing it from so many pollutions. I languish for the sight of turbans and crescents,[2] for the devout call of the muazzin on the lofty minarets. I die in contemplation of the sacred fasts and feasts, the nocturnal

[1] A theorbo was a lute with a double neck which was much used in the seventeenth century.
[2] The symbol of the Ottoman Empire.

joys of Ramadan, the revels and cheerful illuminations of Bairam[3] and the imperial Donanmas. When I think of these things, my soul bursts forth in fervent invocations, and every faculty cries 'Allah, Allah.'

May that Divine and Immortal One hear my prayers and grant me the happiness to see the face of noble Kerker Hassan in an horizon pure and free from the defilement of infidels.

Paris, the 14th of the 2nd moon of the year 1667.

To Mirmadolin

Volume VII, Book I, Letter I

Why was I made a man to endure these cruel agonies, of which no other species of known beings can possibly be capable? Or why at least was I particularly formed of such a constitution as to attract the evils which are scattered up and down the world and piecemeal dropped on the nativities of other mortal men, whilst I alone am made the common sink of human misery? Surely my partial horoscope monopolized the most envenomed aspects of the stars without partaking of the least benign and favourable glance. The planets had laid up an ancient deep reserve of fatal influences which they poured out at large upon the very moment of my birth. Nor could the careful midwife with all her skill and charms defend my tender, ductile, reeking body from the invincible cataracts which flowed upon me from all the envious signs and constellations in heaven.

My whole life has been but one continued tragedy, wherein the various changes of scenes has not relieved me from the least real evil hid behind but only amused my sense with some new pageantry, some fair idea of honour, pleasure or profit; when before the act was done, I found myself cajoled, over-

[3] Bairam is a Turkish word denoting two important Moslem festivals: 'the little festival' celebrates the breaking of the fast with presents of sweetmeats; 'the great festival' celebrates the last month of the Moslem year, a sacred month for making the pilgrimage to Mecca. At both festivals a reception at the Imperial Palace was held.

whelmed in fresh calamities, misfortunes which I never dreamt of.

Oh that the Omnipotent, when from eternal silent thought, He drew the ideas of every specie and every individual being, which He designed for actual existence in the world, had formed me for a tree, an herb, a blade of grass, a stone, a mushroom or any insensible thing, incapable of pleasure or pain, of grief or joy or other passions which hourly thus torment our human race! I had been then a happy neuter to all false shows of happiness and real sense of misery. Oh that I had been an oak, a beech, a palm or cypress of the forest! For then if vegetables have any feeling of their own state, I should be only touched with secret pleasure when the gentle winds should play among my amorous branches and teach my wanton leaves to dance the measures of young harmless love; or when I felt the seasonable rain distilling on my withered bark and from thence sliding to my thirsty roots; or when great Phoebus prints warm vigorous kisses on my cheeks and neck. But if this be too proud a thought, I wish I'd been only some humble shrub, some pigmy plant, some vegetable dwarf, a page unto the mighty trees, subsisting on the drops and fragments of their large banquets, meekly cringing at their feet, whilst I stood safe and free from storms under the shade of their extended boughs in happy low obscurity.

When I pass through the fields and see the harmless sheep browsing upon the tender grass and hear them bleating to their wanton lambs, I cannot choose but envy them a life so void of care and pain. They range and sport at large in flowery meadows near some crystal stream or take the pastures of the mountains, whilst cheerful shepherds tune their pipes and sing in praise of Amaryllis, Daphne, Sylvia or some other nymph; and watchful dogs lie scouring on the plain to give the alarm and chase away sly wolves and other ravenous beasts.

After I've let my envy fix itself a while on these, a warbling melody from neighbouring groves diverts my melancholy thoughts and turns them to new objects. Then I lament my fate in that I was not made a nightingale, a thrush, a lark or any of the feathered choir who with sweet cheerful notes salute Aurora and the rising sun and chirp all day the praises of that source of warmth and life; who vests the earth in green attire; who decks the trees with verdant leaves and fills the world with light. They chirp and fly from tree to tree, from bough to bough, rejoicing in the beams that dart and glide among the moving shades of branches rocked by winds. Their thoughts are taken up in building nests wherein to hatch their young and shelter them from injuries. They have no plots nor politic tricks to undermine each other but pass away their time in innocent security and harmless pleasures.

Methinks the worms and little reptiles of the earth are happier far than I. They crawl and creep about in hollow trees, in clefts of rocks and crannies of the ground to hunt for food and for divertissement. They live at ease without being racked by supernumerary cares and fears. And if some ruder foot of man or beast shall trample them by chance to death, or more malicious hand with stone or other weapon shall wilfully bereave them of their life, 'tis done so suddenly that they have no sense of pain; whereas my life is a constant martyrdom, a long continued series of torments.

I do not complain of the distempers and maladies which afflict my body, though those are sometimes so violent as to make me wish for death that so I might be at ease. But 'tis the fretting anguish of my mind that forces all these sighs and exclamations from me; I am embarrassed in the world, snares compass me round about; my own good nature has betrayed me. Those of my blood conspire against me; they hunt me up and down like a partridge in the wood; they closely pursue my life. The kindness that I have sown spring up in blades of bitter ingratitude and perfidy. My seminaries bring forth aconite [1] and stinking weeds instead of pleasant flowers and wholesome fruits. Tagot has set his foot in all my works. That sly interloping spirit hates to see any good thing prosper or come to perfection. He steals behind us in all our ways, and as fast as we weave any web of virtue, he secretly unravels it or deforms the work with intermixing some threads of vice. I am weary of striving against the current of my fate. Oh that I were as though I had never been! That my soul were drenched in Lethe's forgetful waters, where all past things are buried in eternal oblivion! Then would my

[1] More commonly known as monkshood or wolfsbane, a poisonous plant.

anguish be at an end; whereas I am now rolled about upon a wheel of miseries.

Holy santon, when thou shalt read this, pity me, and amidst thy divine ejaculations dart up Mahmut's soul to paradise on the point of a strong thought, that so at least I may have a moment's respite from my constant sadness.

Paris, the 27th of the 2nd moon of the year 1667.

To the Kaimakam

Volume VII, Book I, Letter II

There is now some probability of a peace between the English and the Dutch, which will also reconcile this crown to that of Great Britain, since the king of France engaged in this war only on account of the Dutch, his allies. The advances towards this accommodation took their rise from the alliance lately concluded between the States of the United Provinces, the king of Denmark, the duke of Brandenburgh and the princes of Brunswick. The king of England protests against the Dutch as the first aggressors in that they had taken above two hundred of his merchant ships before he offered the least act of hostility. Which the States seeming to acknowledge, desire the king to appoint some neutral place of treaty with them and their allies in order to [secure] a peace, the security of navigation and the establishment of commerce for the future.

Here is great joy for the birth of a young princess,[1] of whom the queen was delivered on the 2nd of the moon of January. She is called God's New-Year's gift to France, in regard the first day of that moon begins the year with the Christians. And 'tis common among them to send mutual gifts and presents to one another at that time, which they call New-Year's gifts. And so it seems God Almighty has appeared very modish and complaisant in thus timing the nativity of the royal babe; for which they express their thanks in revelling, dancing, ballads and a thousand other vanities. And these divertissements continue to this time, it being the Nazarene's

[1] Named Maria Theresa, the princess died shortly afterwards.

Carnival, a season consecrated to sport and mirth, to liberty, buffoonery and all manner of comical and ridiculous apishness.

During this time you shall see an infinite variety of odd humours and mimical actions in the open streets according to every man's particular fancy. Here you shall meet with one dressed half in the French and half in the Spanish fashion. On the left side of his head hangs dangling down a long thick curled peruke, which reaches to his breast, whilst on the right you see nothing but his own hair cropped close to his ears. A long moustache as black as jet graces the right side of his upper lip, whilst on the left he is as beardless as a boy of seven years old. And so from head to foot he wears two contrary garbs. One walks with gloves upon his feet and shoes upon his hands; another wears his breeches like a mantle on his shoulders. Here comes a stately coach jogging along with a grave slow pace and drawn by six horses as if some prince or cardinal were in it; when behold there is nothing but a silly ass puts forth his giddy head with flapping ears half drunk with the jolting, unaccustomed motion. Sometimes he brays aloud and then the rabble fall alaughing. A thousand other fopperies there are, not worth thy knowledge. For both the noble and the vulgar are all upon the frolic at this time and indulge their wanton fancies to the height. But 'tis a fatal season for the poor cats, few of which escape the multitude whose peculiar pastime 'tis to toss these creatures in a blanket till they are dead, or else to tie them two and two together by the tails, and then they'll bite and scratch one another to death. The cocks also are generally great martyrs during the Carnival. The rabble have a hundred cruel ways to murder them in sport. All their devices are inhuman and bloody.

They did not learn these profane courses from Jesus or any of the prophets or apostles of God. But they are the relics of gentile vanity in the beginning connived at by the priests, the easier to retain their proselytes in obedience, who would rather have parted with their new religion than with their old barbarous customs. And thus the pagan fooleries were handed down to the posterity of the primitive Christians and were adopted into the family of church traditions. And men are not more zealous for the gospel itself than for these ridiculous profanations of it. So dangerous a thing is it for governors by a criminal indulgence to permit their subjects any liberty which interferes with the fundamental principles of the law; for such a dispensation once granted passes into a precedent, which in process of time becomes of equal force with the law itself. And by such preposterous methods of winning and retaining converts Christianity arrived to the height of corruption 'tis now infected with.

Sage minister, 'twas for this reason God raised up our Holy Prophet and gave Him a new law with power to reform and chastise the infidels. He planted the undefiled faith with scimitar in hand, not palliating or encouraging the smallest vicious practice, but subduing all things by the dint of reason or the keen edge of the sword. God hasten his return, for the prevarications of this age require it.

Paris, the 27th of the 2nd moon of the year 1667.

To Dgnet Oglou

Volume VII, Book I, Letter XII

I know not whether I have reason to rejoice or be sad in my present circumstances, so ambiguous are the events of human life. Even the most blandishing gifts of fortune and such as we are extremely taken with, many times prove like the Trojan horse, only fair and gay in outward appearance, whilst like that deceitful engine of the Grecian craft, they carry an army of hidden calamities within, which in the midst of our secure repose when we least dream of any evil, rush upon us from their concealed and unsuspected ambuscades, put us all in terror and confusion.

However, since I have had a sufficient share of trouble, grief and melancholy, now let other sprightly, cheerful passions take their turn, be the event how it will. I cannot always bear the burden of a loaded spleen, crammed and puffed up with melancholy winds, the embryos or vehicles at least of horrid thoughts, perplexing cares and black despair. Besides, methinks I have a fit occasion to be merry, being by a very pleasing accident at once rid of a great many vain doubts and anxieties (which have disturbed my place for these three or four years) and restored to the charming conversation of Daria, whom thou mayest remember I so passionately loved in the days of my youth.

Know then that one day as I was walking in the streets, I met that lovely Greek in mourning. Surprised above measure at the sight of a person for whom I had formerly cherished so great an esteem, I stood still at first like one thunderstruck. I could not forbear questioning my own senses and giving the lie to my eyes, which assured me it was she. Neither age nor absence had effaced her loved idea from my memory or so much changed her face but that I easily called to mind the object of my amorous desires. Yet my astonishment was such at this unthought of interview that I had not resolution enough to believe myself, and her amazement seemed no less than mine; whilst neither of us had power to speak but stood like fools. Till I, ashamed longer to lose myself in such an effeminate confusion of spirit, first broke silence, not without some rapture and emotion, crying out,

'Is it Daria or her ghost I see? Her fortune blessed or mocked me at the fatal hour? Or do deluding nymphs and fairies haunt the streets of populous cities, walking about in borrowed forms and mixing with the throng of mortals to tantalize our softest hopes with a false show of some dear lover, fiend or person highly wished for, never to be enjoyed? It may be true that Cytherea left her heaven (as Virgil does relate) and in a Tyrian dress met the heroic offspring of Anchises in the fields, amusing him with a disguised semblance of mortality and human race until her heavenly voice discovered that she was a goddess. So used Diana to descend in dead of night and mix the slumbers of Endymion with immortal dreams, stealing soft kisses from the lovely youth and whispering celestial words into his ears more forcible than the songs of Orpheus when he moved the trees and rocks to passions of Platonic love. At other times they would come down and take the air of cool Mount Haemus or the lofty Ida. Thus Melpomene, Clio and the rest of the sacred nine would often visit the refreshing heights of their beloved Parnassus, from whence descending to the shady banks of

Helicon with more than mortal voices would awake and tempt the wanton Echoes to strike up like unisons and join in concert with them, whilst they chant the praises of some demi-god or hero whom they love. But that a goddess, nymph or muse did ever frequent the common crowd of mortals in a city is not to be credited. Therefore, unless I dream, it is Daria I behold.'

My Dgnet, I was running on in higher ecstasies at mentioning of her name but that she smiled and interrupted me with an obliging reservedness and said, 'Mahmut, if you are the man I take you for and would have my esteem, be less passionate and leave off this wild way of raillery. We both are past the vanities of youth. Our years should now retain no remnant froths of early boiling blood and young green foolish passions.'

I took this only for a female banter and essay of women's craft to try the sense and humour of a man. For thou knowest the greatest princess loves a truly passionate address, though not a puling, whining one; besides, 'tis the fashion here in France to use romantic forms of speech when they make love. However, in regard it was inconvenient to lose more time in the open street by this sort of discourse, I invited her to a house where we might converse with more freedom. She accepted the motion and I conducted her to the house of Eliachim the Jew. 'Tis pleasantly situated on the banks of the river Seine and has a fair garden belonging to it. Eliachim happened to be abroad, which gave us a better opportunity of improving the time, without the necessary interruption of salutes, compliments, etc., usual in such a case. And I had the command of his house, as though he had been there himself.

It being in the heat of summer, I led Daria into a little, shady, green retreat in the midst of the garden out of the reach of curious ears, where under the cool refreshing shelter of a wide-spread beech, we sat down and called to mind our former acquaintance and friendship. Daria still retained her native modesty and prudence; neither had the external beauty of her face suffered any greater detriment than what befalls the fairest roses, violets, or other flowers, which even in their most decayed state merit the character of amiable sweetness. However, the lustre of her wit and goodness of her humour supplied all other defects.

I protest, my Dgnet, it was impossible for me to see and not to love again a person whose idea was once so domestic and familiar to my soul. And I was the more animated to make my court when she told me that she was a widow. 'Twas easy to forget or banish from my thoughts her former faithful treachery in acquainting her husband with my amour. Love soon removes all puny obstacles; 'tis ready, prompt and dextrous to find excuses for the greatest faults a friend can ever commit; much more ingenuous to palliate the peccadilloes of a mistress. This generous passion by a peculiar force extirpates all revenge and blots out the memoirs of past unkindnesses. It ever springs and blooms with fresh desires, young vigorous inclination, like to the palm oppressed with weights, it higher grows; 'twould fain increase, dilate and stretch itself to immortality. There is no consideration but that of honour can pretend to match or stand in competition with the divine regards of love. And yet the most exalted human glory often veils this soft passion: the conquerors of the world suffer themselves to be overcome by women. Wonder not therefore that I, who am flesh and blood as well as other men, could not now defend myself from fair Daria's charms.

Excuse me in that I cannot now give thee any farther account of this adventure, being interrupted by a messenger from Eliachim the Jew, who brings me word my mother is very sick and wants my company. Expect another dispatch speedily.

Paris, the 15th of the 10th moon of the year 1667.

To Dgnet Oglou

Volume VII, Book I, Letter XVII

Daria's a queen, a jilt, and I am once more cured of my dotage. There is no trust in woman's beauty, faith or wit; they are deceitful as the fruit of asphaltites,[1] they are perfect riddles and paradoxes, and have more unlucky tricks than cross-grained elves or fairies. When a man, overheated by his amorous passion, thinks to embrace a goddess, he meets with Ixion's fate, and only hugs a gaudy cloud or meteor.

I will not make thee sick with a particular rehearsal of my second folly in being so fond of one who had betrayed me formerly. I will not repeat the vain addresses I made, the kind obliging things I spoke, nor her deceitful answers. I will not tell thee how she drilled me on into her snares, and led me captive in an amorous circle. Content thyself to know that I have been twice her cully; and if ever I am the third time, 'twill be my own fault, as the Italian says. No, my Dgnet, I have done with that false sex. Henceforth forever I abjure all amorous regards of woman; I will shun them, as I would a pestilence. I will either shut my eyes, or turn them another way at least, whenever I meet a female. I will not think of them, but with disdain and hatred. Finally, I am off from them to all intents and purposes.

However, as the Arabian proverb says, that wind blows from an unlucky point of the compass which wafts no good to somebody. So from Daria's false and feigned smiles, I reap some benefit. I have learned a secret which has rid my spirit of a thousand cares, disquiets and agonies.

In the year 1664 of the Christian hejira, I sent a letter to the noble Kerker Hassan, Bassa, our countryman; wherein I informed him of an assassin made upon me in the dark as I was going to my lodgings, and how I killed the ruffian that attempted on my life. I told that generous grandee all my jealousies and conjectures on that subject, how I suspected

[1] That is, women are as treacherous as soft asphalt is to the touch.

some of my enemies at the Porte to have a hand in the design, or else that my Sicilian master was concerned in it. I knew not well what to conclude. But now I am satisfied 'twas Daria's husband, who resenting deeply my former amour with her, which she discovered to me at large, could never be at rest till he saw Paris, where he designed to be the executioner of his own revenge, and lay in wait accordingly for my late returning home; for he was not ignorant of my lodging. His wife knew nothing of his design, he having pretended other business at the city. And 'twas from accidental words in her discourse that I collected this great secret. For when I asked her of her husband's health, she told me he was killed at such a time by night in an alley of Paris, by whom she never yet could learn. But I straight blushed with consciousness and took the hint. I dropped some necessary, careless queries by degrees, and all her answers still confirmed me as to time and place with other circumstances that he must be the man I murdered in my defence so long ago.

I kept this secret locked up in my breast, nor could my doting fondness melt me into such a soft and easy temper as to betray myself to her. But I took inward pleasure at the thoughts of my deliverance from that sudden violent death and from my after cares and fears by this discovery. Henceforward I'll suspect no Mussulman, though my enemy; nor shall I be so fearful of my Sicilian master. No panic terrors shall confine me to my chamber and make me spend my days in fretting and consuming melancholy. I will not be surprised when strangers knock at the gate or when I hear the blustering voices of the parish officers below or the collectors of the king's revenues. Yet these before were dreadful as the Sultan's *khatt i sharif* or fatal warrant when he demands a bassa's head; so forcible is jealousy and suspended thoughtfulness; so black the influence even of misgrounded apprehension and mistaken guilt.

My Dgnet, this mortal life is a dark labyrinth of cross events. Bewildered man gropes up and down; he often trips and stumbles at contingencies; he strays about in thorny rugged paths, not knowing where he is or which way to turn himself. Sometimes an *ignis fatuus* with its deceitful light misguides him in miry places, fens and bogs, where he is in danger of being swallowed up or leads him to the brink of an high precipice, where if he advance but one step more, he is gone beyond recovery; he falls and dashes himself to pieces on under-growing rocks.

Reason is the only clue that can conduct us safe through the windings of the perilous maze. Heaven grant that thou and I may never let go our hold of this so necessary faculty until he has conducted us safe to paradise.

Paris, the 15th of the 12th moon of the year 1667.

To Hamet, Reis Effendi, Principal Secretary of the Ottoman Empire

Volume VII, Book II, Letter III

In this time of wars with Nazarenes, when the Ottoman fury is roused and provoked by infidels, it will not be amiss to expose the nakedness of Europe to the supreme divan, which is on earth the close committee of the court above.

I choose to address my letter to thee in compliance with my former orders, wherein thou seemest passionately desirous to know the present state of Christendom. God give thee a perpetual serenity, scribe of the scribes. Mayest thou never be troubled with a running eye, a shaking hand or the toothache. As for me, I'm a perfect magazine of diseases, a walking hospital, the school of Aesculapius, where the necessary god has scope to vent his skill on all the various kinds of maladies which afflict our mortal race: gouts, fevers, cramps and horrid dysenteries are as common with me as my daily diet.

However, amidst all these afflictions I serve the Grand Signior and my friends with a cordial alacrity, never grudging to sacrifice my ease and health to the interest of true believers.

The face of Europe is much changed since the decline of the Roman Empire and the usurpations of the popes. That once mighty monarchy is now shrunk into a very narrow compass, being shut up within the confines of Germany, which formerly was but a province of the ancient empire. All Italy is revolted. So are the Swiss and the United States of the Low Countries.

The Hans towns,[1] which in time past paid homage to the emperor, have now shaken off the yoke and are become independent commonwealths. Transylvania plays fast and loose with him according as their interest requires. Livonia laughs at his menaces, as appears by the answer they sent to Charles V[2] when he demanded their submissions, and that they would return to their native allegiance, otherwise threatening them with fire and sword. For all the reply they made was that they knew the emperor's horse would be foundered before he could reach the frontiers of their country.

'Tis a general observation that since the reign of Rudolph I,[3] above two hundred principalities and states have fallen off from the empire. And those that yet continue in their obedience, I mean the electoral princes, claim so many privileges, stand so much upon punctilios and prerogatives that there remains now little more of the imperial majesty and power, save the bare title and outward pomp. It is remarkable that within these three hundred years no less than nine German emperors have been murdered and many more have been deposed and banished. To sum up all in a few words, if we survey the present state of the German Empire accurately, if we pry narrowly into its circumstances, we shall find that after all the clatter of his noisy titles, the emperor can call nothing properly his own but his hereditary estate in Austria, which is hardly equivalent to the territories of some lords whom he calls his vassals.

The Germans in general are a rude, unpolished people, greedy of novelties, inconstant, rash, perfidious and very phlegmatic, much addicted to unnatural lusts and incestuous copulations. It is recorded of Barbara the empress, wife to Sigismund,[4] another Messalina,[5] that after her husband's death, her confessor advising her to reform her manners and live more chastely like the turtle,[6] she answered, 'If I must imitate

[1] The Hanseatic League.

[2] Holy Roman Emperor, born 1500 and died 1558.

[3] Holy Roman Emperor, born 1218 and died 1291.

[4] Sigismund (1368-1437), Holy Roman Emperor and King of Hungary, took as his second wife Barbara of the Austrian house of Cilli.

[5] Valeria Messalina, third wife to the Roman Emperor Claudius, was a notorious strumpet.

[6] Turtledove.

the life of birds, why not of a sparrow as well as a turtle?'

Her brother Frederick was much such another, for at ninety years of age he murdered his wife for the sake of a strumpet. And being advised to repent and think of his grave, he said, 'I am now studying my epitaph, which I design shall be comprised in these words:

THIS IS MY WAY TO HELL; I KNOW NOT WHAT I SHALL FIND THERE; WHAT I HAVE LEFT BEHIND ME I KNOW. I ABOUNDED IN ALL DELIGHTS, WHEREOF I CARRY NOTHING WITH ME, NEITHER MY DAINTY MEATS OR PLEASANT WINES OR WHATSOEVER MY INSATIABLE LUXURY EXHAUSTED.'

Drunkenness is said to be the original sin of Germany, from whence it spread itself into other countries. They give this character to a German: that he is an animal which drinks more than he can carry, a tun that contains more than he can express. They tell a story of four old Saxons, who at one sitting drunk as many healths as they could make up years amongst them, which amounted to three hundred. And 'tis recorded of a certain German count that he used to make his children whilst yet infants drink lustily to prove whether they were of his own begetting or no. For if they grew sick after it, he presently concluded them to be bastards, but if they could bear the debauch well, he cherished them as his own true offspring. In a word thou mayest have the same idea of the Germans at this day, as Solyman the Magnificent had in his time, who used to say:

'I fight the Germans above all other people of Europe because they are always at discord among themselves, nor can they ever be united any more than my fingers and toes. They cannot endure labour and are the excessivest gluttons and drunkards in the world. They always maintain a regiment of whores in their camp. Their generals take more pride in feathers than in their military arms.'

In a word the German is so overrun with all kinds of vice that he wants nothing to make him a complete devil but only a little tincture of the Italian qualities, according to the proverb: *Tedesco Italianato e un diavolo incarnato.* A German Italianized is a devil incarnate.

'Tis certain the French have so weakened 'em on one hand

and the Swedes on the other that considering the frequent troubles they meet with from the Hungarians, Bohemians and other tributary nations, besides the intestine feuds of the electoral princes, we need not fear the blunted talons of the eagle, which are scarce strong enough to support her tottering state or prop her from falling into ruin. So far is she from being able to offend her neighbours that she never makes war her choice or takes the field but by compulsion in her own defence.

Illustrious Hamet, I pray God inspire the victorious Osmans with prophetic courage and resolution, and the final conquest of Germany will soon be the prize of true believers.

Paris, the 5th of the 10th moon of the year 1668.

To Mirmadolin

Volume VII, Book III, Letter IV

'Twas a long time before I could find out the true secret of human happiness. I have for many years groped after it in the dark, and when I thought I enjoyed a prospect of it as clear as of things we discern in the light of a midday sun, that sun was little better than the *sol mortuorum* of the ancient Romans, whose beams served only to give a faint mock glimmering to the ghosts that wander on this side of Charon's ferry, and like an *ignis fatuus* to mislead 'em up and down the dark suburbs of Elysium, the fens and marshes of the Stygian lake. So have I straggled all my life through unknown ways, seeking the road to heaven, yet finding nothing but the paradise of fools.

Sometimes I thought by outward works of virtue to purify myself and gain perfection. I was punctual in observing every precept of the law and performed a few acts of supererogation. Considering too much in the fidelity and inviolable fastness of my wings, the force of my religious passions first formed by nature, afterwards improved by pious tutors, I strove to make heroic flights and soar above my guide. But alas! they were mere borrowed wings cemented to my soul only by education, custom and the practice of my fathers, a composition of spiritual wax or glue which could not stand the brunt of hot and fiery trials but soon dissolved in my unwarrantable bold approaches to the sun. So that in fine my wings dropped piecemeal off, and I had the fate of Icarus to fall a victim to my own obstinate zeal and rashness.

Surely our souls are like the Augean stable, which no human power, art or industry can ever cleanse, did not the messengers and favourites of God, like Hercules, teach us the method of opening a canal from heaven and letting in the torrent of the river of purification from paradise.

Our vices, hydra-like, still start young infant heads as fast as we cut off the old. Whereas our virtues are like the Venetian treasure, which being once showed to the Spanish ambassador in many coffers of silver, gold and jewels, the wise Castilian desiring to see the bottoms of those wealthy chests turned up – when it was done – made this remark, 'Your riches have no roots nor grow like those my master does possess in the Indies.'

So are all the boasted excellencies acquired by human discipline, more inanimate and dead than the artificial productions of minerals, metals and stones. No traditional chemistry of men can ever revive a soul that's dead to God. Perhaps some theological Paracelsus,[1] Helmont[2] or Arabian Ifriqui[3] may from the ashes of an original flower raise the fantastic form of it again – I mean the colour and contexture of the leaves – but none of them is able to bestow the vital sap, the seminal juice, the inward virtue of the once prosperous and flourishing vegetable. No mortal can repair what Adam once destroyed. That protoplast has ruined us all.

Well then! Must we despair of remedy? Shall we decamp and sneakingly retire to hell because we cannot take heaven by storm, nor undermine it, nor have recourse to stratagems, nor bribe the garrison or make a party amongst the celestial burghers? No, let us rather lie entrenched within ourselves

[1] Paracelsus or Theophrastus Bombast von Hohenheim (1490-1541) was a famous physician and chemist.

[2] Jean Baptiste von Helmont (1577-1644) was a physician and chemist and in part a follower of Paracelsus.

[3] Perhaps 'Ifriqui' is a corruption of ifrit, which in Moslem mythology is a powerful and clever demon.

till heaven shall voluntarily open its gates and sally forth in love to invite and lead us in.

Oh! Thrice-happy santon, thou hast experienced what I say. My resolution is to follow thee by suffering myself to be gradually abdicated from the world and from my own will. Vouchsafe to instruct me in the method, lest self-love misguide me to my ruin.

In the meanwhile, repose thou in the bosom of God, which is the bed chamber of holy souls.

Paris, the 1st of the 8th moon of the year 1670.

To Muhammad, the Illustrious Solitary of Mount Uriel in Arabia

Volume VII, Book III, Letter VIII

The grand root of the common injustice which men are guilty of in reference to the beasts and of the intemperance with which they corrupt themselves I perceive is a false principle which they have established, denying the capacity and use of reason to all living creatures but themselves.

This error was first publicly maintained by the Peripatetics, Stoics and Epicureans and afterwards by Claudius of Naples [1] out of a particular aversion they had for the doctrines of Pythagoras and Empedocles, two famous patrons of abstinence.

Heraclides Ponticus [2] undertook to explain the sentiments of the former sects and Hermarchus [3] those of the latter. Both of them seem to confide more in the little tricks and arts of sophistry than to use true reason. For at the first essay of their skill they strive to cast a mist in the reader's eyes by dividing the generations of living creatures into such as are endued with the faculty of reason and such as want it. Whereas thou

[1] This philosopher has not been identified.

[2] A fourth-century B.C. Greek philosopher and disciple of Aristotle. Before he came under the influence of Aristotle he had a keen interest in the Pythagorean system.

[3] A disciple of Epicurus, Hermarchus flourished in the third century B.C.

knowest it is an indubitable maxim in the Eastern philosophy that everything which partakes of sense has also reason. For 'tis the mind alone which sees, hears, etc., the body of itself being deaf, blind and void of all sense. It is evident, therefore, that since the beasts do see, hear and perform all other actions of sense they have also what the Greeks call *νοῦς* or the mind in them, which is the very seminary or native seat of reason.

'Tis true, indeed, we cannot affirm that they possess a reason so perfect as ours, since that perfection is required by discipline, which the generality of the brutes want. They have no colleges or schools where the arts and sciences are professed and taught by the rules. Nature is their only school mistress, and they learn her instructions with abundance of promptness and sagacity. They are educated in the open elements as in an academy or university founded by the Creator of all things, where everything they encounter serves as a book to teach them all the knowledge which is necessary to their well-being on earth. And they need no more.

'Tis manifest also that some species and individuals are more capable of learning what is taught 'em that others, even as we discern the same difference among the various nations, families and persons of men. But we do not use to say of inanimate things that this piece of wood is more apt to learn than another, as a dog is more tractable and docile than a hog; nor of immoveable things that this is slower than that; nor of things which want sense that a stone is duller of apprehension than a piece of iron. So could we not probably affirm of animals that one is more crafty and sagacious than another, more provident, chaste, temperate, cleanly and the like epithets, if they were not by nature capable of knowledge and virtue. And yet we daily see all this is true in comparing one species of living creatures with another, nay, and one individual of the same kind with some of its fellows.

When Antipater[4] accused asses and hogs of nastiness, he did not consider how accurately nice and curious the lynxes and cats are, which with so much diligence and care hide their excrements that they can never be seen or smelled again. So

[4] Probably the Antipator mentioned by Diogenes Laertius; he was a stoic philosopher and disciple of Diogenes of Babylon and flourished at the end of the second century B.C.

the swallows teach their young to mute [5] over the brims of the nest. All which are arguments of their prudence and discretion. Doubtless, every animal has its peculiar gift and excellency. One is more quick-sighted than another; this has better ears than that; a third surpasses in the goodness of his smell or the swiftness of his feet. Let not vain man therefore boast and insult as if he were the sole engrosser of all wisdom and virtue, since the beasts of the field, the birds of the air, the fish of the sea with all the generations of reptiles, insects and whatsoever is endued with life and sense possess their shares as well as he.

It is manifest also that there are various principles of folly, injustice and all manner of ignorance, error and vice in human nature equal to what we can possibly find in the rest of the animals whom we so much despise. And 'tis a question whether even the very sea horse, who murders his father and for that reason was by the ancient Egyptians made the heiroglyphic of impiety, may not justly exchange his character with some of human race, who make their parents the continual martyrs to their ambition, pride, envy, avarice and other vices.

I would fain know whether any man would not take it ill to be told he is blind and deaf because he cannot see and hear so quick as some of the beasts? Or that he is a cripple because he cannot outrun a hart? Certainly a strong man deserves that character, though he cannot pretend to match the strength of a camel or an elephant. And shall we then say that the beasts have no reason or virtue because they cannot discover those qualities so artificially as men?

Besides, do not all privations suppose some habits? And is not madness a privation of the habits of reason and prudence? If therefore dogs, bulls, foxes and other animals are known to be sometimes mad, shall we think it less fit to say of them they are out of their minds or wits than to affirm the same of men? And if *compos* or *non compos mentis* are proper expressions of any beasts when it is sober or mad, who that is not deprived of reason himself can deny that they have the possession of that faculty by nature as well as he?

[5] To defecate.

As oft as I trouble thee with letters on this subject, thou mayest conclude I am newly awakened to a sense of my error in not religiously observing the sacred institution of abstinence, which ought to be the natural consequence of these thoughts; for in a word, if it be lawful to kill the animals for the sake of food, I think we may as well turn cannibals and eat the flesh of our purchased slaves or of our captive enemies, over whom we have by the law of nations an equal right as to their life and death as over our beasts.

Abstemious sage, I leave thee to the divine inspirations of the genius which possesses that holy cave; I leave thee to the sacred whispers of winds from Eden and to the sweets of an innocent solitude, which admits no other society than that of angels or beasts.

Paris, the 26th of the 2nd moon of the year 1671.

To Cara Haly

Volume VII, Book III, Letter XII

After all my scepticisms I at this hour believe there is something of us remains immortal and incorruptible when our grosser bodies are dissolved. Call it what you will, an astral body, a ghost, a spirit or anything else; I am sensible some part of us will never die. What signifies the vain dispute of words, the dark resolves of Plato's cave? Let it be substance or accident, matter or form or a result of all, there is still a certain portion of our nature against which the strokes of death and of ten hundred thousand deaths can prevail. We may be changed indeed and masquerade it up and down perhaps through infinite worlds in so many disguises but we can never be annihilated or made nothing. We cannot be excluded from the eternal life of atoms. The loss or absence of the least particle from the universe would either cause the loudest never-ending thunders and lightnings or an everlasting silence, sullenness and darkness. This mighty aggregate and stupendous heap of beings would fall to ruin if there were the least vacuum or the smallest mite missing. Steal but the most indivisible atom from the rest and down comes all the fabric, for one supports another by an inseparable adhesion, reciprocal congruity and mathematical fitness. They are so cunningly hitched and knit together, so closely fastened and indented each with other by the original art or chance which formed the world that all the motions of this grand machine would at an instant stop in such a case, as does a watch when the least tooth is missing from any one of the contiguous wheels. Everything in nature is full and pregnant. Neither can there be any other emptiness save what we think we see in bottles or other hollow vessels, which when they are void of water, wine or other liquor, it is but to be crammed brim full of air, which element insinuates and crowds itself into each diminutive cranny, chink and pore of grosser substances. So if the airy atoms have any hollownesses in them, the smallest vacancy possible is still supplied with its full measure of the pure ether, and that again with some matter more refined, of such there be, or else it drinks full draughts of immaterial essences. And by such a subordinate gradation, human souls, though in themselves perhaps pure incorporeal spirits, are yet fastened and cemented to our bodies. Thus is one being successively and eternally either a syringe or sponge to another. The elements inebriate one another by turns; an universal epicurism and drunkenness reigns.

So the hot stomach of the earth, parched with inward mineral fires, greedily guzzles down the very salt unpalatable lees of the sea rather than be adry; with a thousand thousand gaping throats it gulps the beverage which Neptune's deep and mighty cellar runs withal. It pants and sucks eternally the thick ropy settlements of the Ocean's bottom. These are distilled again in hidden alembics, cylinders and other chemical vessels below, that so the gaping channels of the superficies may be constantly supplied with more refined liquor through the springs and fountains. And yet the globe, not having quenched its thirst with this perpetual draught, continually sips up the rain, a liquor more sublime and pure than all the rest. But this is only on certain holidays of fate, when the celestial powers, the planets, stars and constellations order a Donanma for the vegetable race below to refresh the herbs, the corn and trees with banquets from the clouds. Then the big-bellied tuns above are rolled out of their hidden storehouses and broached; the conduits of the upper region spout and run with plentiful showers and cataracts of nature's seminal juice, the radical all-cheering nectar of heaven. The greedy soil imbibes the sacred strong cascade; each joyful turf is frolicsome, and swallows down large bumpers of the eleemosynary wine. Whilst the least dry and crumbling lump of the late fainting glebe has drops supernaculums enough to revel on, till parti-coloured Iris, the major-domo of these yearly festivals, perceiving the tender seeds and roots are well nigh fuddled with what at second hand they have exhausted from the overladen ground, makes her appearance in the clouds, inviting all the guests to a splendid collation of warm beams and rays with which the sun is minded to regale them.

A grateful soft and cheerful noise was heard throughout the room before. The earth and air were in a merry humour. Well pleased with the debauch, they would have sat till morning at it, being loath to leave their liquor behind 'em or change it for dry meat. But at the sight of Iris every one changed countenance; an universal murmur ran throughout the hall; they were sorry thus to be balked in the midst of their mirth till courtly zephyrs come with their soft compliments and tell 'em it is necessary for their ease and health. Then are the tuns and bottles removed with all the drunken tackle. The table soon is spread and covered with a rich course of glittering charges sent from Phoebus.

That sponging planet only lives by bantering and wheedles. The illustrious figure he makes in the world is always borrowed. He never wore a fashionable dress in his life but what he took up by tally from the first source of lights, for which he's bound to pay so vast an interest that he would necessarily become a bankrupt did he not repair his broken fortune by playing tricks upon the earth. Thus whilst he mocks this sublunary world with his pretended treats, he makes it pay for all with costly exhalations. He plunders the elements, picks the pockets of the earth and robs the treasures of the sea. Nor can he forbear filching something from the air, and when he has stolen enough he slinks away in the dark and flies to the other side of the globe, there to commence new shams and cheats upon the antipodes. And all the while the stars are full as bad as he, for like a brave highwayman, that luminary frequents the public way of heaven by day; he robs in open sight of all the world and leaves a generous viaticum wherever he borrows anything. But the stars, those little bullies of the sky, are perfect night pads, shoplifts and sharpers; they skulk about in the dark through all the private alleys of the firmament and commit a thousand murders, rapes and other violences. Some of their aspects are as venomous as the fatal eyes of basilisks; they carry divers kinds of mortal poisons in their looks, which they disperse at random in this lower world. They strew the earth with hemlocks, aconites and other baneful weeds. They also scatter up and down the more contagious seeds of envy, avarice and a thousand black infernal vices which take root in human souls at our nativities and growing up with us in time bring forth the fatal fruits of death. The ugly race of dragons, serpents, crocodiles and all the reptile generations with everything that's hideous, cruel and destructive on the globe derive their natures, qualities, forms and dispositions from some malignant stars or constellations, if astrologers say true. So do the scaly monsters of the vast abyss and every bird of horrible figure flying in the air. They're all the brood, the emissaries, spies and agents of the powers above, sent down on thievish errands to prey on other animals more innocent than themselves.

There is an eternal cause in nature, whilst everything is either on the hunt or flight. Thus heaven purloins from earth and that from heaven again. When we are first conceived our wandering souls are catched as in a well-baited trap. And when we die 'tis but the soul's escape from one snare to be soon trepanned into another. Perhaps a human body may be our prison again or we may be attracted by some more agreeable embryo. This magnetic star may draw us up to heaven or the wide jaws of all-devouring Orcus[1] may swallow us down into the hungry paunch of hell, which God avert.

Learned Haly, let not thou and I be too solicitous about these things, for all our timorous forecasts are in vain. But considering the secret magnetisms dispersed throughout the

[1] More commonly known as Phorcys, who devoured corpses.

universe and that everything attracts its like, let us take care to qualify ourselves with celestial habits and dispositions and then we cannot fail of being drawn up to paradise.

Paris, the 2nd of the 9th moon of the year 1671.

To Pesteli Haly, His Brother, Master of the Customs and Superintendent of the Arsenal at Constantinople

Volume VII, Book IV, Letter I

I know not well whether it is my part to be sorry or glad when I hear thy son is wild and prodigal, that he is amorous and very much addicted to frolic with women, wine and music, that he frequents the baths and playhouses on purpose to make some interest for his love that he may sometimes get a sight of beautiful ladies and have the pleasure of being admitted into their company; that he haunts the society of foreign merchants, the houses of Christian ambassadors and insinuates himself into the acquaintance and familiarity of all travellers who make any figure in the imperial city.

I protest, it seems difficult in my opinion to determine whether thou thyself hast reason to be grieved at all this or not rather to rejoice as at a presage of his future good fortune, since it is a manifest argument of the greatness of his soul; and let that alone to work out its own way to happiness. Never check a generous spirit, for such are full of the divinity. They are the eagles, the lions, the kings and princes of the earth. Their veins flow with sacred blood; their nerves strut with the milk of paradise. A thousand excellencies possess their hearts and ten thousand perfections take root in their brains. Whatever of precious is scattered up and down in the elements meets in their accomplished nature, as in an epitome or rich compendium of the brightest essences, an extract of all that is valuable, good and lovely in the universe.

Be not discouraged to see thy son amorous of women; 'tis a sign of a good nature. And he is looked upon as a monster or degenerate person who feels no warmths or passions for that lovely sex. Women are sent into the world on purpose to blow up those gentle flames within our breasts, which sublime our grosser mould and make us more refined. Love is a sacred frenzy of the soul, a divine madness, elevating a man up to the pitch of a santon and rendering him the care of the benigner demons. He is everywhere safe, having the favour of gods and men, as the Roman poet expresses it: *Quisque amore tenetur, eat tutusque sacreque.*[1] And had it not been for thy own experience of this noble passion, thou hadst not had a son to complain of. Perhaps it makes him expensive and costly in his manner of living. He would no doubt appear gay and polite in the eyes of his mistresses; he would be generous and magnificent in his entertainments, liberal to his friends and acquaintance, charitable to all persons in distress. And canst thou really blame him for putting in practice so many amiable virtues? Is not this better than to see him of a sneaking sordid temper, addicted to avarice and other ignoble vices? Remember thy own genius when thou wert young; what a passionate delight thou tookest in travelling. Yet this could not be maintained without great charges. Consider therefore that it is thy own blood running in the veins of thy son, which prompts him to a noble way of living. And do not thou imitate those fathers who by their severity teach their children to degenerate instead of making them better or more reformed. They frighten them from the paths of innate virtue for the lucre of their gold, take abundance of pains to instruct them in the methods of covetousness, as if that alone were the zenith of wisdom and virtue, whereas it is in truth the very sink and seminary of all vice.

I will relate to thee a story which I have heard in Paris, which has something in it very singular and remarkable, concerning the affection and care of a father towards his extravagant and prodigal son. This old gentleman had a fair seat about ten leagues from this city, which had belonged to his family for the space of five hundred years. His yearly revenue was very considerable and having only one son, he gave him the liberty of managing half his estate when he came to the age of one and twenty years.

This young spark being of a high spirit was so far from harbouring any thoughts of frugality that he could hardly

[1] Whoever is possessed by love, let him go safely and sacredly.

brook the necessity of living within the compass of his allowance. He addicted himself to gaming, drinking and other lewd courses which in a short time consumed his means and reduced him to great straits.

About the same time his father died and left him the remainder of his estate, giving him all the instructions that are usual in such cases. And among the rest of his sage counsels he charged him, if it should be his misfortune to become a bankrupt again so as to be forced to sell his estate, that he would at least not part with that house which had been so long in the possession of their family. Especially he conjured him to reserve one particular chamber for himself as long as he lived, which was the same where he then lay adying.

'For this,' said he, 'will be a sanctuary for you when you have no other place of refuge in the world.'

After the old man's decease his son fell to his former course of life and, to make short of it, in a few years spent all his patrimony, even that very house itself which he was forced to sell at last for an under-price to supply his present necessities. However, he obeyed his father's last injunction and in the sale of the house made articles for the perpetual claim and use of that chamber to himself.

It was not long before he had consumed the money which he had received for the house, so that now his last support was gone. He tried to borrow of some of his friends and acquaintance, and in charity they supplied him at first with small sums. But when he often pressed them, they grew weary of him and denied to part with any more.

The disconsulate gentleman, overwhelmed with grief and melancholy, returned to his chamber hoping to find some ease in that private recess where he might at least have the privilege of venting his sorrow in sighs and tears.

He passed away some time in this dejected condition when at length he cast his eyes on an old trunk which stood in the corner of the chamber and which he had scarce ever regarded before. An odd curiosity prompted him to rise and look into this trunk, perhaps not so much in hopes of finding any relief there as to divert himself and pass away the tedious minutes. And yet 'tis natural for people in great calamities and misfortunes to flatter themselves with the imagination of unexpected reliefs and to catch at every [moment] the least glimpse or shadow that seems to presage any good. Be it how it will, he fell to rifling the trunk, but found nothing save a parcel of old rags and papers with other remnants and fragments of silk, linen, and velvet, the relics and spoils of his father's wardrobe. This was no booty for him; however, he ceased not his scrutiny till he had quite emptied the trunk when to his no small astonishment, he found these words on the bottom: 'Ah, Prodigal! Hast thou spent all and sold thy house? Now go and hang thyself. There is a rope ready provided for thee in the beam of the chamber.'

The young gentleman, looking to the ceiling and seeing a halter hang there being fastened to an iron ring, was struck with such a damp, that concluding it was the will of fate that he should fulfill the words he found on the bottom of the trunk, he immediately took a chair or stool, and placing it just under the rope, got up and raised himself upon it, that so he might the better reach the designed instrument of his death.

He stood not long musing, for life appeared now insupportable to him. Wherefore putting the halter about his neck, in the height of despair he kicked the stool away. When behold, instead of hanging there, he fell to the ground, the weighty swing of his body having pulled out a piece of square timber from the beam, being that part to which the ring was fastened. Immediately he was like to be overwhelmed and buried alive in a great heap of gold which came showering down upon him out of the hollow place which his father had contrived on purpose in the beam to put this kind of sarcasm on his son, now sufficiently mortified by so many sorrows.

In a word, this made so deep an impression on him that he grew reformed, buying all his estate back again with part of the money, and employing the rest in merchandising, grew to be a richer man than his father or any of his progenitors.

Dear Pesteli, thy son is generous and witty. It is thy part to reclaim him by methods agreeable to his nature. For ruggedness and austerity will make him but the worse.

Paris, the 5th of the 11th moon of the year 1671.

To Dgnet Oglou

Volume VII, Book IV, Letter III

There are a sort of men among the Nazarene ecclesiastics whom they call casuists. These are profoundly versed in the learning of the schools, which (if thou remembrest) honest father Antonio, the old Sicilian priest, our friend, used to term the science of husks: a dry, chaffy sort of knowledge consisting only of empty vapid notions, windy ideas, distinctions made in sand, which may be effaced, altered or formed at pleasure. The very contemplation of these metaphysical trifles is enough to put one in a fever. So subtle is the poison they contain: a spiritual venom which darts like lightning through one's thoughts and soon ferments the soul, boiling our reason up to scum and froth itself away in divine jargon and religious nonsense.

These men will split a hair in divinity to make a scruple or to disannul it. They raise a dust in the eyes of those that give heed to them, and play fast and loose with human reason as it serves a turn. They'll make a hog of a cushion and turn an elephant into a coffee-dish with their enchanting haecceities, identities, quatenuses[1] and the rest of their learned *legerdemain*, the perfect hocus-pocus of the Sorbonne, by which they juggle men out of their senses and frame chimeras far more monstrous than those in the fictions of Ovid or the more early and mysterious poems of Musaeus, Orpheus and Hesiod. They teach men to stumble at a feather in the way of a religious life, yet not to boggle at a millstone or a mountain where interest calls for resolution and speed. They start more difficulties than themselves can answer in the cases of the poor. But where plenty of gold appears, everything is made easy and plain. Mere higglers in religion, quacks and empirics in matters of conscience, murdering a thousand distempered

[1] Logical terms used in scholastic philosophy: haecceity means 'thisness' or the quality which makes a thing unique; identity the quality of sameness in things and quatenus is a longer form of *qua*, meaning in the capacity of.

souls for one they cure; pretending to be guides to paradise, they lead men through uncouth paths and intricate windings till they are lost in labyrinths of error, bordering on the confines of hell. And then they leave them to themselves where, if they make one false step, they go out of their bounds, trespass on the devil's frontiers, and so are either in danger of a precipice or at least of being taken captives by the outlying scouts of the infernal kingdom, from whom 'tis difficult to escape.

There were such as these also among the Jews and gentiles of old, and so there are at this day in all religions men who are severe in punctilios and neglect the more important precepts of the law. Nor can the Mussulmans themselves be free from this embarrassment of the faith and truth brought down from heaven.

If thou observest the grave and supercilious looks of our imams, mullas cadis, etc., thou wilt take 'em for the justest men, the holiest saints on earth. Mark but their discourse, 'tis an abridgment of the Alcoran. They're seen each morning at the first hour of public prayer walking before the mosques or sitting in the royal cemeteries under some melancholy cypress or reading the Book of Assonak [2] or some other spiritual treatise. With eyes cast up to heaven or humbly fixed upon the ground and mimic postures of their hands, they act devotion to the life; yet in their hearts perhaps are studying how to circumvent their neighbours.

Go to these persons for instruction in any doubtful case, they will hamper thee with far-fetched terms and crabbed problems, with formal aspects and tedious circumlocutions; stroking their beards and sighing from deceitful breasts, they will industriously amuse thy soul with dark enigmas and trepan thy sense in snares of insignificant and unintelligible words, striving to make thee believe they are the picklocks of the eternal cabinet if not the privy-counsellors of heaven. Whereas the way of piety is plain and circumscribed with certain noted boundaries. 'Tis hard indeed for a bewildered traveller to find the narrowest gate and first avenue of this sacred

[2] 'Assonak' may be a corruption of *as-sunnah,* which means the practice and traditions of the Prophet. The book may be a collection of Islamic traditions or edifying tales from the life of Muhammad.

path amongst so many gorgeous glittering portals ever standing open and inviting men into the spacious fields of vice. But when he has once entered the obscurer pass, he has nothing else to do but go directly on without turning to the right or the left, only regarding the fixed landmarks of eternal truth, invariable reason and sound morality. To speak plainly, a man's duty is comprehended in a few easy rules, and he that goes to render 'em difficult by knotty, thorny glosses throws stumbling-blocks before the feet of true believers and interrupts their pilgrimage to heaven.

My friend, if any pious scruple trouble thee or me, let us henceforth be our own casuists and not by blind implicit faith enslave our souls to men perhaps more ignorant than ourselves. The law is plain and positive in necessary matters. What need we seek to entangle ourselves more?

If we perform our orisons at the appointed hours, what matter is it whether we observe the six traditionary postures or no? We that are illuminated, I only speak of such. As for the phlegmatic dull multitude, 'tis fit they should be curbed with discipline and made to observe the nice punctilios of obedience. What signifies the old versatile turn of the head from one side to the other as if we thought to catch the Prophet peeping over our shoulders? Or where is the sense of the profounder mystery of poring on our fingers with extended palms, as if we were at school and learning our alphabet, or imitating the clownish rustics of Armenia, who as they work in the fields and vineyards will make a dial of their hand, a gnomon of straw, and lose an hour in steadfast gazing on their dirty fists to know what time of day it is? Then the mysterious resting of our hands upon our knees with other formal ceremonies: what are they all but an external discipline, confirmed by ancient custom and observed for order's sake? This need not trouble thee or me, whenever we have occasion to retrench such indifferent niceties.

Nay, to go farther, if we should neglect the stated periods of solemn adoration, compelled thereto by sickness, travelling or any other necessity, be not disconsolate, as if thou hadst been guilty of a mortal sin. Some supererogating work of charity will cancel ten such faults as that; or at least thou mayest look boldly in the face of God when at another season on thy knees thou makest ample compensation; or by sacred abstinence and fasting dispersest all the mists and clouds of guilt that sat so heavy on thy soul. The times are all alike to Him that is eternal. There's no distinction of day or night with that Immortal Essence, Who made the sun and stars and is Himself the unchangeable source of light.

So if we should address ourselves to heaven without the usual forms of prayer, or any words at all, we have no reason to be sad, as if our orisons were ineffectual and unheard. In the eternal high recess our silent vows and softest whispers of the soul echo as loud as the most bold and noisy clamour of the tongue. There is a rank of spirits among the rest above on purpose made to waft the secret thoughts of mortal men to heaven. We cannot fail of audience there whenever we send the least ejaculation up with firm credentials from the heart.

In a word, believe, my Dgnet, that the supremely Intelligent and Wise chiefly regards the intention and fervour of our minds, the habitual bent of our souls, with the innocent and pious actions of our lives. He is not to be moved (unless to indignation) by the vain tautologies of our verbal orisons, the nauseating crambe of devoutest words common to hypocrites and persons of sincerity, to the most incorrigible sinners and the greatest saints. The humble silence of a heart resigned to destiny is a pacific sacrifice atoning for the greatest sins, attracting choicest favours, smiles and benedictions from the Eternal. This is the discipline of sacred love, the rule of perfect life, the secret chart of the elect whereby they steer their course to paradise.

Which of the prophets was a formal headsman, to number out his orisons at finger's end and offer up to God a short and vain retail of words in recompense of infinite bounties past and in hopes of more to come?

When Muhammad was pursued by cruel infidels and forced to make the wilderness His sanctuary and hide Himself within the hollow of an aged oak, He did not seek to amuse the Eternal with studied forms of speech and human eloquence, or tire the immortal ears with a religious long harangue as if He thought to ensnare the general mercy of the Holy One in trains of artificial and elaborate language, or catch His more particular indulgence in a trap of subtle rhetoric. The harmless saint with heart and face composed, with self-denying thoughts and looks, stood like a statue in the blessed asylum; whilst gentle rivulets of compassionate tears trilled down His cheeks, His soul was pierced with sacred pity to His enemies. He sighed and wished, in short, whatever blameless piety could suggest for Him and them. Angels immediately carried the prophetic vows to heaven. His silent passionate prayer was heard. The cruel persecutors, blinded with impious fury, rushed into the desert; they spread themselves abroad and rode at large. One traitor spurred his horse through thickest webs of low-entangled thorn and underwoods, greedy of the royal and majestic prey, whilst others took the open paths, hoping to overtake the Prophet on the flight. They seemed to swim or fly rather than ride, such was the swiftness of their course. Fierce was the cry, re-echoed from the hollows of the rocks and valleys: 'Mecca for the head of Muhammad.' Some stumbled at the out-creeping roots of trees and broke a leg or an arm by a precipitate fall from off their beasts, whilst others had their eyes struck blind by interfering twigs. One had his turban rudely brushed off and scalp severely shaved by broken stumps of boughs and rows of knotty branches, placed and bent down by fate on purpose to avenge the Apostle's cause on such a miscreant as this. Another could not curb his horse from jumping down into a deep quarry dug in the midst of the wood, where the proud heretic dashed his skull and brains upon the marble pavement at the bottom. So sensible and vindictive are inanimate creatures when a good man, a saint, a friend of God, is wronged. The very sticks and stones and all the elements are touched with sacred sympathies at such a time. The frame of nature feels strange tender passions, fits and qualms of amorous regard. And God Himself, if I may express myself, is roused as from a trance, and snatching up the weapons of His power and wrath, runs like a champion to defend the cause of injured innocence.

But I forget that I am writing a letter and therefore ought to be brief. Besides, what I have said is sufficient to convince thee that I have an idea of religion far different from that which the casuists, whether Mussulmans or Christians, would imprint in men's minds.

If thou canst not think as I do, I condemn thee not. Use thy native freedom, but remember that though men's reasons and opinions vary as do their faces, yet truth is homogeneous, uniform and ever of the same complexion in all ages and nations.

Paris, the 1st of the 2nd moon of the year 1672.

To Cara Haly, Physician to the Grand Signior

Volume VIII, Book I, Letter V

Praise be to God, from whom alone proceed health, long life and immortal happiness. In the whole family of fevers I never was much subject to any, except it were that of love. This indeed is become habitual to me; 'tis grown a perfect hectic; surely 'tis more than second nature. I feel something in the very roots of my essence prompting me to eternal softnesses, wild melting fits of fresh Platonic tender passions; nothing can provoke my hatred but an obdurate surly-tempered fellow, who being the offspring of some bloody butcher, poulterer or greasy cook, his very face portends a present massacre, and all his words breathe nothing else but a continued train of cruel wrongs and violences against the innocent. Pity to him sounds like the news of a famine to a starving man. But if you would make him smile and put him in good humour, tell him how he may get an estate by oppressing the fatherless and widows, or increase his wealth by ruining whole families. Tell him how he may overreach some silly credulous young heir or outwit his neighbour in a bargain. He cherishes a spider in his brain and his heart is full of webs. To such a temper as this I cannot be reconciled; there is an innate antipathy, an immortal contrariety in our souls. My spirit is daunted and retreats within me at the sight of such an one; a languor and faintness seizes my limbs. I am like one that has touched a torpedo.

Surely there is no species of four-footed beasts, of birds, of fish, of insects, reptiles or any other living thing whose nature is not found in man. How exactly agreeable to the fox are some men's tempers? Whilst others are perfect bears in human shape. Here you shall meet a crocodile who seeks with feigned tears to entrap you to your ruin. There a sly serpent creeps and winds himself into your affections, and when he is well warmed with favours, on a sudden he will bite and sting you to death. Tigers, lions, leopards, panthers, wolves and all the monstrous generations of Africa may be seen masquerading in the forms of men. And 'tis not hard for an observing mind to see their natural complexion through the borrowed visor. The physiognomy of vice and virtue are easily distinguished. There are some secret characters in every face which speak the nature of the person. So does Platonic love with eagle eyes soon trace the signatures of what is amiable in the soul. We read the hidden qualities of men at the first glance and hence are lasting friendships often contracted. I love my friends without reserve, and because those are very few among our mortal race, I contract familiarities with the harmless animals. I study like a lover to oblige and win their hearts by all the tender offices I can perform. I bear with patience their wild forward tricks till constant perseverance vanquishes their stubborn humours. Then when we once begin to understand each other aright, they make me a thousand sweet returns of gratitude according to their kind. When I am melancholy, they will soon divert me with one pretty trick or other, as if they were sensible of my pain.

But because my love is large and strong, still seeking to dilate itself, though still recoiling from the degenerate race of men, I go into the fields and woods and make my silent court unto the trees and flowers, and sometimes I converse in raillery with echoes. I languish on the banks of crystal streams and pine away on an old mossy rock. The oak inflames me with a sacred passion when I behold her venerable bulk and shade. I could almost turn Druid for her sake and take my residence up forever in her hollow trunk, where the kind genii of the air would visit me and tell me things to come, for I am in love even with those invisible beings and often tell my passion to them in the woods or on some mountain, where the courteous winds transport my words and waft their secret answers back again. Then is my soul snatched up in sacred ecstasies, because the immortals condescend to talk with me. I often fall into a trance and wake not till the sun is got halfway into the other hemisphere. Then I resolve to pass away the night in this sweet solitude.

Had I the tongues or pens of Cicero and Demosthenes, I could not to the life express the pleasures that I feel at such a time when free and undisturbed I can for several hours behold the motions of the moon and stars. Oh God! What thoughts, what contemplations rise within my breast? My ravished soul is ready to break prison for joy, when it is inspired with certain demonstrations of the world's eternity. Methinks at such a time, I hear the noise and bustle of the worlds above; methinks I see the active busy tenants of the moon and stars trudging about their daily business, even like us mortals here below. Then 'tis I am nauseated by the narrow principles of ignorant superstitious men. I hate to think of ever returning to the city again, there to profane my reason with the vain discourse of self-conceited fools and idiots. I am cloyed with life and wish to die amidst these charming speculations. Thus do I pass the time away till fair Aurora ushers in the rosy-fingered morn. Then I begin to reflect on my duty as a Mussulman and slave to the Grand Signior. I haste to wash myself in the next stream and cheerfully prostrate myself upon the ground, adoring the eternal source of all things. After which, abundantly satisfied with these nocturnal pleasures, I return to the city and to my business, considering that I were not wholly born for contemplation.

Learned Haly, I wish thee consummate happiness in this life and fortunate transmigrations after death, praying also that I may merit one day to enjoy thy company in paradise, where we may discourse these things more at large and in a clearer light than what this earth affords. Adieu.

Paris, the 2nd of the 5th moon of the year 1674.

To Hamet, Reis Effendi, Principal Secretary of the Ottoman Empire

Volume VIII, Book II, Letter XI

The love of women is natural to our sex, and there is no man who at one time or other has not felt the warmths of this amorous passion. But it is strange to observe after what a different manner this flame discovers itself in people of various nations, ages, qualities, fortunes and constitutions. Young men are lascivious and ardent in their love. Old men are ridiculous and formal. The poor man studies to please his mistress by abject submissions and humble obsequiousness. The rich strives to win her by munificent gifts and presents. The vulgar make their court by feasting the coy damsel and regaling her with junket and wine. The noble entertain her with plays, masquerades, ballets and other pompous divertissements.

The ingenious Italian sets upon his mistress with a kind of polished wantonness, not making romantic, whining addresses but with a refined impudence; his eyes, his hands, his tongue and all his actions soon make her sensible where his pain lies. He celebrates her praises in verse and hires music to serenade her. Finally, he never leaves till he gains her or revenges himself on his rival by sending him out of the world, and on her by turning all his compliments into curses and slanders. But if he gets her, he shuts her up forever and makes her chamber her prison.

The headstrong Spaniard burning with desire and impatient of delay, stung with restless concupiscence, behaves himself like a madman. He stamps, stares and raves, walks furiously backward and forward, rolls his eyes after a hideous manner; he starts, stands still, lays his hand upon his sword, looks up to heaven, invokes the saints, talks to himself, threatens the dissolution of all things if he be baulked of his love. In this humour he runs to his mistress, falls at her feet, makes doleful and passionate complaints, throws himself upon her mercy, adores her, and does all things which are proper for a desperate lover. If by these means he enjoys her, he soon grows weary of her and either kills her or prostitutes her secretly for gold. But if he cannot obtain her, then he macerates and torments himself and is resolved to die.

Different from both these is the wanton Frenchman, who courts his mistress after a jolly fashion with songs, dances, music and jests. He is all life and mirth when in her company and abounds with a thousand sorts of comical humours. If he gets her, after a little time the fickle spark is cloyed and falls in love with another. If he fail of his purpose he is not much concerned, for all his love was counterfeit. Yet he makes a show of discontent, he threatens and sputters at her for a while; but this tongue-tempest is soon laid, and a new face produces a calm.

But the phlegmatic German is very hard to be kindled up to this passion, and then needs a great deal of art to blow him into a flame. He is cold and wary, thoughtful and slow, provident and dull. Yet when once touched with this affection, he is very liberal of his gifts, which is the masterpiece of his courtship. If he obtains his mistress, he soon returns to his primitive frigidity, and if he be frustrated, he is but where he was – far from killing himself for a peevish female.

The Frenchman professes more love than he has, the German endeavours to hide the fervour of his passion, the Spaniard persuades himself that he is beloved by his mistress, whilst the Italian takes the nearest course to be beloved by her in reality. The Frenchman loves a pleasant, witty maid, though she be deformed, the Spaniard prefers beauty to wit and good humour, the Italian is for a female of a timorous spirit, whilst the German adores a virago. The Frenchman, by his wandering loves, of a wise man becomes a fool and exchanges his health for a thousand maladies; the German, having profusely spent all in amorous liberalities, at length from a fool, though late, becomes a wise man; the Spaniard undertakes heroic enterprises to please his mistress; whilst the Italian despises honour and everything else that he may enjoy her.

Certainly the greatest men in the world have been subject to this soft passion and have sacrificed their reputation, glory and virtue with their very reason to the regards of love. How ensnared was Mithridates in Pontus by a beautiful woman? How did Hannibal suffer his courage to be enervated with the luxuries of Capua? So Hercules of old left the glorious toils of war and suffered his arms to rust for the sake of his Iole. So Ulysses was captivated by Circe, Achilles by Briseis, and Caesar by Cleopatra. And thou knowest that our annals record strange things of the amours of our glorious monarchs.

There is no nation free from the sentiments of love, yet every age and region vary in their conduct towards women. Here in the West they are all for intriguing and gallantry. They accuse the Mussulmans for having more wives than one and for keeping as many concubines as they please, whilst they themselves have their wives almost in common and lie with every wench that comes in their way. Adultery passes with them for good breeding, and fornication is esteemed as innocent an action as eating and drinking, whereas thou knowest among the true believers these crimes are punished with death. Promiscuous copulation was forbid by Moses, Jesus and Muhammad, and in general by all the prophets. It is a sufficient indulgence that every man may marry four wives and enjoy as many other women as he either takes captives from the enemy in wars or purchases with his money. But these infidels had rather follow the sentiments of the old heathen lawgivers and the examples of idolatrous nations than obey God and his messengers. They applaud Solon, the great lawgiver of the Athenians, calling him a wise man, as he was pronounced by the Delphic oracle, and a generous patriot for procuring harlots to accompany the youths of the city and building a temple to Venus out of the money they got by prostituting themselves.

'Tis certain whores were much esteemed in those days among the Grecians, for the magistrates built them public houses on purpose and free for all comers; they also made laws to protect them from injuries. And so great was the veneration that besotted people had for them that when Perses[1] invaded Greece, the harlots of Corinth undertook to intercede for their country in the Temple of Venus. Nay,

[1] That is, the Persians. Perses, the son of Perseus and Andromeda, was the legendary founder of the Persian nation.

whatsoever extraordinary favour they had to ask of that goddess, it was done by the mediation of the whores. And there seems some reason on their side, since Venus herself was translated to heaven and made a goddess for being the greatest whore and bawd that ever lived. She first taught the Cyprian women to prostitute their bodies for gain.

What a work did Aspasia make, who filled all Greece with whores? For the love of her and her wenches, it was that Pericles began the Peloponnesian War that lasted so many years and is so much talked of in ancient history. There were also learned whores, as Sappho, the mistress of Phaon; Sempronia, Leaena and Leontium, who wrote publicly in vindication of their lewd practice and inveighed against marriage. There were also noble whores, as Rhodope, who built one of the Egyptian pyramids with the money given her by the king; Thais the Corinthian, who was so surprisingly beautiful that she scorned to lie with any but kings and princes. But Messalina, the wife of Claudius Caesar, exceeded them all in the salaciousness of her temper. I will not omit to mention Joan, Queen of Naples, [2] who caused her first husband to be hanged because he could not satisfy her lust. His name was Andrew, son to Elizabeth, Queen of Hungary. Her second husband, to repair the fault of the first, so wasted his strength in the conjugal embraces that in a little time he killed himself. Her third husband was James, King of Majorca, whom she beheaded for lying with another woman. Her fourth and last spouse was Otho, Duke of Brunswick; he lived to see her hanged in the same place where her first husband had by her order suffered the same fate. This was the revenge of Charles, Prince of Dyrrachium, [3] cousin German to Andrew before mentioned. This lascivious Queen would have the company of ten or twelve young men, one after another, the same night.

What shall I say of Semiramis, Empress of the Assyrians; of Pasiphaë, wife to Minos, King of Crete; or of an hundred other royal whores, when it is observable that the most illustrious heroes on earth have sprung from adulterous beds? Witness Hercules, Alexander, Clodoveus, King of the Franks,

[2] Joanna I, *c.* 1327-82.

[3] Dyrrachium is the ancient name for the now Albanian city of Durrës on the Adriatic coast.

Theodoric the Goth, William the Norman, Raymor of Aragon, and many more, too tedious to be recited. Nay, few kings and princes are born of lawful mothers.

Doubtless the infidel nations live in great corruption of manners; they confound and blend together divine and profane maxims, from whence result monstrous and abominable practices and a general uncleanness of life in all things. But the chaste followers of Muhammad have all customs in abomination that defile the soul and rob it of its native purity. We obey the traditions of Ibrahim, Ishmael and the rest of the holy line, who never touched any woman but their own lawful wives and concubines, resting contented with this indulgence of the Omnipotent. We put in practice the law brought down from heaven and the precepts of the Prophet, which forbid all adultery, fornication and incest. We preserve in our veins the pure and unpolluted blood of our fathers, and transmit the same to our children and the posterity to come; that the promises made to Abraham, the glorious Patriarch of the East, may not be disannulled by the sins of his offspring, but may be verified till the day when the moon shall be cancelled in the heavens and all the stars be blotted out.

Oh sage Hamet! we are of a sacred lineage and illustrious pedigree. Our progenitors were the favourites of heaven and lords of the earth by the special benediction of God. The light of the Eternal shines upon the Ottoman house and is reflected from thence on all the empire. I pray heaven that we may not forfeit these privileges by our own folly and cause an ill report to be whispered of us among the angels, saints and prophets, and throughout the precincts of paradise.

I consign thee to the custody of God and thy guardian genius, wishing thee all manner of enjoyments that may consist with purity and innocence.

Paris, the 7th of the 5th moon of the year 1677.

To Dgnet Oglou

Volume VIII, Book II, Letter XIII

I am convinced by long and manifold experience that God and the world and everything appear to man in what figure he pleases. We may make our own optics, though the generality of men take up with those which are prepared for them by their fathers and tutors. We use the prejudices and prepossessions of education, as the Spaniards wear their spectacles even at dinner time for fashion sake, young and old, that they may appear grave and regular. We adhere to the opinions we received in our infancy with a partial stiffness and pride that we may not seem to call in question the wisdom of our ancestors or appear wavering or inconstant ourselves. So the Christian gallants swallow down whole dozen of venomous oysters without saying grace, only because it is the mode, though they will not venture on a crust of wholesome bread without conjuring a blessing on it by making the sign of the cross and squinting two or three magical glances at heaven, seconded by hocus-pocus whispers to complete the charm.

But let thou and I be more rational in our principles and practice. There is no God that will be bantered with vain mummery, or by music be melodiously wheedled out of his eternal reason. No incense can be of proof to nose the sense of the Omniscient, nor the most elegant words delude Him who is perfect in knowledge. He takes no delight in the pompous addresses of the great, nor is He to be moved by the multitude of solemn ceremonies. All that He requires of man is a heart conformable to the Divine Will and actions void of offence.

But the lawgivers and governors of nations observing that there was a certain religious fear and reverence of some divine power, as it were planted in the natures of all men, and considering that this might be improved with good management to the advantage and interest of the commonwealth, they invented set forms of discipline and exterior offices of worship, which they termed holy rites and mysteries. These they fortified with severe laws and sanctions, inflicting grievous penalties on the condemners of the public service performed to the gods. So Hermes Trismegistus first taught the Egyptians; Melissus, the foster father of Jupiter instructed the inhabitants of Crete; Faunus and Janus the Latins; Numa Pompilius the Romans; Orpheus the Grecians or some say Cadmus, the son of Agenor, first instructed that nation in the solemnities which were counted divine and which he himself learned in Phoenicia. He instituted the consecration of images and statues, the burning of incense, the building of temples and altars with the hymns, sacrifices and other magnificent rites by which they honoured the powers above.

Now, that all this religious pageantry was established only for the ends of policy and state is evident from hence: that the chief magistrates took the liberty of making what gods they pleased and of increasing or diminishing their number at discretion. So that in process of time there were reckoned no less than thirty thousand gods in the Roman catalogue, though at first their calendar could show but twenty-five divinities. But when once they had found out a way to distinguish these divinities into several classes or ranks, terming some gods of the greater nations, others of the lesser, having also their tutelar genii, their demi-gods, their rural and household gods, etc., there was no limiting the crafty devices of the priests and rulers in imposing or the superstition of the credulous people in believing and adoring an infinite rabble of new, young and unheard of divinities.

They took also the same freedom to change and alter the established rites and ceremonies, sometimes abolishing the old and primitive institutions and superinducing new ones in their stead or at least adding to the heap of insignificant ceremonies in every age, some mysterious novelty, which might please the people and fasten them in a devouter obedience and veneration of their pious guides and leaders.

Hence sprung the dedication of temples, fanes, chapels, oratories and certain days in the year to the service of particular gods; hence arose the invention and use of so many sorts of vessels of silver and gold and other materials in their sacrifices; of lights, flowers and perfumes; of music, pictures and other decorations; besides the rich and majestic vestments of the priests, their grave and composed carriage, looks and gestures. All designed purely to catch the rude and unpolished multitude in the snares of priestcraft, to strike their unwary minds with an awe and profound attachment for religion; that so being once made thus flexible, they might warp them to what bent they pleased and forever lead 'em in a blind implicit admiration of they know not what.

'Tis certain that religion has this effect on the vulgar to make them more obedient to their governors, just to one another and zealous for the public welfare. I mean the religion allowed by the state, for where the subjects dare to make innovations and schisms, to set up new sects and parties, the greater zeal each faction has for their own way of worship, the more cruel and tragical disorders are generally committed. So fatal a thing it is to be opinionative in religion, to invade the priest's prerogative and to disturb the quiet stream of traditions running in the channel of public faith from one generation to another.

My dear Dgnet, let thou and I shun the devout superstition of bigots and the wanton profaneness of libertines and atheists, adoring one God with sincere faith and a reason void of error. Let us also keep our lives free from all injustice and vice, which will be of more comfort to us than if we had sacrificed every day a thousand bulls.

Paris, the 25th of the 9th moon of the year 1677.

To Kerker Hassan, Bassa

Volume VIII, Book III, Letter XII

Thou requirest an account of the present state of England with a character of their king. In regard there are various rumours among the merchants at the imperial city of certain commotions and rebellious essays of malcontents in that island.

The name of the king who reigns there at present is Charles II, eldest son of Charles I and heir apparent of the British crowns. For his empire consists of three kingdoms which he has in actual possession, besides many vast territories and dominions in America, not to insist on his titular claim to the realm of France.

He is a prince of great wit and policy, nor of less courage where a just occasion requires the discovery of that virtue. He underwent innumerable hardships and misfortunes during his twelve-years exile from his native throne, forced to fly into foreign countries by a prevailing faction of rebels, tyrants and usurpers. Of humour debonair and amorous, much addicted to wine and women, munificent in his gifts and rewards to persons of merit and to those who have the happiness to please him in his recreations, especially to his concubines, who are most of them nobly extracted. By these females he has had several sons, who are all dukes and peers of the realm. He is in peace with all the world abroad, except the Moors of Sally. [1] Yet this Prince cannot be called happy in that he is harassed at home by domestic seditions, factions, plots and conspiracies of his own subjects.

Here is a report that the Roman Catholics of that nation have lately attempted to take away the life of this monarch; whilst others say this accusation is forged by their enemies to render them odious, and that to this end they have suborned false witnesses to swear against them. One does not know what to believe among so many contrary rumours. Neither does it much concern us that are Mussulmans whether party of these infidels be right or wrong.

This Prince, as I have said before, has several nations under his dominion, and 'tis thought he scarce knows the just extent of his territories in America. There is a region in that continent inhabited by a people whom they call Tuscaroras and Doegs. [2] Their language is the same as is spoken by the British or Welsh, a nation that formerly possessed all the island of Great Britain, but were by degrees driven out of it into a mountainous corner of the island where their posterity remains to this day.

[1] Sally or Salli was notorious as a seaport on the Moroccan coast, from which issued the Barbary pirates that harassed European shipping.

[2] By Doeg is probably meant the Onondaga, who along with the Tuscarora tribe formed part of the Iroquois family of North-American Indians.

Those Tuscaroras and Doegs of America are thought to descend from them, being the posterity of such as followed the fortune of one Madoo, a British prince who about five or six hundred years ago being discontented at home, resolved to seek adventures abroad. Wherefore being provided with ships and all other necessaries, he made a voyage towards the West over the Atlantic Ocean, not knowing what would be the event of his undertaking. However, the moon had scarce twice completed her voyage through the Zodiac when an end was put to his [journey] on the sea by landing in America, where he planted a colony of Britains and then returned to his native country. But soon after he put to sea again and sailed directly to the same place. What became of him afterwards is not certainly known, but the inhabitants of that province have a tradition that he lived to a great age and saw his people multiplied to many thousands before he died. For the second voyage he carried over British women with him for the sake of posterity. They show his tomb to this day, with beads, crucifixes and other relics.

It's certain that when the Spaniards first conquered Mexico, they were surprised to hear the inhabitants discourse of a strange people that formerly came thither in curraghs,[3] who taught them the knowledge of God and of immortality, instructed them also in virtue and morality and prescribed holy rites and ceremonies of religion. 'Tis remarkable also what an Indian king said to a Spaniard, *viz.*: 'That in foregoing ages a strange people arrived there by sea, to whom his ancestors gave hospitable entertainment. In regard they found them men of wit and courage, endued also with many other excellencies. But he could give no account of their origin or name.' And Montezuma, Emperor of Mexico, told Hernando Cortez, the Spanish king's ambassador and general in those parts, that his own ancestors landed there as strangers, being conducted by a certain great man who tarried there awhile and then departed, having left a considerable number of his followers behind him. After a year he returned again with a greater company, and that from him the emperors of Mexico derived their pedigree, and his subjects from the rest.

The British language is so prevalent here that the very

[3] Small boats covered with hides.

towns, bridges, beasts, birds, rivers, hills, etc., are called by British or Welsh names. And a certain inhabitant of Virginia (a place subject to the king of Great Britain), straggling not long ago into the wilderness, by chance fell amongst a people who, according to some law or custom of theirs, condemned him to death; when he, in the hearing of them, made his prayer to God in the British tongue, upon which he was released.

Who can tell the various transmigrations of mortals on earth, or trace out the true originals of any people? The whole globe has suffered divers changes, and every particular nation has had its metempsychosis. What grows obsolete and antiquated in one country becomes a new discovery in another. The houses of the living are built on the bones of the dead. Children lay the foundation of their grandeur in the ruin of their fathers. And the generation to come will practise this chemistry on our relics, that are now living; they will extract their fortune out of our ashes.

By the white stone which Adam brought with him out of paradise, and which fell by inheritance to Abraham, Ishmael, and his offspring forever; that stone which at this day lies under the mosque at Mecca and grows black by the touch of sinners: I swear the Arabians are an aboriginal people, a nation established from all antiquity, a stayed race, not canted up and down, hither and thither by every caprice of fortune.

Wherefore be assured, noble Arab, that besides my particular obligations, I honour thee for the sake of thy descent, and purified blood, and pacific temper, wishing for nothing more ardently than the happiness of kissing the border of thy vest in this life, or at least of seeing thee in the paradise of perpetual rest, from whence there are no further transmigrations.

Paris, the 2nd of the 11th moon of the year 1679.

To Dgnet Oglou

Volume VIII, Book IV, Letter VIII

I am as waggish as a janissary that has newly received his aspers! [1] There's more satire in me at this time than there was in Juvenal and Persius. And yet 'tis only the dregs of what I've vented on some learned bigots here in Paris with whom I have been drinking these two or three hours. I tell thee plainly I put off the Mussulman for a while and took my glasses frankly or like a Nazarene.

The discourse we were upon was astrology and the nature of comets, etc. But God tumble me headlong into the lap of Tagot if ever I heard such blockheads, dunces, fools, sots – I know not what to call them properly. Zounds! How can human reason be so debauched? How can man become such an insensible piece of stuff to think as they do? They made me blush for shame or anger. They made me sorry that I was a man to be ranked in the same list with 'em. However, I suppressed my boiling choler; I bit my lips and nails and did everything that patience could suggest (for I used to be a very boon companion in my wine). But at length, as 'tis the fate of all disputers, we grew too hot. There was such a tempest of words and passionate expressions that we could hardly find a grain of sense. At last we fell from words to blows, and I, though old and crazy, held up my head as well as I could.

Thou wilt believe at this age I have no great strength. But I tell thee my courage is the same as when I was but five and twenty; I cannot flinch from provoking dangers. And when I am thoroughly inflamed with wrath, death itself appears to me in the same figure which painters give it; a mere naked skeleton, which I have more reason to pity than fear; if I am afraid of anything, it is of breaking its bones and spoiling its shape, in the clash of my fury. So tender am I even of death itself, the obdurate and inexorable destroyer of all mankind.

One of the company that was a priest and sat right over

[1] Small Turkish coins with which salaries were paid.

against me at the table, threw his four-cornered cap at my head, whilst his next neighbour checked him for his insolence. But he was full of fat and empty of reason or civility, a great hulking fellow that makes a figure like the statue of Pont Ginello at Catania [2] in Sicily, only he is a little taller; but he has a swinging tun of a carcass.

After he had abused me thus he swore if he had the chalice of the altar in his hand he'd do the same thing. Nay, if he had the consecrated wine in it, would turn the blood of Christ into poison as he could turn wine into blood, to be revenged of me.

There was by good chance an Armenian or two in the company (not any of Solyman's gang) who took him up upon his menace. They challenged him severely to answer his words before the Archbishop of Paris. But the cunning priest had more wit in his anger. When he began to reflect on the bad consequences of a summons, he crouched, wheedled, and fawned like a spaniel. So fearful are they of a spiritual court, which is almost as bad in France as the Inquisition in Spain.

Then there was a captain, an old *miles emeritus,* a pensioner, who having not drunk such a quantity of wine many a day, took my part because he sat on my side of the table (for he never saw me before in his lifetime, as I know of). However, the old gentleman showed himself stout and demonstrated that he would stand a push for souls. But there was nobody would oppose him save myself, and I did in *verbo clerici,* not *manu* or *ense militis,* [3] God knows. I prayed the good old man to be pacified; I laid my right hand to my breast and heaved both that and the other joined to heaven. I invocated all the patriarchs and prophets; I bawled at the saints and angels; I summoned God almighty Himself to appear in my vindication. But nothing would do save downright fighting.

To it we went pell-mell. The fellows on the other side of the table were eager; nothing would satisfy them but blood; their rapiers were drawn and they were upon the pass. When

[2] Whatever this statue may have been like it was destroyed along with the rest of the city in the earthquake of 1693.

[3] I opposed him with the words of a cleric, not by hand or by the sword of a soldier.

I started up and cried out aloud, 'Gentlemen, 'tis the wrong minute for ye to fight in; Mars is in the eighth house in conjunction with Saturn and in quartile with the sun, a very malevolent aspect.'

Upon this they grew all madder than before.

'Damn that astrologer,' says one.

'Curse upon his stomach,' says another.

Till at last they all fell foul upon me; only my side-captain stood up stiffly for me. I did what became a man, but 'tis to his bravery I owe my life. For one of the opposite sparks made a full pass at my breast, which the noble old captain parried with a sudden shot of his arm athwart and a dexterity which I can never admire enough.

I that had neither sword nor skill in the science of fencing thought it my part to expose my body between my seeming friends and enemies, since all the occasion of this quarrel was on my account as an astrologer. I leaped upon the table and seized upon the sword of my captain's antagonist. I smiled upon him at the same time and convinced him that I was not in anger. I twisted it out of his hand with a complaisant violence. And then the strife was appeased. For 'twas not he that begun the quarrel, any more than my old captain, but the priest was wholly in the fault, who straggling out of his sphere, pretended to set up for an astrologer and tell us things that would not square with reason.

My Dgnet, thou knowest me and all my inclinations. Thou art sensible that I cannot stoop to the magisterial dictates of error, nor the bold impositions of ignorance. Let 'em approach as near as they will to truth on the backside, they are the further off from attaining it. And so let thou and I enjoy ourselves in perfect tranquillity.

Paris, the 17th of the 5th moon of the year 1681.

To Cara Haly

Volume VIII, Book IV, Letter XIII

I am now arrived to a great age and have rubbed through many fatigues in my lifetime. I have stood the brunt of a thousand perils and undergone much hardship; pains and afflictions have invaded me in body and soul. Labour, persecution and grief have been the portion of my past years. Now I would fain live at ease if 'twere possible.

Therefore I have recourse to thee my old friend who hast often afforded me thy counsel in time of need. I do not address for fashion sake or to discover the vast esteem I have for a physician whose skilful prescriptions have so often saved my life. No, no, I'm really in want of aid, and no man but thyself can cure me.

It is not easy for me to define my distemper, since 'tis heterogeneous and complicated of many different maladies. However, it is fit that thou shouldst be informed of the particular symptoms and the causes as far as I can guess at 'em, and I can do no less than make thee in part my confessor.

Methinks I feel the reversion of my youthful vanities inherit the entail of my past pleasures, which is certainly nothing but pain and torment. Those agonies which I laughed at in other men are now fallen to my own share. The comedies of my greener years are become the sensible tragedies of my weather-beaten age.

Whilst I sweat, frown and make a thousand grimaces at the anguish given me by the gout, stone, strangury, cholic, cramp and other acute diseases, which excruciate me by turns; I think the divine Nemesis has appointed some devil for an inquisitor and tormentor of every bone, vein, artery, nerve, muscle and gut in my body. Surely, I'm laid in the first pickle of nature's wrath; I wish it may be the last, for I do not in the least covet her ill will.

Then I have my successive intervals of dropsies, asthmas, dysenteries, fevers, consumptions and God knows how many more species of sickness. Yet sometimes I am as seemingly well in health as Morogli Zudistan, the old aga, that lived just by the obelisk in the hippodrome,[1] who ran away from his father in his youth and served seventeen years in the wars of Persia; lived till he was eighty-nine years old, yet never was let blood, took physic or was sick in all his life.

I protest 'tis hard for me to guess at my own constitution or to find out the original of those different habits in my body. Yet I have a feeling sense of that myself, which I cannot express to another. Sometimes I think there is some native and radical venom in my body, derived from the influence of malignant stars that had the dominion at my birth, though how or why it should be so, I am altogether ignorant. Neither can an astrologer with all his schemes and heavenly figures convince me which of the constellations or planets did me the fatal injury. I give no credit to their antiquated tales of trines, conjunctions, oppositions, quartiles and the rest of their Egyptian jargon. I believe there may be something true and sacred at the bottom of astrology, but 'tis covered with a heap of rubbish, rules and observations. And they that take most pains, dig deepest and make the narrowest search into the ruins of that noble science shall for one genuine pearl find a thousand counterfeits, for one truth a thousand errors. It fares with astrology as it does with religion, which is cantonized into innumerable sects and factions, each positively asserting that they have the only incorrupt laws of God; whereas if you make a strict scrutiny, you shall find a very little sincere piety but abundance of profaneness, hypocrisy and superstition.

Well, let it be how it will, whether the stars have any hand in the plot of human events or no, whether Saturn or Mars be malevolent or benign planets, it matters not much; no more does it to hear what they prate of all the various aspects and configurations of the other stars. This I am sure of, that I endure a great many pains which, let them be derived from above or below, are very troublesome.

'Tis possible that all or most distempers which afflict human bodies in so many different kinds may be but the effects of

[1] The Atmidan or hippodrome of old Constantinople mentioned above on page 45.

one original indisposition or ataxia in our animal spirits, or some hereditary contagion in our blood, or seminal pests in our humours; which Proteus-like appears in different forms masquerading it up and down our bodies in the disguise of fevers, agues, phthisics, coughs, consumptions, rheumatisms, pleurisies and a thousand more. Or perhaps our vitals are not sound. Some fall or knock or other accident in our infancy might put us out of frame, or the debaucheries of youth may leave their sting behind them to chastise our riper years and teach us wisdom before it is too late.

I tell thee, in short, all my maladies as I conjecture owe their original to an ill-tempered spleen and vitiated hypochondria. This, as I said before, I can easily feel within myself but can hardly express the manner how it comes to pass with that accuracy as is requisite to make another sensible of it. Only in general terms I suppose it has made me extremely melancholy at some times and as excessive merry and frolicsome at others, both which passions, thou knowest, have an ill influence on the heart, midriff, pericardium, liver and lungs. This I have found by frequent and long experience, though I will not undertake to describe the mechanic operation of these contiguous vitals one upon another, especially to thee who art the most accomplished and curious anatomist of this age. Suffice it to say that I have perceived within myself the violent and forcible contraction or dilatation, heating or cooling of any of these interior principal parts to be very pernicious to my health, having an immediate influx on all the rest and so the blood, wherein is contained the very essence of this mortal life.

My dear physician, our bodies are perfect machines and subject to the like mischances. If but a straw, a pin or any such diminutive trifle get between the wheels of a watch, 'tis presently disordered in its motion. The whole frame of the artificial mechanism is either at a stand or goes too slow or fast or at least unevenly. So the smallest irregular passion in any of the chief members of our bodies, disturbs and violates the peace of all the rest; it spoils their harmony and makes them jar just like a viol when some blundering hand has new turned the pegs after a skilful musician had put the instrument in tune.

Besides, there is a strange chain of consequences without. Our passions hurt not ourselves only but others, and we receive again the revenge of the damages we give. For there is an eternal circulation of justice in the world. The whole universe is but a piece of clock-work, where one motion begets another to infinity, and one stop in the meanest wheel would put all the rest to an equal stand. We mortals are parts of this grand mechanism and have our particular shares in the disasters that happen to the whole. I for my part by many casual jolts of misfortune, the designed bruises of enemies and the corroding teeth of time am almost worn out. If thou wilt by thy skill restore me again and put me in frame, the praise will be thy own. Otherwise the first artist must even take me to pieces, dissolve this useless mass, and when I am thus reduced to my original element, he may new mould my ductile substance and hammer it to what fashion and end he pleases.

Only I beg of him rather to make me any four-footed beast than a Spaniard, a Dutchman or a Jew among men, for these are the scandals of the human race.

Paris, the 2nd of the 3rd moon of the year 1682.

To Dgnet Oglou

Volume VIII, Book IV, Letter XVIII

This letter comes to thy hand by the same post with one to the Kaimakam; therefore, I pray thee be quick in executing the contents of it. I have not one friend in the seraglio whom I dare trust with such a secret. Thou art my only refuge at a juncture which requires fidelity, prudence and a dextrous conduct in diving and searching into a certain mystery, which, for aught I know, may concern my life.

To tell thee in short, Nathan Ben Saddi, the sultan's agent incognito at Vienna, a Jew by descent and religion, is, I fear, privately murdered by some order from the Divan. But for what reasons I know not; unless it were in compliance with the old maxims of the sublime Porte, which seldom suffers any slave to go to his sepulchre in peace who has served the Grand Signior many years in any eminent station. He has been missed at Vienna these eight weeks; and within a day or two after his first absence, the body of a dead man was found floating on the Danube, but so disfigured with wounds, as it could not possibly be known who he was; which gives me the greater suspicion that it was he. And if so, I may expect to be served so myself in a little time; for my turn is next.

Therefore, if thou hast any love or friendship for me, be watchful on my behalf. Attend the whispers of the court and observe the language of those who discourse with their fingers' ends.[1] The cast of the eye many times discovers the secret sentiments of the heart. So does a shrug of the shoulder, a pout of the lip or any other artificial gesture. They are all significant and expressive of what affection and thoughts we harbour within. Thou knowest how to act mute upon occasion, as well as any in the seraglio. I conjure thee to use great dexterity, and no less expedition in unravelling this secret. Feign to know something more than thou dost, that so thou mayest really learn what I would have thee know concerning Nathan's fate and mine too, if possible. Let no cold indifference make thee neglect this due care of thy friend's interest and life. We were born to serve one another with mutual zeal and fidelity. The good offices thou dost me are but lent to be repaid again with others whenever opportunity presents itself. But these arguments are superfluous. Thou needest no spurs to do a generous action. I know thou lovest me and wilt be active at this juncture on my account.

In full and entire confidence of this, I take my repose under the shadow of the divine mercy, begging God to afford thee a shelter in time of peril; and that when thou and I have weathered all the tempests of this mortal life, we may triumphantly enter the part of paradise and enjoy one another in eternal felicity.

Paris, the 6th of the 11th moon of the year 1682.

[1] The deaf mutes who are the personal bodyguards of the sultan.

FINIS

SELECTIVE BIBLIOGRAPHY

First Editions of *The Turkish Spy*

MARANA, GIOVANNI PAOLO, *L'Espion du Grand Seigneur*. Vol. I. Paris, 1684-86. The first edition of the French *Turkish Spy*.
— *Letters Writ by a Turkish Spy*, trans. (?). Vol. I. London, 1687. The first translation of Marana's French version.
— *Letters Writ by a Turkish Spy*, 'Second edition'. 2 vols. London, 1691. This publication reprints the 1687 translation in the first volume and contains the first appearance of the second volume with the lying preface containing 'Saltmarsh's' letter.
— *Letters Writ by a Turkish Spy*. Vol. III. London, 1691.
— *Letters Writ by a Turkish Spy*. Vols. IV and V. London, 1692.
— *Letters Writ by a Turkish Spy*. Vol. I. London, 1693.
—*Letter Writ by a Turkish Spy*. Vols. VII and VIII. London, 1694.
— *Letters Writ by a Turkish Spy*. 8 vols. London, 1694. The first complete English edition.
— *L'Espion dans les Cours des Princes Chrétiens*. 4 vols. Cologne. 1696-97. The French translation of the English editions.

Later Editions Consulted

— *L'Espion Turc*, 6 vols., Cologne, 1715-16. In the 'Preface' the editor avows that this edition is a translation of the English version.
— *Letters Writ by a Turkish Spy*. 8 vols. London, 1730.
— *Letters Writ by a Turkish Spy*. 8 vols. London, 1734.
— *Letters Writ by a Turkish Spy*. 8 vols. Dublin, 1736.
— *Letters Writ by a Turkish Spy*. 8 vols. London, 1741.
— *Letters Writ by a Turkish Spy*. 8 vols. London, 1748.
— *Letters Writ by a Turkish Spy*. 8 vols. London, 1801. This is the last printing of the letters.

Studies

A., F. R.: Correspondence, *Gentlemen's Magazine,* new ser. XIV, (1840), 142-143.

CORNEY, BOLTON, 'On the Authorship of the Turkish Spy', *Gentlemen's Magazine,* new ser. XIV (1840), 465-469.

CRISAFULLI, ALLESSANDRO, 'L'Observateur oriental avant les *Lettres persanes*', *Lettres Romanes,* VIII (1954), 91-113.

D'ISRAELI, ISAAC, *Curiosities of Literature,* Boston, 1833, II, 123-126.

DUFRENOY, MARIE-LOUISE, *L'Orient romanesque en France, 1704–1789,* Montreal, 1946, I, 155-162.

— Correspondence, *Gentlemen's Magazine,* new ser. XV (1841), 149-151.

HALLAM, HENRY, *Introduction to the Literature of Europe,* London, 1872, IV, 332-335.

MARTINO, PIERRE M., *L'Orient dans la littérature française au XVII*e *et au XVIII*e *siècle,* Paris, 1906, 284-291

MCBURNEY, WILLIAM, 'The Authorship of *The Turkish Spy*', *PMLA,* LXXII (1957), 915-935.

NICHOLS, JOHN, *Literary Anecdotes of the Eighteenth Century,* London, 1812, I, 413-414.

R[EPTON], J.: Correspondence, *Gentlemen's Magazine,* new ser. XIV (1840), 260-263, 374-378.

RIMBAULT, EDWARD F., 'Who Translated the "Turkish Spy"?' *N & Q,* ser. 1, I (1850), 334.

'ROBERT MIDGELY', *Dictionary of National Biography.*

TUCKER, JOSEPH, 'On the Authorship of *The Turkish Spy*: an *État Présent*', *Papers of the Bibliographical Society of America,* LII (1958), 34-47.

— '*The Turkish Spy* and its French Background', *Revue de Littérature Comparée,* XXXII (1958), 74-91.